New Edition

Jesus the Christ

CONTEMPORARY PERSPECTIVES

New Edition

JESUS
THE CHRIST
CONTEMPORARY PERSPECTIVES

BRENNAN R. HILL

WIPF & STOCK · Eugene, Oregon

Dedication

To the four Maries in my life

Acknowledgments

My thanks to Xavier University for granting me a sabbatical
during which I could revise this book.

Gratitude also to the librarians at Xavier University
for their generous assistance.

Special appreciation to my wife, Marie,
for her excellent suggestions and proofreading.

And finally, I want to acknowledge my many students who have helped
me understand the person of Jesus more deeply.

Wipf and Stock Publishers
199 W 8th Ave, Suite 3
Eugene, OR 97401

Jesus, the Christ
Contemporary Perspectives
By Hill, Brennan R.
Copyright©2004 by Hill, Brennan R.
ISBN 13: 978-1-62564-643-9
Publication date 2/15/2014
Previously published by Twenty-Third, 2004

Table of Contents

Introduction

Since I first published this study of Jesus in 1991, there has been a tremendous upsurge in the study of Christology. Recent excavations at places like Sepphoris, Capernaum, and Jerusalem have produced new perspectives on Jesus' social, political, and religious milieu. Books such as *Excavating Jesus* by John Crossan and Jonathan Reed and the work of Sean Freyne in Galilee now offer a wealth of material on the places where Jesus lived and worked.

The last decade has also seen some monumental studies on the historical Jesus by scholars such as John Crossan, E.P. Sanders, Paula Fredericksen, James Charlesworth, and John Meier. This research yields many new insights into the teachers and healers of Jesus' day, and helps us to see the uniqueness of Jesus' work in context. There is also a new interest in the prophetic tradition and its relevance to Jesus, as well as to the many oppressive and unjust situations of the contemporary world. Jesus is more than ever seen as a nonviolent rebel, struggling to bring about a kingdom of love and peace in a world where cruelty and violence prevailed.

Biblical criticism continues apace and offers an abundance of background and interpretative insights into the parables and the miracle stories. Raymond Brown has produced monumental studies of the birth and passion stories. Kenan Osborne and Gerald Collins have written influential studies on the resurrection.

The number of significant women's voices has also grown. Scholars such

1

as Elizabeth Schüssler-Fiorenza and Elizabeth Johnson have made extraordinary contributions to Christology. Moreover, there are now a growing number of women scholars developing Christology in the context of Asia and Africa. They especially speak for the women in these areas who suffer from poverty and oppression.

Eco-theology has also developed significantly in the last decade. Theologians, ethicists, and church leaders have come to more clearly see the links between the Jesus tradition and concern for the earth. Significant documents have come out of the bishops' conferences in Central America, the United States, the Philippines, and Europe. They call for a strong connection between the gospel message of Jesus and concern for the earth and its resources. In addition, the movement of eco-feminism has brought many women's voices into the dialogue.

There is still much discussion on what salvation really means, but the most debated topic has been the uniqueness of Jesus as savior. The contributions of scholars such as Paul Knitter, Jacques Dupuis, and Mark Heim, as well as the publication of the Vatican document *Dominus Jesus,* have produced a heated debate that has many interfaith and ecclesial implications.

Liberation theology continues to evolve. We have come to realize how this theology has roots in the Black Theology in America. While there is no longer the flood of writings coming out of Central and South America, the living of this theology still goes on in the base communities. Inspiration from Jesus Christ the liberator has also spread to the different political, social, and religious contexts of Asia and Africa.

Many theologians are attempting to address the limitations of the early council definitions on the divinity and humanity of Christ.

Renewed interest in the historical Jesus has brought with it a fresh interest in the human Jesus. Christians are beginning to wake up to the realization that Jesus led an authentic human life as a person of faith, an individual with weaknesses and failings, and one who struggled nonviolently to promote the authentic kingdom of God.

Many point out that it has been over sixteen centuries since the Church has dedicated a council to discuss Jesus. It has been suggested that the time has come to gather the people of God from around the world and proclaim the richness of belief about Jesus that has developed over the centuries in theology, biblical studies, spirituality, liturgical experience, prayer, interfaith dialogue, daily living, and the struggles for peace, justice, and the integrity of the earth.

Given all the developments in Christology, it became clear to me that the time had come to write a new edition of this text. This, of course, required extensive reading of the scholarship on Jesus produced over the last decade, and the integration of the newer perspectives into my text. I have chosen to rewrite the book in an informal style, which should be simpler and easier to read than the earlier work. At the end of each chapter, I have noted my sources, books that I would recommend for further reading. I have also included a list of films that I have found to be useful.

Writing a book on Jesus has always been a moving and graced experience for me. I have written other books, but they were about "topics." A book on Jesus is about a person, the very person who is the heart of the Christian tradition and experience. It is about an extraordinary individual who lived, died, and was raised by God: a person whose Spirit now dwells in the hearts of his disciples and their communities. Doing research on such a person gives one new glimpses into his personality, his unique search for God, his struggle to understand and believe. At times I have had sudden glimpses of him in library stalls, or while reading the insights of scholars, or in the eyes of my students as I taught this material.

I have come to realize that the true center of Christianity is not a set of doctrines, a code of laws, a number of sacraments and rituals, church officials, or such controversies as birth control or which parishes should be closed. All of these have their importance, but the center of Christianity is a person—Jesus Christ. Without him, his life, his teachings, his risen presence among us, the other aspects of church life are without meaning and purpose. All discussion on Christian faith must begin and end with Jesus, the one who is the Christ.

CHAPTER ONE

People and Places in the Life of Jesus

People are usually shaped by the places where they grow up and by the persons who surround them. Jesus was no exception. He was a Jew who grew up in Palestine, an eastern Mediterranean area that was subject to Roman domination. Jesus was from a largely rural area in the northern province of Galilee, and worked for many years in and around a tiny village called Nazareth. Jesus' little village was a stone's throw from the bustling city of Sepphoris and was also near the main trade route.

Throughout his life, Jesus was surrounded by the political and religious figures of his time, ranging from the reclusive Essenes, zealous revolutionaries, elite Sadducees, scholarly Scribes, hard-working Pharisees, and many other figures of his time. Tyrannical leaders like Herod Antipas, Pontius Pilate, and Caiaphas held sway during Jesus' life, and ultimately ordered his death. Much can be learned about Jesus by comparing and contrasting him with these figures.

In this chapter we are going to examine Jesus' social and political environment, as well as some of the kinds of persons who surrounded him. We do this in order to come to a better understanding of the elusive historical person, Jesus of Nazareth.

Sources

Our sources for reconstructing the historical Jesus are limited. There are a few outside sources, such as the Roman historians Pliny the Younger, Tacitus, and Suetonius, as well as the Jewish historians Josephus and Philo. Rabbinic materials after the destruction of Jerusalem are also useful, although we are not sure how much of this applies to the time of Jesus. All we can gather from these non-Christian sources are some statements acknowledging that Jesus existed and had followers.

Our primary sources are the four canonical gospels. These, as we know, were written by Jesus' followers decades after his birth, and are constructed in light of their faith in Jesus as the Christ. In 1948 and the years following, the Dead Sea Scrolls of the Essene community in Qumran were discovered. These scrolls contain documents from this religious community, as well as many other Jewish documents. These resources provide invaluable insights into the wide diversity of Jewish beliefs and lifestyles at the time of Jesus. In 1945 the so-called Gnostic gospels were found in Nag Hammadi in Egypt. These gospel texts and fragments are not recognized to be part of the Church's official canon of scriptures, yet many scholars use them as important resources for discovering what diverse Christian communities believed about Jesus. Finally, both past and present archaeological discoveries have offered valuable insights into the past history of Palestine. Extremely revealing "digs" have been done most recently under the Temple mount, as well as in Sepphoris, a city near Nazareth. All of these resources can help us in our search to better understand the person Jesus.

Palestine

Jesus was a Jew from the ancient area of Palestine, where his people, the ancient Hebrews, had lived for thousands of years, going back to the days of Abraham, Isaac, and Jacob. This area had been conquered by the Hebrew tribes that then, under the leadership of Saul, David, and Solomon, coalesced into a nation.

The Hebrew nation suffered a long series of conquests, first by the Babylonians in 539 B.C., and then by the Persians, Greeks, and finally the Romans about fifty years before Jesus' birth.

Though dominated by Rome, the Palestine of Jesus' day was relatively independent. Rome preferred to control its conquests remotely through loyal local leaders if possible. As long as the taxes kept coming into Roman coffers and the borders were kept stable, the Romans did not see a need to rule with a strong military presence.

During Jesus' time, the Herodian family held authority in Palestine. Herod the Great, who ruled for thirty-three years and died around the time when Jesus was born, had been appointed king by the Romans. He had been a loyal soldier who had fought Jewish civil wars on the side of the Romans, and Rome knew that he would be a strong leader and a loyal instrument for Roman imperialism.

No doubt Jesus heard many negative remarks about the tyrannical rule of Herod and his family over Palestine. The Herodians, first of all, were not considered to be authentic Jews, but were rather viewed as "half-breeds" from Idumea. Herod the Great's lavish lifestyle, which included a series of ten wives and a sumptuous existence in palaces built from taxes ruthlessly extracted from the people, caused a great deal of resentment among the Jews. Moreover, Herod's taxes supported an enormous building program, which included monuments, theatres, sports arenas, baths, fortresses, and even entire new cities. Much of this construction aped the Roman culture and was done to impress the Emperor. Herod did make an attempt to appease his people with a lavish reconstruction of the Temple in Jerusalem, but the heavy burdens that this placed upon the people only generated further resentment toward him. His ruthless behavior, including the murder of his own wives and children when they became a threat to his power, further repulsed Herod's subjects.

When Herod the Great died, the Romans divided his kingdom among his three sons: Archelaus was given Judea, Samaria, and Idumea; Philip ruled over the areas north and east of the Sea of Galilee; and Herod Antipas took over Galilee and Perea. Since Jesus was a Galilean, Herod Antipas would figure in his life and even his death. Though the period during Jesus' life was relatively free of rebellion, it was this minor prince, Herod Antipas, who executed Jesus' mentor, John the Baptist. Herod also figures in Luke's passion story, where he mocks Jesus before his crucifixion. Luke also reports that Jesus spoke of Herod Antipas as "that fox"(Lk 3:32).

Archelaus proved to be a cruel and disastrous leader in Judea, so much so that his subjects went to Rome and persuaded the authorities to depose him and send him into exile. The Romans decided to place a Roman prefect in charge of Judea, who would reside in the Herodian palaces at Caesarea and Jerusalem. One such prefect was Pontius Pilate, who gained infamy for decreeing the death of Jesus.

Pilate was widely known for his brutality. The gospels tell us that Pilate had some of Jesus' fellow Galileans killed while they were offering sacrifice (Lk 13:1). On another occasion, Pilate had some Jews beaten to death for protesting the use of temple money to build aqueducts. Eventually, Pilate's barbarities were reported to Rome and he was summoned to the capital to account for his atrocities. After that, Pilate disappeared from history, and we have only legends that possibly he was executed by Nero or that he took his own life.

A Man from Galilee

Jesus was known to be a Galilean, that is, a person who hailed from the northern province of Palestine. All Jesus' apostles, with the possible exception of Judas, were also from Galilee. Since this province was not under the direct rule of Rome, Galileans were known for their strong sense of independence. Galilee's distance from Jerusalem, the center of Jewish religious authority, placed Galileans out of reach of the Sanhedrin, the Jewish ruling body. Furthermore, the province was rich in farm products, lumber, fruit, wool, figs, olives, and fish; and Galilee's access to the key trade routes in the north provided its citizens with ample opportunities for commerce.

Galileans had a reputation for being cocky and rebellious, and this province was at times the flash point for revolutionary activities. Many of its residents had lost their lands during the Roman occupation, and were now required to forfeit large portions of their harvest to the landowners and to pay exorbitant taxes. Although Jesus lived during a rather peaceful period, he would have witnessed some incidents of rebellion. Around the time of Jesus' birth, a rebel called Judah the Galilean broke into the arsenal in Sepphoris, the capital of Galilee, stole weapons, and led an uprising. The Romans retaliated by burning much of Sepphoris, and either crucified or sold into slavery thousands of rebels. Again, when Jesus was about ten, Judah led another rebellion against a Roman census and unjust taxes. Finally, forty years after Jesus' birth this rebellious spirit exploded in the great uprising against Rome in 66 CE. The Romans slaughtered the Jewish rebels and destroyed Jerusalem in 70 CE. Early in the second century Rome put down one final rebellion.

Some scholars today describe Jesus the Galilean as a rebel. Though Jesus' strategies were nonviolent, still he was confrontational and aggressive in his criticism of oppression and injustice. In the gospels, Jesus carries himself as one who is independent, critical-minded, and a strong advocate for the down-and-out. His firm commitment to a "kingdom" of justice, particularly for the poor and downtrodden, no doubt made him many enemies and was partly responsible for his execution.

He seems to have led a nonviolent revolution that threatened both Jewish and Roman authorities committed to violence, and disappointed those who longed for a warrior leader who would restore the glory of Israel.

Since many Galileans lived in rural areas, they often had the reputation of being "hicks" or "country types," and Jesus has been traditionally portrayed as being from a poor peasant background. Most Galileans lived in ghettos as poor tenant farmers or shepherds. Many had been relocated by the Romans from the coastal areas and had lived in their own homeland as refugees and tenant farmers. Jesus the Galilean probably shared in the anger and resentment that was widespread among his oppressed people.

Nazareth

Jesus grew up in Nazareth, a village so obscure that it was never mentioned in the Hebrew Scriptures. Nazareth was situated among the hills of southern Galilee, a fertile area where tenant farmers worked hard to bring in two harvests a year from the rich alluvial basins, and where herds of sheep and goats could be pastured on the green hillsides.

Nazareth was a Jewish ghetto of perhaps five hundred people, whose forebears had migrated there a century earlier. It was isolated and clannish, and its people lived close to the edge, struggling for subsistence. Perhaps in the everyday challenges of this tiny village, Jesus learned the importance of equality and community. It is also possible that, in the face of heavy taxation and the demand for a large portion of the crop from the landowners,

Jesus would identify with the poor and oppressed.

Life in Nazareth was quite simple, yet arduous. The narrow dirt streets were lined with square one-roomed houses, each having a yard for a few sheep, a goat, and perhaps a donkey. The houses, made of fieldstone and with thatched roofs, were clustered together so that resources could be shared with neighbors and extended families. (This context must have been foundational for Jesus' later teaching on the love of neighbor and service to others.)

Sanitation was primitive, disease endemic, and life expectancy short. Water was scarce and had to be carried from local wells. The diet was simple, consisting in local grain, fruit, figs, vegetables, and the occasional meat. In times of drought there was a shortage of food and water. These conditions generated a system of local care for the less fortunate, especially the elderly, the disabled, and diseased. (Could it have been in this environment that Jesus learned to reach out to outcasts, and the needy, and to bring healing to the disabled?)

Though a Jewish ghetto, Nazareth did not exist in total isolation. It was in fact near several urban areas and the main trade route. As mentioned earlier, Sepphoris, a sophisticated Hellenistic Jewish city, had been destroyed in reprisal by the Romans, and rebuilt by Herod Antipas. During Jesus' youth, the city had a population of about 8,000 people, mostly Jews who lived well in Roman style. Sepphoris was located just about four miles from Nazareth and may have provided Jesus opportunities for work as well as cultural enrichment. Tiberias was another urban area only twenty miles from Nazareth.

The pastoral tone of Jesus' public teaching would indicate that he was more influenced by rural life than urban. While Jesus certainly could hold his own with the learned in Jerusalem, in fact he showed little inclination to preach and teach in urban areas with all their hierarchical authoritarianism and materialism.

When Jesus was a young adult, he moved to Capernaum, a fishing village of about 1,000 inhabitants on the Sea of Galilee. Perhaps he first moved there to find work, and then made this the location where he would select his disciples and set up the center for his ministry. In any event, it was here that Jesus began his public ministry, which was largely confined to the hillsides of Galilee.

Educational opportunities in rural Galilee were limited. Tiny synagogue schoolhouses were available to only a few, and most of the population was illiterate. Most likely Jesus' education was gained at home and at synagogue meetings until he was of age, namely, twelve. Jesus obviously did not have the opportunity to attend one of the fine rabbinic schools in Jerusalem. He may have known enough Hebrew to read the Torah, and if he wrote at all he left no record. His native language was Aramaic, and he possibly knew enough Greek for business transactions. The brilliance of Jesus' later teaching leads us to believe that he had a great deal of natural intelligence, and that possibly he received some excellent teaching at home or in the synagogue school in Nazareth.

Jesus grew up and lived among rural peasants, and worked for eighteen years with his hands as a craftsman. He is described as a "*tekton*," which can refer to an artisan in wood or stone. The social strata of the time in descending order was comprised of rulers, priests, retainers who worked for those in power, merchants, peasants, artisans, and outcasts, including beggars and slaves. Jesus, as you can see, was very low in the pecking order. Most likely he had to seek jobs in construction in the neighboring towns and cities. Much of his work would have been arduous, working outdoors in the sun with wood, stone, and clay. Tools were primitive, and the hauling of wood, sometimes from great distances, as well as the cutting, was grueling labor. Jesus' appearance, therefore, would have been rugged, his face leathered and tanned by the sun, his frame well-muscled, and his hands calloused from hard work. His Middle Eastern skin and eyes would have been dark. His stature, typical of the time, would probably have been slightly over five feet in height.

Jesus was a devout Jew. He would have honored the Sabbath and the Jewish feasts, and he would have discussed the Torah while working in the fields at harvest time, at the table fellowship meals, or on the rooftops in the cool of the evening. He would have attended the local synagogue meetings for liturgical prayer and study. (No synagogue structure has been excavated in Nazareth). Jesus' public teachings reflect a deep wisdom and understanding toward his religion, as well as a feverish desire to reform it. Common sense tells us that he did not arrive on the scene in his public ministry as a master teacher and healer without having prepared himself well through extensive study and experience beforehand.

Jerusalem

The Book of Ezekiel (38:12) describes Jerusalem as "the center [or navel] of the earth," and at the time of Jesus Jerusalem was the still the center of Judaism. The city symbolized the culmination of the exodus into the promised land and the days of glory when King David ruled the nation. It was the "Holy City," where Yahweh dwelt in the Temple, the center of Hebrew worship, authority, and education.

The Roman eagle dominated Jerusalem more than in Galilee because the province of Judea was under the direct control of a Roman procurator. Especially on the great feasts, troops of the empire, many of them Gallic, German, and Italian mercenaries known for their brutality, were visible throughout the city. Anyone who had doubts about who was in charge had only to look at the crosses outside the city, on which hung those convicted of sedition or rebellion.

It is not known how many times Jesus went to Jerusalem. The gospel of John indicates that Jesus made three visits as an adult. The synoptic gospels refer to only one adult visit. Two gospels recount a visit with his family when Jesus was twelve. Although there was a law that required male Jews to make a pilgrimage to Jerusalem three times a year for the feasts of Passover, Pentecost, and Tabernacles, it is doubtful that this law applied to a province as distant as Galilee.

Jerusalem was about one hundred miles from Nazareth, a trip usually taken with a slow-moving caravan for a week or more. There were dangers aplenty on this journey. Brigands and robbers lived in the hills, waiting to pounce on the pilgrims bringing their tithes to Jerusalem. (The well-known story of the good Samaritan gives an account of such an attack.) There was also the danger of skirmishes with hostile Samaritans, or attacks from the wild animals that then roamed the deserts.

For Jesus, a visit to Jerusalem had its negative aspects. Here in the metropolitan area lived the wealthy absentee landlords who held high mortgages on the lands of his people. Here dwelt the infamous customs and tax officials who were so oppressive to his neighbors. And the Sanhedrin, with its many unreasonable edicts and harsh punishments, was also located in the big city of Jerusalem.

A rural workman like Jesus must have experienced culture shock when he joined the hundreds of thousands of visitors for the great feasts in

Jerusalem. In the enormous marketplace merchants hawked their wares. Traders from the great port in Tyre displayed precious glassware and the renowned purple dyes. Fine white linen and scarlet woven materials had been brought from Babylon. Huge caravans of camels moved into the city laden with spices and exotic products from Mesopotamia. Many fish merchants sold dried fish from the Sea of Galilee. Jesus must have been stunned to see slaves sold on the auction block, and must have looked wide-eyed at the chariot races, the wild animal shows at Herod's Hippodrome, and the latest musicals and dramas at the theatre. The spectacles of sumptuous banquets, exotic dancing, and open prostitution must have been disturbing to this simple craftsman from the north.

Jesus would no doubt have looked forward to visiting with friends and relatives who would gather in Jerusalem for the feast. Perhaps at times he stayed with his friends Martha, Mary, and Lazarus in nearby Bethany. If that were not possible, he would have to either battle the crowds for scarce accommodations in the city or pitch a tent outside the city and walk to the festivities.

The main attraction for the devout Jew in Jerusalem was the Temple, the place where Yahweh dwelt and the center of Hebrew worship. The Temple visited by Jesus was the so-called Second Temple. The First Temple of Solomon was destroyed by the Babylonians in 587 BCE. This magnificent Second Temple was built by Herod the Great and had been completed about ten years before Jesus was born. (Workers continued to decorate this Temple until its destruction by the Romans in 70 CE.)

At the Temple Jesus would have seen the high priests and Sadducees appointed by Rome and often known for their corruption. They lived in magnificent villas on the hillsides, and walked about in the finest materials from India, bedecked in precious jewels. Revenues poured into the Temple coffers from tithes, from the sale of sacrificial animals and birds, as well as from the required exchange of "unclean" foreign money for the half-shekels required for the Temple tax. The huge profits enabled these Jewish leaders to live extravagantly and support several wives, along with many slaves and servants. The gospels recall one occasion when the chaos and corruption in the Temple court pushed Jesus over the edge. He trashed the money tables and drove the merchants and animals out of the Temple court. (The significance of this event will be discussed in the chapter on the trial and execution of Jesus.)

We have so far seen how specific places provided a context for Jesus' life and formation. Now we shall examine some of the religious figures who were contemporary with Jesus, and by comparison and contrast gain further insight into the uniqueness of his personality and message.

Religious groups

Information about the nature and status of all the religious groups existing during Jesus' life is not available. While there were many groups active at that time, Josephus, the Jewish historian, describes only three: Pharisees, Sadducees, and Essenes. His descriptions are sketchy, at times conflicting, and often skewed by his own prejudices. The gospels offer considerable material on the Pharisees and scribes, little on the Sadducees, and oddly never mention the Essenes. The rabbinic sources available were written much later than Jesus' time and therefore have limited value as resources. Especially with regard the Pharisees and Sadducees, these sources tell us little about their origins, beliefs, or social structures and render any definitive reconstruction most difficult except by way of speculation. With these limitations in mind, let us attempt to describe some of the groups that existed in Jesus' time.

Pharisees

Pharisees have acquired a bad reputation over the centuries. The standard dictionary definition of a "pharisee" is one who is a hypocritical, self-righteous person. This negative image is derived largely from the gospels, where they are described as "blind guides," "frauds," "white sepulchers," and even as individuals who work for the devil. Even later rabbinical literature presents a disparaging picture of the Pharisees, putting them in seven categories and praising only the last. They are described as pompous, foolish, and filled with false humility.

Many scholars today point out that the extremely negative view of Pharisees found in the gospels might come in part from a period later than the time of Jesus, that is, the time after the destruction of Jerusalem. During this period, the Temple, the Jewish state, and the parties and sects were obliterated, with the exception of the Pharisees. Judaism moved north to Jamnia, where it reinvented itself, and gave the leadership over to rabbis and Pharisees. It was these pharisaical leaders, including Paul, who cast the Christians out of the synagogues as heretics and hunted them down. These later Pharisees, who prevailed during the times in which the gospels were composed, seem to have been written into the gospels as the enemies of Jesus. At the same time, the gospels do seem to reflect strong memories of conflicts between Jesus himself with some of the Pharisees of his own time.

The word "pharisee" is derived from the Hebrew word *perushim*, which means "the separated ones." This has been traditionally interpreted to mean that the Pharisees saw themselves as the elite and stood aloof from those who did not follow the law. More recent scholarship reveals that the Pharisees of Jesus' time were not separated from the people, and were closely identified with the working people. The Pharisees had trades themselves, and often represented a more common sense and flexible approach to the law. At the same time, the Pharisees were careful observers of the law, especially the dietary, purity, and Sabbath laws. They valued community and table ministry and seemed to have a strong support among the people. They used this popular support to gain political influence with the officials of government and temple.

Jesus had much in common with the Pharisees. Like many of the Pharisees, Jesus was a tradesman without formal scribal training. Like them, Jesus was more a practitioner of the law, one who preferred to serve the poor and outcasts than engage in scholarship. Jesus also shared the Pharisees' preference for a simple lifestyle. He shared their appreciation for table ministry, for conversion of the heart, and viewed acts of love and justice as of higher value than the priestly cult in the Temple. He would have agreed with the Pharisees in their Jewish belief in the afterlife, and would have sided with those Pharisees who were nonviolent in their opposition to Roman rule.

Still, Jesus had his points of disagreement with many of the Pharisees. He challenged them as the accurate interpreters of the law, did not place the same emphasis on the scribal oral tradition, and was not as rigid when it came to observing purity regulations and Sabbath laws. Jesus preferred to teach his own version of the law on his own authority, and laid the foundations for the eventual setting aside of the Torah and the scribal tradition for his own oral tradition.

As to following the law in everyday life, Jesus displayed even more liberal views than the Pharisees. He shocked and angered some of them by his willingness to cure on the Sabbath. Moreover, he went beyond their open table ministry and included prostitutes (the story at Simon the Pharisee's house) and tax collectors. Jesus also went beyond the Father God of the Pharisees and called God by an even more intimate name, Abba.

While many Pharisees saw disease and disabilities as punishments from God, Jesus taught a God of wholeness and extended his hands in healing miracles. Jesus' growing support from the common folk, as well as his founding of a community bent on reforming Judaism, would have been threatening to the social and political position of many of the Pharisees. The Pharisees prided themselves on the support they received from the common folk, and were most cautious about their political links to the establishment.

The synoptic gospels tell us that as soon as Jesus began his ministry, the Pharisees took strong opposition to him. The earliest gospel, Mark, presents the Pharisees and scribes as Jesus' chief opponents in Galilee. We are told that the Pharisees plotted with the Herodians for Jesus' death after he healed on the Sabbath (Mk 3:6). In the gospel of John, the Pharisees, along with the Jews and chief priests, are the most important opponents to Jesus. (This contrasts, however, with Luke's view (13:31), where some Pharisees warn Jesus that Herod is seeking him.)

The Scribes

The scribes during the time of Jesus held positions ranging from mere copyists to religious intellectuals and scholars, even to advisors of the royal court. Since scribes did not make up an official party of their own, some scribes belonged to the Pharisee sect and a good number of them were also priests. Jesus, while he shared their commitment to the Jewish tradition and practices, differed from the higher scribes significantly in that he had no formal training as a scholar. Jesus did not belong to any official group in the hierarchical structure of his religion, including the priesthood.

Some higher scribes viewed themselves as the successors to the prophets. Others were official teachers, who organized scribal schools where they passed on their esoteric and secret knowledge of the law. These were the creators and teachers of the oral law, which was viewed as being equal to the Torah. Ultimate authority was given to this tradition and it had to be learned and passed on precisely as formulated by the scholars. In Mark, the scribes treat Jesus as a subordinate and even condemn him as a blasphemer when he forgives sins (Mt 9:3). Jesus in turn challenges the social standing of scribes and contradicts their teaching.

It was not easy to become one of the elite among the scribes. One had to be a male from a well-to-do family and apprentice under a master scribe for years. During these years the candidate acted as servant to the teacher, while studying carefully every word and gesture of the master regarding the laws of Sabbath and purification. Once finished, the candidate could be ordained as a scribe, and henceforth would be venerated by the people and worthy of the highest places of honor at feasts and in the synagogue. Matthew's gospel indicates that such scribes had governing power, by virtue of their association with the chief priests and elders. At times, these scribes are portrayed as joining forces with the Pharisees as opponents to Jesus.

Once again, Jesus can be seen in stark contrast to such scribes. Jesus apparently had no formal training in any of the exclusive rabbinic schools. He was a teacher without portfolio, and instead of quoting from the scholarly opinions and the oral law, he taught on his own authority, using homey stories and parables. Jesus selected his own disciples, both male and female, largely from the uneducated working classes. His teaching was open to the masses along the roadsides and seashore. And rather than call his disciples servants, he called them friends. Jesus taught his followers to disdain places of honor, and sent them to humbly serve others, especially the poor. Jesus placed the law of love and mercy over the scribal laws, and freely associated with outcasts and sinners.

The gospels contain evidence of the deep animosity that some of the scribes felt toward Jesus. They slander him and attempt to trick him in debate. Scribes are among those in the arresting party in Gethsemane, and in the group that presents Jesus to Caiaphas for judgment. They accuse Jesus before Herod, mock him on the cross, and persecute the disciples.

Not all the scribes were hostile toward Jesus; indeed, some seemed to be among his admirers. One addresses Jesus as "Teacher," and offers to follow him as a disciple. Another admires Jesus' answers to the Sadducees when they tried to ridicule his teaching on the afterlife with a question about a woman who had been married seven times. Jesus commends the scribe for his insights and says that the scribe is "not far from the kingdom of God" (Mk 12:28–34).

The Sadducees

Jesus stands more in contrast to the Sadducees than to any other group of his time. Although sources tell us little about them, it appears the wealthy aristocracy in the Jewish society of Jerusalem could be counted among the Sadducees. Included in their number were the high priests, elders, and nobles of the community in Jerusalem. Some Sadducees led patrician families who controlled the wealth and land of Judea and Galilee. They might be compared to the privileged few families in many societies today who control the wealth and power and live off the labors of the underclass and minorities. Jesus, on the other hand, was from peasant, working-class stock, a man of simple means who worked many years with his hands before he became a wandering preacher. He viewed wealth as an obstacle to holiness, taught the value of "power for," rather than "power over," and advocated a life of detachment and simplicity.

Josephus describes the Sadducees as boorish, heartless individuals who followed the letter of the law and imposed harsh sanctions on those who disobeyed the laws of the Torah. They are portrayed as competitive and hard to get along with. Many of them seemed to have been strict and literal in their interpretation of the written law, and thus rejected the oral law of the scribes and Pharisees, along with interpretations of the law outside of their influence. No doubt they would have disapproved of Jesus' freedom in teaching an oral law of his own, as well as of his liberal views on the observance of Sabbath and purification laws.

For the Sadducees in governing positions, the greatest good was sustaining the Temple and its rituals, even if it meant collaborating with their Roman occupiers. Jesus seems to have valued authentic Temple ritual also, but for him, love was supreme. He cautioned his followers not to judge, to reach out to sinners with mercy and compassionate service. He strongly condemned the hypocrisy of oppression, whether it be on the part of his own religious leaders or the Romans.

Ironically, in spite of their rigid dedication to the Torah, the Sadducees seemed to have been quite materialistic in their approach to religion. They viewed their wealth, success, and power as signs of God's blessing. This earthly life was all important to them, since they did not believe in the resurrection of the dead or a divine providence that intervened in human life. Jesus' message on the blessedness of the poor, the resurrection into eternal life, and God's intimate everyday care for all, especially outcasts, would probably have been strongly opposed by most of the Sadducees.

Some of the Sadducees were part of the governing body of the Sanhedrin, the highest political and religious body in Judaism, led by the Roman-appointed chief priest. Other members of the ordained class, the scribal Pharisees, were on the Sanhedrin, but were no match for the wealthy and Roman-connected Sadducees. Still, the Sadducees had to be cautious of the Pharisees, because of their strong support from the common folk. Jesus' alliance with some of the Pharisees may have been problematic for the Sadducees.

The gospels tell us little about the relationship of Jesus with the Sadducees. Their exclusiveness would have given Jesus little opportunity for contact with them. The gospel of Mark recounts the Sadducees questioning Jesus before his passion, and challenging his views on resurrection. We do know, however, from the passion stories, that the Sadducees considered Jesus to be a dangerous person, and they are portrayed as key figures in his condemnation and crucifixion.

The Zealot movement

It is unlikely that there was an organized Zealot party during Jesus' lifetime, yet there does seem to have been a revolutionary movement among his contemporaries. This movement advocated the violent overthrow of the Roman occupiers, along with their Jewish collaborators. It erupted from time to time, but for the most part smoldered underground until the 60s. At that point, violent revolution broke out and continued until the final stand of the rebels at Masada in 73 CE.

Jesus may have shared some of the sentiments of those in the Zealot movement, and seems to have chosen an apostle from their number, Simon the Zealot. Jesus would have agreed with these rebels in their dedication to the one God, and their rejection of the pagan view that Caesar was divine. Jesus told his followers to give Caesar the coin of tribute and nothing more. He would have opposed the brutal oppression of his people by the Romans and shared the Zealot dedication to opening the way for the true reign of God. He could have shared their motto taken from Elijah the prophet: "With zeal am I zealous for the Lord God of Hosts."

Where Jesus and the Zealot movement parted company was in the area of violence. Jesus taught his disciples to turn the other cheek to violence and to love and pray for their enemies. His was not the warrior God who wrought vengeance on enemies, but the God of love, mercy, and forgiveness. He could never have supported the holy wars of the Zealots, where acts of terrorism were seen as the will of God. Jesus supported confrontation, aggressive action against oppression, vigorous dedication to the cause of the poor, but gave no support to violence! For Jesus, the reign of God was recognized within by the presence of peace, justice, mercy, and love. He taught his disciples to not even carry a staff, and told them to put aside their swords.

The Essenes

Both Josephus and Philo mention the Essenes, but we have known little about them until the late 1940s and early 1950s, when a collection of their manuscripts (the so-called Dead Sea Scrolls) were found in caves where the Wadi Qumran flows into the Dead Sea.

The Essenes were a group of sectarian Jews who lived a strict monastic life. Some think that they had their origin in the Hasidim during the time of the Maccabean revolt; in any event, they remained in existence for about 200 years. The Essenes broke off from mainstream Judaism because they did not recognize the legitimacy of the Temple priesthood, and established themselves as the true remnant of Israel. They set up their own priesthood and rituals, and lived in the expectation that several messiahs would come exclusively to them on the final day. Their largest monastery was at Qumran, but they had many other communities throughout the cities and towns of Palestine. There were possibly several thousand Essenes during the time of Jesus. They were quite hierarchical in their structure, and legalistic to the point where they seriously punished members who broke communal laws.

It is quite possible that Jesus encountered some of these austere monks as they silently moved in their white robes from one community to another. Jesus would have admired their fervent commitment to the one God, Yahweh, their esteem for Moses, their dedication to the Torah, and their commitment to truth, humility, and justice. He would have shared their concerns for the coming of a messiah, their struggle with Satan, and their anticipation of the coming of the endtime. Their regard for table fellowship, poverty, helping the poor, as well as their dedication to prayer and hard work would also have won Jesus' admiration. It is possible that he heard of their call for repentance from his mentor, John the Baptist, who might well have been influenced by the Essenes.

But there are many areas where Jesus would have taken exception with the Essenes. Jesus recognized the validity of the Temple and its priesthood, even though he was critical of its corruption. Jesus wanted to reform Judaism and bring it to its most authentic traditions, and not to break from it and start a new sect.

Jesus would have also differed from the Essene approach to community. Jesus' discipleship included females and males, married and single, the healthy and handicapped, and all traveled about as brothers and sisters. In contrast to the hierarchical model among the Essenes, and indeed in his own religion, Jesus developed a fellowship of equals, where the first is to be last and the servant of all. Jesus never punished the members of his group, even when they betrayed or abandoned him. He would also have opposed the Essenes' contempt for those outside the community, especially the rich. Jesus, though he valued poverty, persistently taught love of rich and poor, friend and enemy alike. His movement openly welcomed all children of God, especially outcasts.

Neither would Jesus have shared the Essenes' rigid adherence to the Sabbath laws. The Essene would not help a friend or animal on Sabbath, where Jesus felt quite comfortable extending a healing or forgiving hand to an outcast or one suffering on the Sabbath. Nor would Jesus accept the Essene's apparent acceptance of violence toward enemies. Jesus stood strongly for nonviolence and taught his followers to love their enemies and to pray for those who persecuted them.

The main community of the Essenes at Qumran was annihilated by the Romans during the revolution in the 60s and 70s CE. Apparently the last of them died alongside the revolutionaries at Masada, possibly perishing in a mass suicide. The Essenes ended in death and destruction. Jesus' life also came to a brutal and violent end, but his followers experienced him raised to new life and his movement now numbers in the billions.

Summary

Jesus of Nazareth was a person of his time, a Jew who grew up in Palestine during difficult times of occupation. As a Jew, he shared in the devotion and fidelity of his people to Yahweh and the Hebrew tradition. Jesus was most likely deeply affected by the oppression, unrest, and periodic rebellion in his native province of Galilee. The small village of Nazareth where he was raised, the town of Capernaum where he lived as a young adult, and the metropolis of Jerusalem all played roles in his formation.

We have seen how Jesus might be compared and contrasted with those of other religious figures of his time. The gospels often use these figures as straw men against which they highlight the teachings and actions of Jesus Christ. Looking back, the gospel writers, and the communities that they represent, see Jesus as a Jewish reformer who stresses a unique perspective on the Jewish tradition, one which sees God's rule as one of love, peace, and nonviolent resistance to oppression. It is a strong position against religious corruption in the forms of greed, empty ritualism, self-righteousness, and hypocrisy. Jesus confronts absolutism, legal rigidity, and hierarchical structures that exclude the poor and outcast. Jesus advocates nonviolence, the acceptance of a loving, liberating covenant with Abba, and a covenant lived out in prayer and sacrifice. Jesus stands uniquely on his own, a singular individual introducing the beginning of a new movement in religious belief and practice among his people.

Questions for reflection and discussion

1. Discuss how the place(s) where you grew up influenced you.
2. In what ways did Jesus reflect the image of a Galilean?
3. What feelings do you think Jesus had toward the occupation of his country by the Romans?
4. Discuss the image of Jesus that you had as a child. Has that image changed?
5. How would living and working in Nazareth have influenced Jesus?
6. Compare and contrast Jesus with the Essenes, Pharisees, scribes, and Sadducees.

Sources

Borg, Marcus J. *Jesus, a New Vision: Spirit, Culture, and the Life of Discipleship.* San Francisco: Harper & Row, 1987.

Freyne, Sean. *Galilee, Jesus, and the Gospels: Literary Approaches and Historical Investigations.* Philadelphia: Fortress Press, 1988.

Horsley, Richard A. *Archaeology, History, and Society in Galilee: The Social Context of Jesus and the Rabbis.* Valley Forge, PA: Trinity Press International, 1996.

Horsley, Richard A., with John S. Hanson. *Bandits, Prophets, and Messiahs: Popular Movements in the Time of Jesus.* Minneapolis: Winston Press, 1985.

Jeremias, Joachim. *Jerusalem in the Time of Jesus: An Investigation into Economic and Social Conditions during the New Testament Period.* Philadelphia: Fortress Press, 1969.

Malina, Bruce. *The Social World of Jesus and the Gospels.* London: Routledge, 1996.

Mason, Steve. "Chief Priests, Sadducees, Pharisees, and Sanhedrin in Acts." In *The Book of Acts in Its Palestine Setting,* edited by Richard Bauckham. Carlisle, UK: Paternoster Press, 1995.

———. *Josephus and the New Testament.* Peabody, Mass.: Hendrickson Publishers, 1992.

Murphy, Frederick J. *The Religious World of Jesus: An Introduction to Second Temple Palestinian Judaism.* Nashville: Abingdon Press, 1991.

Riches, John. *The World of Jesus: First-Century Judaism in Crisis.* New York: Cambridge University Press, 1990.

Saldarini, Anthony J. *Pharisees, Scribes and Sadducees in Palestinian Society: A Sociological Approach.* Wilmington, DE.: Michael Glazier, 1988.

Sanders, E. P. *The Historical Figure of Jesus.* London: Penguin Press, 1993.

Stegemann, Ekkehard, W., and Wolfgang Stegemann. *The Jesus Movement: A Social History of Its First Century.* Translated by O. C. Dean, Jr. Minneapolis: Fortress Press, 1999.

Stemberger, Günter. *Jewish Contemporaries of Jesus: Pharisees, Sadducees, Essenes.* Minneapolis: Fortress Press, 1995.

Zeitlin, Irving M. *Jesus and the Judaism of His Time.* New York: Polity Press, 1988.

CHAPTER TWO

Searching for the Historical Jesus

The Jesus movement began with people following a certain historical person, Jesus of Nazareth. Our modern demand for historical accuracy, along with the availability of modern scholarly tools to uncover the past, have created a strong impulse among many contemporary scholars to attempt to reconstruct the Jesus of history. There is a drive today to get behind the myths, the doctrines, and the theology and rediscover Jesus as he walked along the dusty roads of Galilee, or sat at table drinking wine with his friends. Scholars have searched the deepest layers of the gospels, archaeologists have dug beneath the earth to times past, and novelists and filmmakers have searched their imaginations to somehow recapture Jesus the man.

As we have seen, our sources about Jesus are limited, we have very little factual information about Jesus. We have no statues or drawings of the actual Jesus, so we really don't know what he looked like. Since we have nothing that he wrote, and because many of his "sayings" are later formulations, we have few of his exact words. We know little or nothing about the first thirty years of Jesus' life, and we are not even sure how long his ministry lasted, since the gospels differ on this.

We are certain about some things. Jesus was a Jew who was born during the reign of Augustus and around the time when Herod died, in 4 BCE. We know that Jesus' close disciples were Jews, and that the movement he began was initially composed of Jews, who continued attending synagogue and Temple. Jesus grew up in the tiny village of Nazareth in the northern province of Palestine, called Galilee. His parents were Mary, a peasant woman, and Joseph, a craftsman, who passed his trade on to his son. In Jesus' public life, he was known to be an itinerant teacher who spoke much about the reign of God and called people to conversion. He was also known as a miracle worker, an exorcist, and a friend to the downtrodden. His words and actions apparently alienated some of the religious and political leaders of the time. Jesus was arrested in Jerusalem, condemned to death, and crucified outside the city. Shortly after Jesus' death, his followers claimed to experience him as raised from the dead, and started a movement that came to be known as the Way, and then as Christianity.

Approaches to the gospels

Reconstructions of the historical Jesus from the four canonical gospels vary widely, depending on how the gospels are approached. Those who believe the gospels were written by eyewitnesses to Jesus' life hold that these accounts are actually historical records of what Jesus said and did. Any discrepancies among the gospels are solved by putting the gospels together in what is known as a "harmony." Efforts to harmonize the gospels go back as early as Tatian in the second century, are found in the writings of some of the later church fathers, and continue on into modern times.

This literal approach to the gospel actually makes little distinction between the Jesus of history and the Christ of faith. Here it is assumed that the Jesus of the gospels was the messiah, the Son of God, and the savior all along. Although Jesus knew of this, his disciples were slow in catching on.

Here, Jesus as the Christ actually walked the roads of Galilee. The literal approach to the gospels, then, accepts the stories of Jesus' birth, miracles, death, and resurrection to be divinely inspired and thus historically accurate accounts of what happened.

This approach was behind the many "lives of Christ" that were written in the 1940s and '50s. The most well-known authors of these "lives," Fulton Oursler, Ferdinand Prat, Giuseppe Ricciotti, and Fulton J. Sheen, were all persons deeply devoted to Jesus Christ and the Catholic faith. Each wrote a creative biography of Jesus, even at times recreating his inner thoughts and feelings. Nevertheless, these accounts, inspiring as they may be, are based on assumptions about the gospels that are no longer held to be accurate. It is unlikely that such a "life of Christ" will ever again be attempted by a Catholic scholar.

Biblical criticism

The modern scientific approach to the Bible places the Scriptures in their historical context and uses the critical tools of textual analysis to study these writings. The Reformation prepared the way for this movement by giving priority to Scripture over tradition and by challenging the Church's authority to interpret the Bible. Then the Enlightenment, with its emphasis on reason, research, and scientific analysis, gave further impetus to a new scrutiny of Scripture. The critical approach began with the work of a French priest, R. Simon (1638-1712), who analyzed the various styles of Hebrew in the Pentateuch and then questioned Moses' authorship of these books. This critical method began to flourish in the nineteenth century in Germany, a time when there was an intense interest in linguistics, the history of religions, and researching the vast amount of data discovered in the Middle East following the French and British conquests there.

There was much excitement surrounding these new discoveries about Scripture. Source criticism revealed that many oral and written sources underlay the gospels. It was discovered that Mark was the first gospel and the source, along with a collection dubbed Q, for the gospels of Matthew and Luke. The gospel of John, accepted as the last of the canonical gospels, was seen to stand on its own. The gospels were now understood to be highly complicated literary and theological statements written decades after Jesus' death. The progress of this scientific approach continued to develop and expand. Redaction criticism examined the arranging and editing of materials by the author. Form analysis discovered a wide variety of literary forms that were used by the authors. And more recently, literary criticism has begun to study Scripture strictly as a unique genre of writing. The liberation movement has led to a re-examination of the Scriptures by oppressed groups, including people of color, women, and the poor.

Catholic biblical scholarship has had a stormy history. Some Catholic scholars embraced this approach in the last century, but were severely censured for their views. Others persisted, until Catholic scholars were forbidden to use the historical-critical approach to the Bible in 1907 by Pius X. Catholic biblical research was shut down from then until 1943, when Pius XII gave permission for this approach to be used. Catholic biblical studies came under attack once again in the United States during the 1950s, but were ultimately approved by the Second Vatican Council. The historical-critical approach to the Bible is now standard among Catholic scholars.

The search for the historical Jesus

In its beginnings, biblical criticism produced some extreme conclusions with regard the historical Jesus. In the eighteenth century H.S. Reimarus (d. 1768) was the first to separate the Jesus of history from the Christ preached in the early church. In his *Fragments*, which was published posthumously, Reimarus shocked his readers by maintaining that Jesus was nothing other than a deluded failure, a frustrated revolutionary who was crucified crying out in despair and anger. According to this theory, the "Christ" notion was a fraudulent scheme perpetrated by the first disciples. The disciples stole Jesus' body, and then made up stories about the resurrection in order to attract a following. Reimarus was a confirmed rationalist, unable to accept the supernatural. He hoped that his theories would discredit the stories of the supernatural in the gospels as well as the subsequent doctrines about Jesus being the Christ.

Reimarus' "repulsive caricature" caused an uproar among scholars, and strenuous efforts were made to more authentically reconstruct the historical Jesus by scholars like David Strauss (d. 1874), Ernest Renan (d. 1892), Adolph Harnack (d. 1932), and many others. Their methodology was generally similar: to set aside the dogmatic teachings of the early church about Jesus, and with what was left reassemble a portrait of Jesus as he really was.

Generally the result was a failure, in part because they began with the assumption that the gospel of Mark was the historical account of Jesus' words and deeds and could serve as the basis for true information on Jesus. In 1901 W. Wrede undercut this approach by demonstrating that Mark's gospel was also a highly theological interpretation of Jesus and his mission.

Albert Schweitzer (1875-1965), the famous musician, theologian, and medical missionary in Africa, exposed the futility of the nineteenth-century search for the historical Jesus. He pointed out that the searchers had failed because of their mistaken assumption of the historicity of Mark's gospel, and because of their false assumptions and prejudices. Schweitzer accused these scholars of projecting nineteenth-century views back into the gospels and thus making Jesus out to be a teacher of ethics, a social worker, and even a German philosopher.

Having said this, Schweitzer went on to draw his own portrait of Jesus, based on the conviction that anticipation of the apocalypse was central to Jesus' message. Schweitzer portrayed Jesus as a heroic but deluded preacher, who proclaimed the coming of the last days. When Jesus realized that the end had not come, he went to his death hoping that his crucifixion would somehow bring about the coming of the kingdom. Schweitzer's cogent exposure of the failure of liberal Protestantism to reconstruct the historical Jesus, as well as his own failure to do so, discouraged scholars from the "search" for some time to come.

Can the historical Jesus be recovered?

Many scholars have concluded that the historical Jesus cannot be reconstructed. Here we will examine the efforts of two scholars from the last two centuries: David Strauss (d. 1874) and Rudolf Bultmann (d. 1976).

David Strauss was a young scholar at Tübingen University who decided that the rationalists' discarding of the supernatural in the gospels was irrelevant. He believed that the supernatural stories in the gospels were myths surrounding Jesus, a preacher of little significance. For Strauss the heart of the gospel was not a person, but an idea—that the divine and the human are joined in reality. Jesus had no importance of his own; he was merely a symbol of this central idea. The mythical stories of Jesus' birth, death, resurrection, and supernatural events in the gospels therefore tell us little of Jesus, but rather elaborate this central notion concerning the divine and the human.

Young Strauss became the most controversial figure in Germany in the 1830s. He was dismissed from his university position and his career was ruined. For a time Strauss attempted to again win favor by conceding that Jesus was a great genius. Ultimately he came to a sad end, still maintaining his original position that little could be said about the historical Jesus other than that he was merely an insignificant preacher, a symbol of the eternal idea that the human and divine are joined.

Rudolf Bultmann is a household name in biblical studies and has had wide influence on both Catholic and Protestant scholars on the question of the historical Jesus. Bultmann was one of the architects of modern form criticism, which maintained that the gospels are largely made up of disconnected anecdotes (forms) and that these forms, which are not necessarily the historical words and deeds of Jesus, carry forth the Christian message (*kerygma*). Bultmann, especially in his early work, took that position that all we can know for sure is that Jesus lived and died, and that is sufficient historical basis for the message. The message is all important, not the person conveying it.

Bultmann took his cue from Strauss and argued that the early Christian communities used the myths of the gospels to convey the message of God that came through Jesus. He disagreed, however, with Strauss' position that the central Christian message was the union of the human and the divine. For Bultmann, the Christian message has to do with how to live an authentic human life. On this point, he was influenced by the thought of the existential philosopher, Martin Heidegger (d. 1976), on authentic human living. Bultmann argued that authentic human living is a gift from God and that the way to be open to this gift is to accept the Word of God as witnessed in the gospels. The gift, the invitation to faith, is contained in the gospel *kerygma*.

Bultmann's Lutheran approach to faith as a blind leap allowed him to be indifferent to the need for historical knowledge about Jesus. For Bultmann, faith was the core of Christian life, and therefore the historical facts about Jesus are not only inaccessible, but are irrelevant. It is sufficient that Jesus existed and served as the source of the *kerygma*.

The process of "demythologizing" became synonymous with Bultmann's work. This does not mean that he dismissed gospel myths as fairy tales to be discarded. Rather, Bultmann revered the gospel forms as the means through which the early church witnessed to its faith. Rather than debunk these forms, Bultmann attempted to translate them into contemporary language so that the gospel message could be heard today. He was suspicious, however, of the historicity of the gospel material, for he held that this material was heavily influenced by other ancient religions, gnostic sources, and the theological controversies of the early church. In his later period, Bultmann did concede the existence of a fuller historical core of the words and deeds of Jesus in the gospels, but he never gave in on the centrality of the message.

Some of Bultmann's own followers, led by Ernst Kasemann, claimed to find much more historical material in the gospels and launched what was called the "new quest" for the historical Jesus.

In 1953, Kasemann warned that the Christ could become a myth without a historical Jesus. He granted that the early church proclaimed belief in the Christ of faith, but at same time showed considerable interest in the historical person who was behind this belief. Kasemann offered scholars new critical tools and criteria for reclaiming the historical material in the gospels. He initiated a new era of searching for Jesus as he lived and taught. For the last half of the twentieth century, this search has been carried out with vitality and intensity by a host of scholars. The search has yielded a wide variety of images of Jesus. Jesus has been portrayed by credible scholars to be a prophet of the endtime, a revolutionary, an Essene, a Pharisee, a Galilean holy man, a magician, a wandering Cynic, and as a Jew who lived on the margins of his religion.

Why is the historical Jesus important?

Scholars pursue the discovery of the historical Jesus for many reasons. Some are historians and understandably find it valuable to locate Jesus in his own time frame. Others are social scientists and are intrigued with re-creating the context surrounding this teacher from Nazareth. There are biblical scholars, who peel back the layers of the gospels searching for memories of what Jesus said and did. And finally, there are scholars and theologians who search for foundational reasons for Christian faith and a linkage between the Jesus of history and the Christ of faith. Here we will examine some of the salient reasons why the historical Jesus might have importance to people of faith.

To appeal to a contemporary mentality

This age has been described as an age of information. Technology especially has made an enormous amount of information available, and we are constantly faced with the challenge of sorting out and critiquing the authenticity of data. This same challenge applies even to the area of Christian faith. Though faith is a gifted invitation to respond to a relationship with God, for many the response must be made reasonably and reflectively. Many today would resist following Jesus unless they could be reasonably certain about the authenticity of his life and teaching.

This is also an age of personalism, which values relationships, intimacy, and community. Perhaps some nineteenth-century rationalists could be satisfied with following an ideology, a message, or an institution. Today many are more inclined to view faith as following a person, one who in fact established and continues to dwell in a real community. Since the Christian movement seems to have begun with people following a person, many want to authentically carry on his tradition. They are not, therefore, satisfied with a Jesus who is some vague phantom of the past, but want to be assured that they are following a real person who lived a fully human life in history.

Finally, in what some call a post-modern age, wherein some challenge the very possibility of the historical, there are those who reject such relativity and disconnection with the past. They want at least an approximation of history and assurance that those who lived before us, including Jesus, can be identified as real individuals in a real historical context.

To provide continuity and wholeness in our understanding of Jesus Christ, biblical scholars and theologians have provided so many varying images of Jesus that one can have the impression that these could be different persons. There is the actual Jesus as he lived in Palestine, the historical Jesus as reconstructed by scholars, the post-resurrection Jesus who was experienced by his followers, the Christ of faith who has been described in the doctrines of the community and worshiped in ritual, and finally, the Christ of glory who is to come in the final days. There is Jesus the rebel, the pacifist, the liberator, the wonder-worker, and the Lord of the televangelist.

This wide range of images can be confusing to the believer who wishes to relate to Jesus as friend and savior. Without the Jesus of history, a real flesh and blood person, the doctrines and titles can well become an ideology. Jesus of Nazareth must be known in order to keep our understanding of Jesus the Christ rooted in reality. Just as we need more than the Lincoln memorial to carry on our admiration for Abraham Lincoln, we need more than doctrines and myths to sustain faith in Jesus. In both cases, a real historical figure who lived a truly human life of integrity must have existed.

To provide a basis for myth and doctrine

The myths and teaching of the gospels can easily be reduced to fairy tales or religious fabrications unless they can be rooted in the words of the real person of Jesus. The faith of the early church did not begin spontaneously from a vacuum after the resurrection. Post-resurrection faith is a validation of what had been experienced earlier in Jesus of Nazareth. During his life many "believed" in him, trusted in him, loved him, and uniquely found in him the power of God. They had already decided to answer his call to conversion and discipleship. This was all validated and transformed to a new level after the resurrection, but nonetheless the foundation remained as real and as historical experience. The gospels' myths are attempts to share this experience. Though these myths can be larger than life, they become useless if they are not based on the early followers' real experience of a living person.

To keep us in touch with the distinctiveness of Jesus

It seems preposterous to assume that the phenomenon of Christianity, which has so profoundly shaped countless lives as well as human history for two thousand years, can simply be traced back to a rather ordinary carpenter. It seems equally unlikely, as some scholars set out to prove, that Jesus was a typical Pharisee, magician, or even Zealot of his day. It is more reasonable to suppose that Jesus was a unique individual in history, a man of genius, an individual who seems to defy comparison. The very fact that after two millennia believers and scholars still carry on a vigorous search to capture some glimpse of who he was bears witness to his significance. Jesus was a unique religious reformer and teacher, who initiated an extraordinary movement that still bears his name today.

To provide a norm for evaluating interpretations of Jesus, not only biblical scholars and theologians but also artists, novelists, poets, sculptors, filmmakers and musicians attempt to portray Jesus. In modern times, he has been portrayed as an anti-hero, a confused craftsman making crosses for the Romans, a flower child, a deviant prophet hatching a Passover plot, or the product of hallucinations brought on by the eating of mushrooms. Some have argued that he was not a Jew, and others even deny that he ever existed. While many of these images of Jesus can be dismissed as fantasies, it is still valuable for the Christian community to possess a substantial understanding of the real identity of the historical Jesus as a norm that can be used to critique distortions.

Other current and more substantial proposals that Jesus was a liberator of the poor or an advocate for women also have to be substantiated in history if they are to be of value. Liberation theology has shown how Jesus struggled for justice and freedom and was in solidarity with outcasts. Scholars have linked Jesus' crucifixion with his dangerous sayings against religious and political corruption. Feminist scholars maintain that Jesus opposed the hierarchical structures of his time and established equality in his following. These images of Jesus, if they can be validly linked to the historical Jesus, can indeed revolutionize the future of Christianity and redirect the efforts of the Church.

A basis for Catholic faith?

At this point, it might be useful to look at a sampling of prominent Catholic theologians to see how they link the historical Jesus with Christian faith. We will examine the approaches of Karl Rahner, Hans Küng, Edward Schillebeeckx, David Tracy, and Roger Haight.

Karl Rahner maintained that Christian faith is grounded in the historical events of Jesus' life, death, and resurrection. Otherwise, he cautioned that these events could be seen as mere myths created by faith. According to Rahner, Christians need a personal Jesus Christ who sustains faith, and not simply some doctrine or notion put forth by faith. For him, therefore, the miracles and the resurrection are real events that serve as the very foundation of faith. Rahner holds that historical knowledge of Jesus does not generate faith, but it does provide a ground for such faith. To demonstrate his position, he goes back to the early Christian believers, who after the resurrection had a new transcendent comprehension of historical events. After their experience of the risen Lord, these believers saw their earlier experiences of the historical Jesus in a new light.

Hans Küng discusses the historical limitations of the gospel. He points out that the gospels are primarily testimonies of faith rather than historical accounts. The gospels invite us to believe and be saved, not to investigate the facts of what really happened during the life of Jesus. At the same time, Küng is convinced that these faith accounts are based on very real memories of what Jesus said and did. The early communities did not arbitrarily invent Jesus' words and deeds. Rather they witnessed in faith that they now knew better than in Jesus' lifetime who he really was and what his life meant. At the same time, the early authors felt free to create sayings and stories that would reflect their faith, always remaining true to the original experience they had of Jesus of Nazareth. For Küng there is a definite continuity between what was preached and what really happened.

Even though Küng values the historical layers in the gospels and holds that they can be recovered through research, he does not maintain that historical material provides a reason for faith. Such history helps us take stock of our tradition, maintain faith concretely, and share our faith with others. While he values the link with Jesus as he was in actual life, Küng holds that the primary concern of faith is how Jesus meets and challenges us in the here and now.

Edward Schillebeeckx, who has written the most extensive Catholic account of Jesus Christ in modern times, is deeply concerned about the value of the Jesus of history. It is his position that when the early Christians speak of their faith in Christ, they are at the same time referring to their memory of Jesus of Nazareth. The magnificent images and titles that they attribute to Jesus are in light of both their past and present experiences. For Schillebeeckx, the "matrix" of the gospels is both the firsthand experience of the followers of Jesus as well as the continuing fellowship that they were experiencing with his Spirit. His position is that all faith articulations about Christ, if they are to be valid, must somehow be based on the original memories of the words and deeds of Jesus of Nazareth.

Schillebeeckx has a profound regard for biblical criticism and uses its findings as a basis for his own Christology. Still he cautions that such scholarship should not hope to find some neat core of historical material that is untouched by doctrine. Schillebeeckx warns that if the doctrinal tradition is removed, as was done by the nineteenth century rationalists, we will be left with a kind of vague phantom-like Jesus. The Jesus of the gospels, he asserts, must be acknowledged as the Christ. Jesus of Nazareth and Jesus the Christ are one and the same person.

The driving force behind Schillebeeckx' theology is that Christian faith is not a commitment to an ideology or even a doctrine, but to a person, Jesus Christ. While this commitment is to the glorified Jesus of today, it is also linked to the Christ-event of the early communities and to the experience many had of the earthly Jesus. It was this earthly life that was acknowledged and empowered by God through the resurrection.

David Tracy, an American theologian, describes the primary norm of faith to be not the historical Jesus but the apostolic witness to Jesus as remembered and proclaimed by the original followers. Tracy stills values the Jesus of history as a secondary norm of faith and says that it helps us hold on to what is subversive and dangerous in the memories of Jesus. In other words, our understanding of the historical Jesus keeps us in touch with the radical dimension of Jesus' message, a dimension that can be lost as the doctrinal tradition develops. Doctrinal development must always be measured against the historical words and deeds of Jesus. The historical Jesus is also valued as a reference for reform and renewal.

Tracy does not make the Jesus of history the primary norm of faith, but he maintains that enough about Jesus can be recovered to serve as a rational basis of faith. Tracy deeply respects the work of exegetes, but he observes that there are too many versions of the Jesus of history to allow any of these to be the norm of faith. Therefore, he concludes that faith primarily is a response to "the event of Jesus," as witnessed in the past and experienced in the present. The confessed Jesus Christ is therefore Tracy's primary norm for Christology, and only secondarily the historical Jesus of Nazareth.

Roger Haight, another American, holds that very few theologians today base their Christology (the study of the faith doctrines surrounding Jesus Christ) on the historical Jesus. He agrees with the commonly held position that faith should not be based on or caused by historical evidence. Nevertheless, he recognizes that the ongoing search for the historical Jesus is having its effect on the study of Christology. First of all, Jesus research reinforces the notion that Jesus is the subject matter for Christology. There will always be an ongoing curiosity as to who Jesus was, since the later *kerygma* in the gospels is based on interpretations of this person. Secondly, Jesus research can affect the imaginative portrayal of Jesus in our liturgical, catechetical, and devotional dedication to the Christ. Finally, the study of the Jesus of history can clarify our understanding of Jesus' self-awareness and distinguish this from the later expressions of his identity. A deeper understanding of both of these areas offers new possibilities for a broader notion of salvation and new possibilities for interfaith dialogue.

It seems clear from this overview of Catholic theologians that historical material on Jesus does not generate faith, nor can it be the object or norm of faith. No evidence of any kind can serve as the basis for faith. Yet the Catholic tradition finds no contradiction between faith and reason, and therefore values recovery of the historical words and deeds of Jesus, and the memories of him that underlie the gospels. This historical material renders faith reasonable.

Christian faith is in the risen Lord, but the risen Lord is identified and in continuity with the historical Jesus, along with his teachings and actions. Fresh interpretations of both the Jesus of history and the Christ of faith can assist Christians in applying the gospel to today's questions.

An emerging portrait

Biblical scholarship has now joined hands with theology, anthropology, archeology, the social sciences, historical research, and other disciplines to assist in the search for the historical Jesus. Added to this, the arts, mysticism, the imagination and celebrations of the faithful, as well as the struggle for liberation in many countries, have all added to the picture. The portraits vary, and there are numerous reconstructions, yet they usually share a significant amount of common ground. Here for your consideration is a proposed portrait of this mysterious, yet amazingly vivid figure.

Jesus (Yeshua, Joshua) of Nazareth was a real human individual, a person of flesh and blood who lived some two thousand years ago. He was an Eastern Mediterranean Jew who lived most of his thirty-some years in Palestine in the tiny hamlet of Nazareth in the southern part of the province of Galilee. Jesus was from peasant stock, and came from a large family of brothers and sisters, whose parents were a carpenter named Joseph and a Mary (Miriam). His most notable sibling was James, who eventually became the head of the Christian church in Jerusalem.

Jesus may have been partially or wholly illiterate, and left no writings behind. For most of his life, Jesus worked as an artisan, which placed him in one of the lowest classes at that time. This profession would have given him a rugged appearance. Jesus possibly worked in nearby Sepphoris and Tiberias, where he might have been influenced culturally. As a young adult, Jesus moved to a fishing village, Capernaum, where he selected some of his followers to assist him in his mission. These early followers were largely rustic and uneducated fishermen. He went on to select other followers, which included women, a tax collector, a Zealot, and people from all walks of life.

As a human person, Jesus shared the same emotions, physical pleasures, thought processes, and ability to choose freely that are common to all. He had the normal human limitations to his intelligence, and thus experienced ignorance and the struggle to learn and discover the truth. He had to deal with confusion, doubt, and even failure. Jesus, as portrayed in the gospels, says little about himself and does not seem to be aware of being messiah or of having a divine identity.

Jesus was a traditional Jew, who accepted and cherished the religion of Israel, along with its traditions, feasts, and rituals. He studied the Torah, attended synagogue, and went on pilgrimage to the Temple in Jerusalem. He recognized the priests and teachers of his time, and followed the traditional laws with regard to the Sabbath and purification. His passion for Judaism moved him to set out to reform and renew his religion by recovering its best elements.

Jesus seems to have been a disciple of John the Baptist, and was especially influenced by John's eschatological message and his call to conversion. Jesus was baptized by John in the river Jordan. The gospel writers reflect a certain early embarrassment about John's influence on Jesus, and that is perhaps why they portray John as a blood relative and one who acts as a precursor and witness to Jesus. After John's execution, Jesus began his own mission, which was carried out largely in the rural areas and small towns of Galilee. He entered public life as a charismatic teacher. His teachings were not scholarly, but were largely conveyed in intriguing parables, proverbs, powerful one-liners, paradoxes, and hyperboles.He taught with an authority of his own.

The rule or reign of God was at the heart of Jesus' teachings. This was a common theme among Jews, who believed that God had chosen them in a special way and would one day restore the glory of the nation. Generally this view was eschatological, focused on a glorious endtime. Some Jews were more apocalyptic in that they believed in a fiery and destructive ending that would consume all of Israel's enemies. Jesus' own version of the kingdom was unique in that he seems to speak from an unprecedented intimacy with God and hoped for the endtime to come soon. Jesus admitted to not knowing the specific time for the end, and he seldom followed the doomsday approach to this kingdom. Jesus taught that this same kingdom was at hand and could be furthered through peaceful resistance to injustice and oppression. He was a nonviolent revolutionary, committed to freeing people from that which prevented them from experiencing the love and compassion of God.

Jesus' extraordinary intimacy with the Creator seems to have been sustained by dedicated prayer and contemplation. Jesus called God "Abba," and he called others to share in this intimacy along with him. As a Jew, Jesus perceived all reality to be the creation of a loving and saving God. He revealed a rule or reign of this God that is universally inclusive, loving, forgiving, compassionate, and just. He taught that the rule of God must, and indeed will prevail. In this plan, all people are children of God, and the oppressed and exploited are blameless and in a special way blessed by Abba. Jesus selected twelve apostles to symbolize the renewal of the tribes of the nation of Israel, which he hoped was uniquely breaking into history through his mission of renewal.

Jesus called his people to conversion, a radical return to the best of their traditions and a repentance for their infidelity. He protested when the reign of God was often mistakenly reduced to mere legal observance and ritual. He condemned the hypocrisy connected with such a perspective, and demonstrated his rejection of such legalism by placing love and service over mechanical Sabbath observance and slavish adherence to purity laws. Jesus empowered the destitute and the outcast to obey the law of love and to recognize their true dignity as children of God.

Jesus taught in the prophetic tradition, similar to Elijah, in that he was an itinerant leader of a community and a miracle worker and exorcist, who exposed exploitation and oppression, and predicted dire consequences if justice was not observed. He insisted on the equality of all and raised up women, children, the disabled, the poor and those who had been rejected as "sinners." He welcomed to his table outcasts, which at the time included gamblers, prostitutes, tax collectors and shepherds. Jesus was not an ascetic, but a person who was generally "out and about." His enemies perceived him to be a drinker and glutton, a friend to outcasts and sinners.

Jesus performed miracles and mighty deeds, which displayed God's power over evil and the presence of God's reign. Through healings and exorcisms of evil spirits, Jesus demonstrated that the rule of God was at hand and powerfully present in the world. These wondrous acts also demonstrated that God was indeed at work in Jesus' teachings and actions. At first, the response to Jesus' mission was wildly enthusiastic. This enthusiasm, as well as the radical nature of his teachings and prophetic actions, seemed to alienate and alarm some of the Jewish and Roman leaders of the time. Jesus' healings on the Sabbath, his triumphant entry into Jerusalem, and his cleansing of the Temple also played a role in his condemnation.

Ultimately, Jesus was arrested in Jerusalem and crucified, falsely accused of being a blasphemer, seditionist, and false King of the Jews. He died on a cross outside the city, apparently facing death with courage, forgiveness, and persistent fidelity to his mission. After Jesus' death, his followers began to experience him as being raised from the dead. They came to have faith in him as their messiah, savior, and the Son of God. These disciples established a new community within Judaism, but eventually this group became separated from its mother religion and took on an identity of its own, first as the Way, and then as Christian churches.

This is a credible if brief portrait of Jesus of Nazareth, who came to be recognized as the Christ. Modern biblical studies have revealed a progressive development in the personality of Jesus as well as in his followers' perception of him. Jesus gradually becomes the Christ and is revealed to his followers as such. There is a distinction between the historical Jesus as he lived and was experienced during his life, and the individual who was raised up, exalted, and revealed as the anointed one of God. At the same time, both Jesus and the Christ are two dimensions of the same life. Christians do not follow an idea or a doctrine. Rather they follow a flesh-and-blood person who in his life, death, and resurrection was revealed to be the Lord.

The search for his identity will continue and the results will never be definitive. Nevertheless, both the historical Jesus and the Christ of faith remain integral to the Christian tradition. Gerhard Kittel put it well earlier in this century when he wrote:

> The Jesus of history is valueless and unintelligible unless he be experienced and confessed by faith as the living Christ. But, if we would be true to the New Testament, we must at once reverse this judgment. The

Christ of faith has no existence, is mere noise and smoke, apart from the reality of Jesus of history. The two are inseparable in the New Testament.

Summary

Most scholars have rejected past views that little or nothing can be learned about the historical Jesus, and at the same time there are few who think that a "life" of Jesus can be written by harmonizing the gospels. In the last several decades there has been a keen interest in rediscovering the historical Jesus through the process of biblical criticism, archaeology, and the study of the social and political background of the time. It is now considered both useful and possible to develop a fairly comprehensive portrait of the man Jesus, who lived such an extraordinary life over two thousand years ago, and who came to be acknowledged by countless people as the Christ.

Questions for reflection and discussion

1. Compare and contrast the literal approach to the Scriptures with that taken by biblical criticism.
2. Explain the distinction between the historical Jesus and the Christ of faith.
3. Do you think it is valuable to search for the historical Jesus? If so, why?
4. What is your portrait of the historical Jesus? Does that differ from the portrait suggested in this chapter?
5. Explain how resurrection faith affected the portrayal of Jesus in the gospels.

Sources

Charlesworth, James H., ed. *Jesus' Jewishness: Exploring the Place of Jesus within Early Judaism*. Philadelphia; New York: American Interfaith Institute; Crossroad, 1991.

Crossan, John Dominic. *The Historical Jesus: The Life of a Mediterranean Jewish Peasant*. San Francisco: HarperSanFrancisco, 1991.

———. *Jesus: A Revolutionary Biography*. San Francisco: HarperSanFrancisco, 1994.

Fredericksen, Paula. *Jesus of Nazareth, King of the Jews: A Jewish Life and the Emergence of Christianity.* New York: Knopf, 1999.

From Jesus to Christ: The First Christians (videocassette). Directed by William Cran. Co-produced by Frontline and Invision Productions, Ltd. PBS Home Video, 1998.

Horsley, Richard A. *Jesus and Empire: The Kingdom of God and the New World Disorder.* Minneapolis: Fortress Press, 2003.

Keck, Leander E. *Who Is Jesus?: History in Perfect Tense.* Columbia: University of South Carolina Press, 2000.

Meier, John P. *A Marginal Jew: Rethinking the Historical Jesus.* 3 vols. New York: Doubleday, 1991-2001.

Schneiders, Sandra Marie. *Written That You May Believe: Encountering Jesus in the Fourth Gospel.* New York: Crossroad Publications, 1999.

Sloyan, Gerard. *Jesus in Focus: A Life in Its Setting.* Mystic, CT.: Twenty-Third Publications, 1983.

Wink, Walter. *Jesus and Nonviolence: A Third Way.* Minneapolis: Fortress Press, 2003.

Wright, N. T. *The Contemporary Quest for Jesus.* Minneapolis: Fortress Press, 2002.

Films

Godspell (DVD). Directed by David Greene; 103 min. Columbia Tri-Star, 2000.

The Greatest Story Ever Told (DVD). Directed by George Stevens; 225 min. MGM Home Entertainment, 2001.

Jesus Christ Superstar (videocassette). Directed by Norman Jewison; 107 min. MCA Home Video, 1987.

Jesus of Montreal (*Jésus de Montréal*) (videocassette). Directed by Denys Arcand; French with English subtitles; 119 min. Orion Home Video, 1993.

Jesus of Nazareth (videocassette). Directed by Franco Zeffirelli. Family Home Entertainment, 2002.

The Last Temptation of Christ (videocassette). Directed by Martin Scorsese; 163 min. MCA Home Video 1989.

Search for Jesus, The. (ABC, Peter Jennings).

CHAPTER THREE

Teacher and Prophet

Jesus is revered as one the great teachers of history. Looking for comparisons, one thinks of Moses, the powerful teacher of the law to the Hebrews some 1400 years before Jesus; or of Siddhartha Gautama, who 500 years before the time of Jesus, wandered through India teaching a reform of Hinduism. Or Jesus might be compared with Socrates, a philosopher who was executed by the Athenians in 399 BCE, or with the equally renowned Plato, who was taught by Socrates.

In all four gospels Jesus is addressed by both friends and enemies as "teacher," probably a term of respect rather than an official title. Teaching was obviously an important element in Jesus' mission, and yet his style was so different that it is difficult to situate him among other teachers of his time. First of all, the descriptions of similar teachers are from later sources, and we are not sure if these descriptions apply to teachers of Jesus' time. Nevertheless, it is useful to contrast and compare Jesus with what we know of other teachers of his period.

The Cynics

Jesus has been compared with the wandering Cynic teachers of his time. The Cynics were Greek-influenced philosophers, who went from city to city living and preaching countercultural values. They were teachers who embraced poverty, having only a staff and knapsack, and by this lifestyle declared themselves freed from societal strictures. The Cynics were not so much scholars as they were wise commentators on life, and their message was one of common sense, and opposition to oppression and hypocrisy. Their teachings were often considered to be radical and unorthodox, and they urged their listeners to live close to nature, be independent, and to think and live for themselves.

Certain parallels with Jesus are obvious in that he also valued simplicity, nature, freedom, and independence; and he sternly opposed oppression and hypocrisy. Jesus, of course, was neither a Greek nor did he represent any school of philosophy. His distinctness is also seen in his drive to reform his own Jewish religion. Rather than teach individualism, Jesus taught the importance of community and discipleship. Love was uniquely central to Jesus' message, and he extended his message largely to his own poor rural audience, rather than directly challenge the lifestyle of urban areas.

The Sages

Others compare Jesus with the rabbinic sages of his time. Hillel, a contemporary of Jesus, who died when Jesus was a boy, was a prominent teacher of the time. Hillel was well-liked for his gentleness, concern for the impoverished, and dedication to peace. His "School" was often in opposition to that of another well-known sage, Shammai. Hillel's inclusive and liberal views, as well as his support of the oral law, gained him much popularity among the people. Hillel's teaching on loving neighbor as the self, on flexibility toward the law, on not being judgmental, as well as his advice about not being anxious for the future, are similar to the teachings of Jesus. Still, Hillel was educated in a formal rabbinic school in Jerusalem and was therefore much more concerned with passing on the oral and written traditions surrounding the Torah than was Jesus. Philo was another famous sage of the time. He resided in Egypt and attempted to integrate Jewish and Greek thinking, a matter of little concern to Jesus.

Jesus differed from the sages in that he had no formal academic training in a rabbinic school. He did not concern himself so much with the oral and written tradition, but rather conveyed his own message about the kingdom on his own authority. Jesus preferred to teach through parables rather than quote opinions of the rabbinic schools. Moreover, he did not seem to belong to any one school of thought, nor did he set out to establish an elitist rabbinic school of his own or to integrate his Jewish thought with the philosophies of other cultures.

Jesus' teachings stand in stark contrast to the militant and exclusive teachings of the Essenes. His was an inclusive and merciful movement, which stood in stark contrast to the hierarchical structures and systems of punishment in the Essene communities. Jesus' passion was to bring Judaism back to the best of its traditions on love and justice, and not to deny the legitimacy of Temple Judaism, as did the Essenes. Jesus' followers were for the most part commoners, women and men, the respected and the outcast. Jesus' disciples were not subject to a careful testing process; and he viewed his followers as his friends, his collaborators, and commissioned them to share in his mission of spreading the good news of an egalitarian kingdom to the world.

A teacher of the Torah?

We know that Paul declared Christ to be the "end of the law," and that Christianity eventually moved away from the formal Torah. Questions therefore arise with regard Jesus' teaching concerning Torah, and whether or not he was attempting to start a new religion or simply reform Judaism. Matthew's gospel has significance here. Jesus tells the crowds that the teachers of the law and the Pharisees are authorized interpreters of Moses' law and that the people should follow everything that they are told. At the same time, Jesus warns: "but do not do as they do, for they do not practice what they teach" (Mt 23:1–3). Clearly, Jesus here is calling for reform in the actual practice of the law. In another key passage, Jesus says: "Do not think that I have come to abolish the law or the prophets; I have come not to abolish but to fulfill" (Mt 5:17). It is evident from these passages that Jesus taught his early followers to value their Jewish heritage, to remain authentic followers of the Torah, and to continue Temple worship.

Jesus taught his fellow Jews that love of God and neighbor was central to their tradition, and he insisted that love took precedence over blind and rigid obedience to the law. He had strong words on how hypocrisy was a contradiction to love. Though determined to reform Judaism, Jesus does at times go beyond the Torah on his own authority. He uniquely forbids revenge, oaths, lust in the heart, and divorce.

A unique Jewish teacher

Jesus had a distinctive style of teaching. At times he seems to work within the wisdom tradition of his religion, especially in his use of proverbs. His wisdom statements sometimes come in the form of memorable one-liners: "Repent and believe in the gospel"; "the Sabbath is made for man, not man for the Sabbath"; "the first shall be last and the last first"; "love one another as I have loved you;" "love your enemies"; and "turn the other cheek."

At times, Jesus' teachings are paradoxical, as when he tells his followers that they should be as little children, and that they should hate their parents. On other occasions, he uses hyperbole, as when he tells his disciples to cut off their hand and pluck out their eyes to avoid sin, or when he says that it is easier for a camel to fit through the eye of a needle than for a rich person to enter into the kingdom of God. None of this was simply folksy wisdom. Jesus was always challenging his listeners toward radically new ways of thinking and acting, turning them toward a new vision of life. Rather than give definitive answers, Jesus taught his audience new ways to search for answers. Surprise and challenge are often characteristic of his methods of teaching.

Parables

Jesus commonly made use of parables in his teaching. Parallels to Jesus' parables are found in the Hebrew Scriptures and in later rabbinic writings, further indication that he honored Jewish teaching forms. Some scholars also find influences from the Hellenistic-Roman literature, which would reinforce the notion that Jesus' teaching reflected the melting pot of cultures in the Mediterranean area.

In the last century there has been a wide range of studies of the parables from many different points of view. First of all, it is generally agreed that the parables, though they include editing by later communities, in their deepest layers come from Jesus himself. The parables therefore provide a surprisingly rich resource for coming to a better understanding of the historical Jesus. They give us a window into his own search for understanding, as well as into his efforts to share his vision with others. This moved the great biblical scholar Joachim Jeremias to remark that "we stand right before Jesus when we read the parables."

Biblical critics over this last century have labored over the parables in order to peel back the layers of interpretation added by Christian communities and gospel writers in order to discover the original messages. Other scholars have attempted to translate the language of the parables into more contemporary categories so that they can address modern concerns. Literary approaches had abounded; these have examined the parables as poetic works of art, or as metaphorical language. In this literary purview, the response of the reader to the parable is the prime focus, rather than the original historic context. Others have turned to the social sciences, and with new discoveries about the ancient Jewish and Mediterranean world have offered fresh insights into how Jesus' parables challenged the oppression and exploitation of his time. More intense studies of ancient cultures are revealing that traditional interpretations of the parables often miss the mark.

Though related to other parables of his time, Jesus' parables are unique. First of all, Jesus did not use them in the traditional fashion to teach biblical and scribal writings. Rather, he invited the listener to grapple with the story and come to new understandings. Jesus challenged conventional standards, and contradicted attitudes and practices that had long been accepted. In his stories things are often stood on their head. In the good Samaritan parable, the "good" (the priest and Levite) are "bad," and the "bad" (Samaritan) ends up being "good." In the story of the prodigal son, the indulgent son is celebrated while the faithful son is discounted. All the while, a father, who should be filled with wrath and indignation, runs to lovingly embrace his lost son. The parables subvert established hierarchies, expose injustice that has gone unnoticed, and often make outsiders into insiders. They reveal the surprising and unexpected interventions of God in ordinary events. God's wisdom is not ours!

The word "parable" is related to the word parabolic, which means to be placed alongside of for purposes of comparison. The parable, then, is to be put alongside of reality in order to challenge assumptions and suggest new insights and beliefs. The parable is always open-ended and can be reinterpreted and re-understood in terms of new circumstances.

Today we see many oppressed people in the world placing these stories alongside their experience and receiving from them a new vision of wholeness and freedom.

The kingdom

There is a consensus among scholars today that the central theme of Jesus' teaching was the kingdom of God, sometimes referred to as the rule or reign of God. The notion of the kingdom of God is treasured within the Hebrew tradition. Martin Buber, the Jewish philosopher, maintained that the realization of God's all-embracing reign is "the Alpha and Omega of Israel." The "kingdom" is a belief that is derived from God's function as creator and sustainer of all reality. The prophet Isaiah proclaimed the good news of the peace and salvation that flows from God's powerful reign over the world: How beautiful upon the mountains are the feet of the messenger who announces peace, who brings good news, who announces salvation, who says to Zion, "Your God reigns" (Is 52:7).

The reign or rule of God, properly understood, is one where love and mercy prevail. (It is a misconception that the God of the Hebrews was predominantly a God of fear.) God's constant and eternal love are common themes throughout the Psalms and other books of the Hebrew Scriptures. The psalmist proclaims: "For your steadfast love is before my eyes, and I walk in faithfulness to you" (Ps 26:3). This loving leadership, whereby God protects and strengthens Judah is extended especially to the poor: "For he did not despise or abhor the affliction of the afflicted" (Ps 22:24). Jesus was convinced that these Jewish beliefs were at the very heart of his religion, and he felt called to both teach and live these teachings no matter what the cost.

In its purest meaning, the kingdom of God refers to the revelation of God's loving and saving presence during the course of human events. It is the manifestation of God's will to save all humankind. It is the recognition that God is in charge, and that the signs of God's rule are love, peace, victory over sin and evil. The Hebrews recognized the power of God's rule when they were liberated from slavery and brought to the promised land. Ultimately it became their mission to reveal this plan of freedom to all people.

Jesus preached the reign of a loving saving God in the context of his own time. In the Mediterranean area, where honor and shame took on such significance, his people were often dishonored and put to shame. There was much "anti-kingdom" for Jesus to experience. First of all, the Hebrews believed that their land belonged to God, and had been given to them to share. Now their land was occupied by a foreign power. The land for the most part had been turned over to the greedy rich, and most of Jesus' people worked as tenant farmers, barely subsisting. Gone were the days of the Jubilee year, when land was redistributed and debts forgiven. A hierarchical system of grinding authority prevailed, centered in far-off Rome and delegated to Herodian princes or Roman prefects in the provinces of Israel. Legions of brutal mercenaries were posted in centers throughout the country, ready to respond to any disturbance or uprising with lethal force. The Herodians and many of the Jewish leaders in Jerusalem collaborated with the Romans in the exploitation of their own people in order to maintain power and wealth. A corrupt system of patronage forced people to sell their souls for some semblance of security.

The vast majority of Jews lived in the rural areas. They had no legal rights and struggled daily in an atmosphere of fear. Failure to pay the exorbitant taxes and land rentals could result in exile into slavery, imprisonment, or even death. Immorality could be punished by stoning. Travel was always dangerous because of thieves and rebels who hid in the mountains. Throughout Jesus' homeland there existed a whole culture of the outcasts: prisoners, the disabled, the diseased, the destitute. Greed, hatred, violence, and oppression of the weak had supplanted love and justice and peace.

Out of this cauldron of suffering, Jesus stepped forth with his call for repentance, a radical change in behavior, a realization that God's rule must and will prevail. God's rule was at hand, and sometime soon a major breakthrough of divine power was coming. Perhaps without knowing it, Jesus himself ushered in this apocalyptic event through the power of his life and message. The world would never be the same once Jesus' gospel message was revealed.

Jesus threw down the gauntlet to the kingdom of evil, the reign of Satan. He exposed the corruption of the Temple, the hypocrisy of some of its leaders, the greed of the rich, and the shame of the oppressor. Jesus called his disciples to an alternate lifestyle of poverty, detachment, and gracious service. He refused to participate in the system of patronage and rejected collaboration with the Romans, advising his followers to limit their compliance to the payment of the forced tax to Caesar. He declared how difficult it was for the greedy rich to be part of the kingdom and called for them to give their goods to the poor. Jesus condemned those who laid heavy burdens on the backs of his people. He physically attacked the corrupt money changers and sellers at the Temple and the corrupt system for which they worked.

This humble preacher from Nazareth dared to challenge the political-religious structure of his time, and proposed a counterculture. Jesus called for freedom and equality and an end to absolutist teaching, hierarchical oppression, and exclusion. Jesus called for an end to the violence and told his followers to turn the other cheek and to love and pray for their enemies. He raised up and empowered the impoverished, the downtrodden, called them blessed, and predicted that they would be first rather than last. Jesus brought healing to the infirm, and peace to those with evil spirits, thereby revealing a God of mercy.

Jesus preached a kingdom where the true God is Yahweh, and not an emperor, a Herodian king, or a high priest. This God is neither a warrior God who conquers for his people through violence, nor a vindictive God who sends squalor, disabilities, or diseases. Jesus' God forgives, even enemies. The God of Jesus is a loving Father, Abba, the very source of love, peace, justice, and healing. "Prepare yourselves," Jesus proclaimed; this God intends to rule creation. As a devout Jew, Jesus shared the perennial hope that God would intervene and save his people from enslavement. Somehow he saw his own mission as the new breaking in of this saving power, a new dawning of salvation. He signaled this dramatic and inevitable breakthrough of God's power through miracles and through the paradigmatic images of heavenly banquets and wedding feasts.

Now and not yet

There was an urgency in Jesus' message about the kingdom of God. God's saving presence was "at hand" and "in your midst." He told his audience to focus on the concerns of today and not be anxious about the future. The power of the Father could be experienced in children, in the birds and lilies, in the poor of Spirit, all of whom depended on the Creator.

At the same time, Jesus alluded to the future dimension of the kingdom. A time of fulfillment is ahead, "coming." Yahweh is transcendent, a "God ahead of us," drawing all of creation to fulfillment and completion. Jesus urged his disciples to live "in between times," struggling for peace and justice, and at the same time to trust that ultimately God's future will prevail.

A challenge to alternate views of kingdom

Jesus' vision of the kingdom stood in opposition to many of the alternate views of his day. The Essenes had chosen to withdraw from society to await the coming of their own messiah in closed, alienated communities. Jesus, in contrast, proposed an embracing of life, an inclusive love of friend and foe, a communal expectation of the salvation of all. Some of the Pharisees and scribes, while not withdrawing from society, formed exclusive fellowships and hoped to usher in the kingdom through meticulous observance of the law and ritual. Jesus preached the primacy of love and service over legalistic obedience. The rich land owners and wealthy Sadducees identified the kingdom with their success and wealth, thanking God for their blessings. Jesus warned them that their greed kept them from entering the kingdom and told them to give to the poor and follow him.

Rooted in the Abba experience

Jesus did not preach some abstract kingdom, but rather spoke of a kingdom that he had intimately experienced in his own life. In the deepest layers of the gospel there are memories of Jesus' unique and incomparable experience of intimate loving union with God. This Abba comes to him as he rises from sleep to pray on his own. This loving parent is described as coming to Jesus at his baptism and transfiguration saying: "This is my Son, the Beloved, with whom I am well pleased" (Mt 3:17; cf Mt 17:5). This same Abba receives Jesus' spirit in death: "Father, into your hands I commend my spirit" (Lk 23:46).

A call to conversion

Jesus' mission was to embody this experience and to invite others to share in it. He summoned people to a conversion to this friendship with God. "The time is fulfilled, and the kingdom of God has come near; repent, and believe in the good news" (Mk 1:15). Jesus called out for people to turn their lives around and be open to the prevailing power of God's love and forgiveness. This was not some distant kingdom brought about through external observance, empty sacrifices, or violent revolution. This was God's plan to free his people from fear, shame, and exploitation. God stands with and hopes to free the marginalized from the political, religious, and economic forces that crush them. Jesus promises such freedom: "So if the Son makes you free, you will be free indeed" (Jn 8:36). It is a freedom brought by the power of love, compassion, and forgiveness.

Parables of the kingdom

As we saw earlier, Jesus often used parables as a vehicle for challenging his listeners to think in new ways and come to new awareness. Many of his parables wrestle with the mysteries of God's kingdom. The parables use everyday situations as metaphors for a kingdom, that is in fact beyond complete description. They use the real to lead to some inkling of a kingdom that is beyond reality.

Each parable attempts to grapple with some dimension of God's kingdom. The parable of the mustard seed (Mk 4:30–32) suggests that the kingdom is tiny but fruitful. The parable of the prodigal son (Lk 15:11–32) helps the listener to deal with the awesome truth that God loves everyone with an unconditional love and "runs down the road" to offer forgiveness. The parable of the persistent widow (Lk 18:1–8) reveals how the power of prayer is effective in bringing about the kingdom. And the parable of the Pharisee and the tax collector grapples with the teaching that humility and truthfulness are the way of the kingdom, and not proud self-righteousness. The parable of the good Samaritan presents the irony that the outcast is first in the kingdom, while the self-righteous are the last.

The Hebrew notion of God's vengeance is addressed in some of the parables. The man without a wedding garment is cast out into the outer darkness, and the servant is punished for burying his money instead of investing it. In the last judgment scene in Matthew, the sheep are separated from the goats, and one group is rewarded while the other punished.

But the memories of Jesus and his teachings about God more characteristically portray a God who is loving and forgiving. Jesus himself punishes no one who is a sinner. When he returns to his disciples after the resurrection, there is no revenge for their betrayal and cowardice, only the words "Peace be with you." If anything, punishment seems to be self-inflicted on those who refuse to follow Jesus, as in the case of the rich young man, who cannot give up his possessions. It is "hardness of heart" through which people turn from God and as a result cut themselves off from salvation.

This deliberate choice to reject God is perhaps what Jesus symbolizes in his teachings on "judgment," "outer darkness," and "gehenna." The "judgment" is our own doing.

The prophetic mission

The ancient Jewish prophets played a key role in the religious history of Israel. They served as the nation's conscience and visionaries. By the time of Jesus, the prophets of old had not been around for hundreds of years and were sorely missed. The scribes claimed to be the successors of the prophets, but often lacked the passion and vision to stir their people. The occasional eccentric claiming to be a prophet would march a group out into the desert to await the endtime. Such individuals were generally dispatched quickly by the Romans. Many of Jesus' time longed for the good old days of Moses, Elijah, or Jeremiah, charismatic figures who kept the vision of God's people before them.

Prophets, though well-remembered, were not always popular in their own day. They constantly reminded the people how they had strayed from the truth and warned of dire consequences in the future. The prophets of old often portrayed God as angry and vengeful, a punisher who visits wrath on those who are evil, and who ushers in apocalyptic destruction on those who are unfaithful. Thus some of Jesus' contemporaries were looking for a militant prophet who would lead them to free Israel from the Romans and restore the glory of Israel.

Contrary to popular understanding, the prophets were not predictors of the future, nor were they microphones for God. They were human beings, who were inspired to look at the human situation from the Creator's perspective. They were a combination of poet, patriot, and moralist, people who spoke out against the abuses in society. They were outraged at the apathy toward evil and threatened judgment if changes were not made. At the same time, the prophets showed a love toward their people and offered them a hopeful future it they returned to the ways of God.

The prophets criticized the conventional wisdom of their times and offered inspired alternatives. Moses, the greatest of the Hebrew prophets, challenged the Egyptian domination and slavery of the Jews, and led his people to freedom and justice. Isaiah warned the people of Jerusalem that they would be severely punished if they did not care for the poor and defenseless in their midst. When the Hebrews were overrun by the Assyrians, the prophet Isaiah hoped that this would serve to purify his people, and he reiterated that God would always be compassionate and faithful to his people.

The ancient prophets were able to excite their people with powerful symbols and dramatic language. They stirred them out of apathy and called them to conversion. At the same time, the prophets identified with the suffering of their people, which enabled the prophets to move their audience to transform their lives. Since prophets were so stinging in their condemnations and radical in their message, they usually offended the powerbrokers. Most of the prophets came to tragic ends.

We can see parallels in the lives of today's prophets. Martin Luther King, Jr., stood up to American racial prejudice, gave his people new dignity, and fought for civil rights. He helped transform racial attitudes, but as a result made many enemies and was eventually murdered. Nelson Mandela challenged the evil system of apartheid in South Africa and demanded equality and justice for his people. Ultimately, apartheid was dismantled, but by that time Mandela had spent most of his life in prison.

John the Baptist

As mentioned earlier, the Jewish people had not seen a genuine prophet for some time and many longed for one. Suddenly, John the Baptist burst on the scene: a desert ascetic who wore animal skins and ate locusts and honey. He was outraged at the immorality of the royalty and the hypocrisy so rampant among his people. John brought a message of judgment and a threat of punishment to those who had been unfaithful to Yahweh. He called his people to repentance, and summoned them to come into the Jordan River to be washed clean. Apparently John even dared to charge Herod with immorality, and for that he was arrested and beheaded.

John the Baptizer was indeed a prophet in his own right and was likely an important mentor for Jesus himself. The gospels tend to bypass this, and in an effort to demonstrate that only Jesus is the savior, they stress John's role as the forerunner of Jesus, the one who prepares the way for his mission. Both Jesus and John called their people to repentance and alerted them to the kingdom, but John's fire and brimstone approach stands in stark contrast to Jesus' accent on mercy and forgiveness. John's reclusive asceticism also differs from Jesus, who was known to eat and drink with sinners, and who valued community.

Jesus the prophet

Clearly Jesus was considered to be a prophet in his day. In Mark's gospel Jesus is thought to possibly be John the Baptist returned from the dead (Mk 6:14), or Elijah, or possibly a new prophet. In Matthew the crowd describes Jesus as "the prophet Jesus from Nazareth" (Mt 21:11), and in Luke they proclaim that "a great prophet has risen among us" (Lk 7:16). When Jesus asks his own disciples how he is perceived by others, they tell him he is thought to be one of the prophets.

Jesus seems to recognize his prophetic role. Like past prophets, he seems to be aware of a special calling to speak and act through divine power. In the synagogue in Nazareth, he identified his mission of liberation with that of Isaiah (Lk 4:21). When his authority is challenged in Nazareth, Jesus remarks: "Prophets are not without honor, except in their hometown, and among their own kin, and in their own house" (Mk 6:4).

There were distinctive marks to Jesus' prophetic mission. Unlike other prophets, he did not attempt to offer credentials with phrases like "Thus says the Lord." Nor did he claim to have experienced ecstatic states, visions, or some dramatic call to speak for God. Instead, Jesus spoke on his own authority, always attempting to share his search for God and his unique intimacy with God with others. At times the gospel writers have Jesus speak of judgment and punishment, but more often he proclaims God's constant and eternal love for his people. Jesus' message is generally not one of wrathful vengeance but of gracious mercy, especially toward sinners and those on the margins of life.

Jesus brings the "good news" of salvation to his people through his preaching as well as through his mighty deeds. At first his preaching caused amazement and astonishment in the audience. They had heard about God's love before, but never had they seen this truth so vividly proclaimed and lived so fervently as in this carpenter from Nazareth. Here was a man, who was not only a gifted preacher, but one who actually lived his message, and who through his miracles demonstrated that the power of God was its source.

Jesus' personal gifts, power, and message called for a radical decision. A person either had to accept his message or declare him to be a false prophet and an agent of the devil. Jesus was too much a force to be simply ignored.

From the beginning of Jesus' ministry, some of the religious leaders of the time chose to condemn him rather than change their perspectives and behavior. After all, they had it all sorted out "correctly." The wealthy and the powerful were the righteous, while the vast majority who worked in the grinding heat, struggled with debts, taxes, sickness, and disabilities were those in need of salvation. Jesus turned the whole system on its head. He called the destitutes and the nobodies "blessed," and condemned the greedy oppressors who lorded it over them politically and religiously. His message took aim at the corruption in the Roman and Jewish political, social, and religious systems. Moreover, Jesus' mighty deeds of healing demonstrated that God's power was on the side of those who were victims of these systems. In this kingdom, the blind, the crippled, the destitute, and the outcast were at the center of God's concern and love. The gospel writers clearly use the prophetic model as a kind of template to organize the words and actions of Jesus' mission. His teachings are often framed in prophetic tones, and his miracles are commonly described as signs that divinely validate his message. Symbolic actions are the hallmark of Jesus' prophetic ministry.

The gospels describe Jesus as an eschatological prophet, one who predicted the endtime. Contemporaries of Jesus had differing views of what this endtime meant. For some, it meant that a military messiah would lead them to victory over the Romans and restore the kingdom of Israel. For others, it meant the apocalyptic destruction of the world as they knew it, and the ushering in of a new messianic era where Israel would be restored and would draw all nations to itself in peace. It is debatable where Jesus himself stood on all this. It is likely that he sensed that a turning point in history was at hand. Perhaps he "saw" that the corruption and violence of his time would ultimately lead to the destruction of Jerusalem and the Temple. At one point, Jesus shed tears over the city, lamenting that if his people would only listen to his message of love and nonviolence, the devastation could be avoided. Was this story simply the gospel writer, who had already witnessed the destruction of Jerusalem, projecting back in time? Or did Jesus actually have a sense of what would happen to the city if the oppression, exploitation, hypocrisy, legalism, violence and self-righteousness were not ended?

The new Moses

Moses was the greatest of the Jewish prophets, and in the gospels Jesus is portrayed as the new Moses. In Matthew's nativity story Jesus is saved from a slaughter of children by Herod, just as Moses was saved from a similar slaughter by Pharaoh. Like Moses, the infant is in exile in Egypt and then "comes out," now free to live in his homeland (a mini-exodus). Like Moses bringing the law of God from Mount Sinai, Jesus preaches his Sermon on the Mount. In John's gospel, Philip, who was recently called by Jesus, tells his brother: "We have found him about whom Moses in the law and also the prophets wrote, Jesus son of Joseph from Nazareth" (Jn 1:45). It is possible that the accounts of Jesus calming the storm and walking on the water are stories that parallel Moses' parting of the Red Sea.

In the tradition of the prophets

In Luke's gospel, Jesus begins his ministry in the tradition of Isaiah. In the synagogue in Nazareth, he takes up the scroll, reads the passage where the prophet explains how he has been anointed by God to preach to the poor, and bring freedom and healing. Jesus said: "Today this Scripture has been fulfilled in your hearing" (Lk 4:21). Jesus' neighbors are so infuriated that they want to kill him! Avoiding the danger, Jesus proceeds to carry out the mission that he announced in the synagogue throughout the gospel stories.

In a later chapter, Luke portrays Jesus raising the only son of a widow from the dead, which is reminiscent of a similar miracle by Elijah. The people are frightened by this miracle and cry out: " A great prophet has risen among us" (Lk 7:16). Luke later points out that Herod is concerned that Jesus is Elijah returned or one of the other ancient prophets. At Luke's transfiguration scene, both Moses and Elijah are seen to be conversing with Jesus. A voice from heaven then proclaims that Jesus is more than a prophet—he is God's own Son. These examples give further evidence of how closely Jesus' followers came to see him as part of the prophetic tradition.

Jesus' baptism

John the Baptist is portrayed in gospels as the one whom Isaiah prophesied would prepare the way. His prophetic mission was to make the way straight for another prophet, Jesus. John proclaims that his baptism is of water and looks forward to Jesus' baptism with the Holy Spirit. At Jesus' baptism,

John is portrayed as feeling unworthy to baptize Jesus. But Jesus insists and is baptized, and his prophetic mission becomes immediately validated by Abba. A voice from the heavens says: "This is my Son, the Beloved, with whom I am well pleased" (Mt 3:17). In the gospel of John, the Baptist gives his final testimony to Jesus: "He whom God has sent speaks the words of God" (Jn 3:3). Once John is executed, Jesus goes out into the desert and prepares for his own mission.

The cleansing of the temple

In the synoptic gospels Jesus rode into Jerusalem on a colt never before ridden and is honored by crowds who spread their cloaks and leafy branches on the road. They welcomed Jesus as one coming in the name of the Lord, as a son of David coming to restore the kingdom. A humble carpenter riding on a donkey stands as a parody of the glorious entrances that Roman officials made into the city on decorated steeds. Jesus' kingdom of love and peace would stand in stark contrast to the kingdoms of wealth and power. Later this challenging entry into Jerusalem would contribute to Jesus' condemnation. This kind of "King of the Jews" was not acceptable.

Jesus' first act in the city was prophetic: he drove out the merchants and money changers, shouting that they had made a house of prayer into a den of thieves. This symbolic cleansing challenges the high priest families, who lived off the huge profits from the Temple sales and taxes, and enjoyed luxurious lifestyles, while so many of their people struggled for subsistence in the rural areas. When the chief priests and scribes hear of this they want to kill him but fear the crowds who are astonished at Jesus' teaching. Quietly and ominously, they leave the city under the cover of darkness to hatch a plot.

The synoptic gospels cite this incident in the Temple as a turning point in Jesus' ministry. It was the last straw for his enemies, and his crucifixion would soon follow. Jesus had healed the lame and the blind in the Temple, and it was there that children cried out: "Hosanna to the son of David." Now Jesus had the audacity to challenge the corrupt marketplace on the Temple grounds. This incident is portrayed by the gospel writers as a prophetic sign of Jesus' execution, as well as a sign of the fall of Jerusalem and the destruction of the Temple, which they had truly witnessed in their time. Jesus would die within days after this cleansing of the Temple, and by the time the gospels were written, forty years later, the Temple, the entire city of

Jerusalem, and the Judaism of the high priests and Sandedrin would be destroyed.

In John's version, where the cleansing of the Temple occurs at the beginning of his ministry, Jesus is described as being filled with a zeal reminiscent of the ancient prophets, as he clears his Father's house of the merchants and money changers. When Jesus says; "Destroy this temple, and in three days I will raise it up" (Jn 2:19), the story prophetically points to the destruction of the Temple as well the death and resurrection of Jesus. This statement is brought up in Jesus' trial.

Signs in John

John's gospel focuses on signs that reveal the authenticity of Jesus' prophetic role. At Cana, when his mother informs him of the lack of wine, Jesus is not ready for his mission. Then, apparently on her behalf, he turns water into wine and saves the wedding feast. The gospel tells us that this was a sign that revealed Jesus' glory and brought his disciples to begin to believe in him. On another occasion in Cana, Jesus promised to cure the son of a royal official, possibly a prophetic sign that his mission would go beyond Judaism.

The story of the multiplication of the loaves and fishes to feed a large crowd is reminiscent of the exodus story where Hebrews were fed manna in the desert. After being fed, the people proclaim: "This is indeed the prophet who is to come into the world" (Jn 6:14). But in this case we are told that Jesus knows that they have misread his role and want to carry him off as a king. To avoid this, Jesus withdraws to be alone on a mountain.

In the intriguing story of the man born blind, Jesus declares that he is the "light of the world" and restores the man's sight. When the man goes to the Pharisees to show them, they are incredulous, saying that the cure was a sin because it was performed on the Sabbath. When they ask the cured man what he thinks of Jesus, he says: "He is a prophet" (Jn 9:17). When he persists in this belief in Jesus, they say: "You are that man's disciple; we are the disciples of Moses." The man persists in his belief and Jesus personally reveals himself to him as the Son of Man.

Other prophetic signs

Other incidents in the gospels are presented as similar prophetic "forthtellings" of what is to come. The choice of the Twelve symbolizes that Jesus is attempting to shape a new Israel with twelve new tribal heads. The primacy given to Peter points to the future leadership within this reform. Jesus' selection of women and outcasts as disciples points to his desire for equality within his community. And his cure of the Syro-Phoenician's daughter and the servant of the Roman centurion indicate the extension of the gospel message of salvation beyond Judaism to the Gentiles.

The last supper

The gospel accounts of Jesus' final meal contain many prophetic words and gestures. In Mark's version, Jesus takes the bread from the passover meal, blesses and breaks it, identifies it with himself, and then shares it with his disciples. He then takes a cup of wine, gives thanks, and identifies the wine with his blood "which is poured out for many" (Mk 14:24). Then Jesus says that he will not drink wine again until he drinks new wine in the kingdom of God, a clear prophetic statement about the future. In Luke's account, Jesus says he will not eat the passover meal itself "until the kingdom of God comes" (Lk 22:18).

John's account of the time leading up to the passion is markedly different. At Bethany, Jesus interprets his friend Mary's anointing as a sign of his burial. Just before the supper, the gospel writer compares the Jews' disbelief in Jesus to their earlier rejection of Isaiah. At the supper itself, the washing of the feet is featured instead of the breaking of bread, to accent the humility and service that are to be the hallmarks of the Jesus movement. Extensive discourses by Jesus at the meal contain many prophetic statements. Jesus speaks of the coming of the Spirit with love and peace. The image of the vine symbolizes the unity that is Jesus' ideal. Jesus then prays for oneness in the world and closes with the words of the last of the prophets: "I made your name known to them, and I will make it known, so that the love with which you have loved me may be in them, and I in them" (Jn 17:26).

The last days

The gospel accounts of Jesus' final days are replete with prophetic overtones. In Mark's account Jesus acknowledges that he is the messiah and predicts his coming in the future. With appropriate irony, Pilate persistently refers to Jesus as "King of the Jews." The soldiers dress Jesus accordingly and mock him as a King. The title is then affixed to his cross. The son of David is to reign over suffering, sin, and death. As Jesus dies, someone offers him a sponge soaked in wine and says: ""Wait, let us see whether Elijah will come to take him down." When Jesus finally expires, the temple veil is torn from top to bottom as a symbol of the divisions in later Judaism over Jesus. A Gentile centurion testifies: "Truly this man was God's Son" (Mk 15:36–39).

Luke adds some interesting details to the passion. When Herod returns Jesus to Pilate, Luke gives the curious detail that from that day forward Herod and Pilate were friends. This can only be a creation of the gospel writers and symbolized the peacemaking so characteristic of Jesus' prophetic mission. When the women of Jerusalem weep along the way to Calvary, Jesus prophetically tells them to instead weep for themselves and their children. Only future generations will even begin to understand the tragedy of this death. From the cross Jesus murmurs words of forgiveness, even as he is mocked as messiah and king, symbolizing the future saving power of this event. Then Jesus promises paradise to the criminal on his right, another prophetic statement of his saving power. In this account, a Gentile centurion glorifies God and declares Jesus to be innocent, a harbinger of the future of the community.

John's account of the passion introduces new prophetic themes. When Jesus is arrested in the garden, he refers to himself as "I am," an obvious allusion to the future belief in his divinity that will commence after the resurrection. In an exchange with Pilate, Jesus acknowledges that he was born to be a king, but that his kingdom is not of this world. Jesus then says: "Everyone who belongs to the truth listens to my voice" (Jn 18:37). Once again Jesus is crucified as King of the Jews, but before he dies he gives his mother to his beloved disciple, a symbol of the beginning of the community. A sprig of hyssop, the same plant used to anoint the doorposts of the Hebrews with the blood of the lamb before the exodus, is used to offer Jesus wine. Jesus takes the wine and completes his sacrifice with the words: "It is finished" (Jn 19:30).

Summary

For Christians, Jesus is the greatest of all teachers and the last of the ancient prophets. Though parallels can be drawn between Jesus and other teachers of his time, he stands as unique in the way his life, words, and actions carried the word of God to the world. His message on the kingdom is beyond comparison. Jesus also stands in the honored tradition of the prophets. But here, Jesus is also distinctive in that he taught with his own authority and in his many symbolic actions went far beyond the ancient prophets. Perhaps Jesus' followers first recognized him as an outstanding prophet, and then only after the resurrection came to see him as the Christ, their messiah and savior.

Questions for reflection and discussion

1. Discuss a teacher who had a significant influence on you. What were some of the characteristics of this teacher?
2. Which teachings of Jesus are important to you?
3. Dramatize several parables in groups and discuss the meanings of these parables.
4. What is the main function of a prophet? Who are some important prophets in recent history?
5. What is your understanding of the kingdom of God?

Sources

Charlesworth, James H., and Loren T. Johns, eds. *Hillel and Jesus: Comparative Studies of Two Major Religious Leaders.* Minneapolis: Fortress Press, 1997.

Carter, Warren, and John Paul Heil. *Matthew's Parables: Audience-Oriented Perspectives.* Washington, DC: Catholic Biblical Association of America, 1998.

Crossan, John Dominic. *The Historical Jesus: The Life of a Mediterranean Jewish Peasant.* San Francisco: HarperSanFrancisco, 1991.

Ford, Richard Q. *The Parables of Jesus: Recovering the Art of Listening.* Minneapolis: Fortress Press, 1997.

Fuellenbach, John. *The Kingdom of God: The Message of Jesus Today.* Maryknoll, NY: Orbis Books, 1995.

Gowler, David B. *What Are They Saying about the Parables?* New York: Paulist Press, 2000.

Hooker, Morna D. *The Signs of a Prophet: The Prophetic Actions of Jesus.* Harrisburg, PA: Trinity Press International, 1997.

Longenecker, Richard N., ed. *The Challenge of Jesus' Parables.* Grand Rapids: W. B. Eerdmans Pub. Co., 2000.

Malina, Bruce. *The Social Gospel of Jesus: The Kingdom of God in Mediterranean Perspective.* Minneapolis: Fortress Press, 2001.

McKenna, Megan. *Parables: The Arrows of God.* Maryknoll, NY: Orbis Books, 1994.

Neusner, Jacob. *A Rabbi Talks with Jesus,* rev. ed. Montreal: McGill-Queen's University Press, 2000.

Perkins, Pheme. *Hearing the Parables of Jesus.* New York: Paulist Press, 1981.

―――. *Jesus as Teacher.* New York: Cambridge University Press, 1990.

Robbins, Vernon K. *Jesus the Teacher: A Socio-Rhetorical Interpretation of Mark,* with a new introduction. Minneapolis: Fortress Press, 1992.

Westermann, Claus. *The Parables of Jesus in the Light of the Old Testament.* Translated and edited by Friedemann W. Golka and Alastair H. B. Logan. Minneapolis: Fortress Press, 1990.

Witherington, Ben, III. *Jesus the Sage: The Pilgrimage of Wisdom.* Minneapolis: Fortress Press, 1994.

CHAPTER FOUR

Worker of Mighty Deeds

On Pentecost Peter stood before the crowd gathered in Jerusalem and proclaimed: "You that are Israelites, listen to what I have to say: Jesus of Nazareth, a man attested to you by God with deeds of power, wonders, and signs that God did through him among you" (Acts 2:22). This passage gets to the heart of the meaning of Jesus' miracles. Miracles were presented as actions of God's power, which gave the divine stamp of approval to Jesus and his mission. They were explosive events, which revealed that Jesus was an instrument of God's energy, a prophet of the Creator's rule over the world. After the Lord's resurrection, these mighty deeds reassured his followers that he was indeed the Son of God and Savior.

According to the gospels, miracles were a significant part of Jesus's mission. There are in the gospels thirty-one different miracle stories, including six exorcisms, seventeen healings including three raisings from the dead) and eight nature miracles (including wondrous feedings, calming storms, and walking on water). And in the synoptic gospels, all such miraculous activity is carried out in one year! This is unprecedented in Jewish religious history.

In this chapter, we will look at some notions about the nature of miracles, discuss miracles in ancient cultures and religions, and suggest the meanings attached to some of the miracles in each gospel.

What is a miracle?

The *Oxford English Dictionary* defines "miracle" as "a remarkable and welcome event that seems impossible to explain by means of the known laws of nature and is therefore attributed to a supernatural agency." This definition is meant to describe the miracles in the Bible, as well as many events depicted in the literature of Buddhist, Hindu, Islam, Sufi, and other religions. It also points to events in the lives of religious figures, the many healings associated with religious shrines, the experiences of God's power that is required in the Catholic canonization process, as well as the often private and yet nonetheless amazing experiences that people of faith have everyday.

This dictionary definition is not, however, one which the biblical world would recognize. In the prescientific era, the Hebrews had little notion of "the laws of nature." In fact, the ancient Hebrews did not use the word "nature," because they saw all reality as "God's creation." The Hebrew God was a God of history, always active in the creation. For the Jews, all reality came from the hand of God, including sunsets, floods, or plagues. The only exceptions were physical afflictions and disabilities, and those were commonly believed to come from the power of Satan.

There is another problem with the modern dictionary definition of miracle. It seems to be based on a dualistic perspective, viewing the world as a split-level reality with natural and supernatural levels. From this point of view, if an event cannot be explained by natural causes, it is attributed to supernatural causes. By way of contrast, the world today is approached holistically by people of faith as one reality with many dimensions, including the material and the spiritual. Miracles today, then, are events that go beyond any reasonable explanation and are therefore considered by people of faith to be acts of God.

Miracles are extraordinary events that go beyond ordinary experience. As described in the synoptic gospels, miracles are wondrous events that accompany Jesus' teaching, They are amazing deeds that demonstrate God's power over Satan and teach that God's kingdom is at hand in the mission of Jesus. This is especially apparent in John's gospel, where miracles are "works" of the Creator and "signs' that point to the divine identity of Jesus. They are signs that God is at work through this humble preacher from Nazareth, healing, forgiving, and bringing new life. All four gospels present these amazing events in stories, stories often based on original experiences, but embellished with theological meaning relevant to the early communities.

Skepticism toward miracles

Throughout history, many individuals have had serious problems with the phenomenon of miracles. The great Roman writer, Cicero, thought it ridiculous to believe that the gods intervened through miraculous actions. In the gospels, some of the religious leaders in Jesus' time were of the mind that such powerful acts on his part could only come from Satan. This position actually moved Jesus' enemies to conspire to kill him because his cures were thought to be expressions of evil powers.

In the modern era, Thomas Jefferson held that miracle stories were simply part of the "rubbish" under which the great moral teachings of Jesus were buried. Jefferson considered himself part of an "enlightened" generation, which considered it absurd to think that the God in the heavens would go against his own reasonable laws of nature. In the same period, the great French writer, Voltaire, wrote that it is inconceivable that an infinitely wise God would set the rules for the world and then choose to violate them. Other eighteenth-century scholars followed the arguments of David Hume (d. 1776) that human experience is the ground of human knowledge; and since miracles are beyond the human experience of the laws of nature, they are not credible.

With the appearance of the modern scientific age, which deals in facts, observation, mathematical demonstration, and clear proofs, miracles came to be relegated to the level of myths of the ancient past. For many today, the theories and findings of modern science better serve to explain the workings of reality than belief in the power of God.

Diverse views among biblical scholars

Some biblical scholars have also rejected miracles. Rationalist scholars, who denied the possibility of the supernatural, viewed miracles as mythical stories placed in the gospels to teach or even to deceive. Even scholars who have approached the Scriptures with faith have had their doubts about miracles. Bultmann, a leading Protestant biblical scholar, maintained that it is impossible to be part of the modern world of science and still believe in miracles. He held that miracles are merely part of the mythology used to convey the teachings of Jesus on how to live human life. His views have been very influential on many biblical scholars.

On the other extreme in biblical studies, there are fundamentalists who take the Scriptures literally. The so-called Creationists maintain that the creation stories are in fact scientific accounts of how the world came to be, and that the miracle stories of the gospels are exact historical accounts of the miracles that Jesus performed. Television evangelists generally take the miracle stories literally, and attempt to re-enact them through their own cures before the cameras.

The literal approach to Scripture is common among Christians, in spite of the fact that the critical historical approach is now prominent in scriptural studies. (This approach was officially approved by the Catholic Church in 1942 and was reconfirmed by the Second Vatican Council.) Many of the clergy, both Protestant and Catholic, still continue to preach about miracles from the literal perspective, and many Christians, even with college degrees, seem to be unaware of the contextual approach to the Scriptures and miracle stories.

The middle ground

The majority of biblical scholars accept a certain historical basis for some of the miracles, but recognize that the miracle stories were developed, and even at times created, in order to present the faith of the early communities. Most scholars acknowledge that the historical event is not the central issue in the miracle stories, and that it is impossible to determine the facts of what actually happened in every miracle story.

The biblical scholars who write from the position of faith are willing to grant the possibility of the miracles, since all things are possible with God. There are scholars who both accept and understand modern science, and yet at the same time realize that science often discovers more mystery than it explains. In other words, science continues to discover the open-ended complexity behind the so-called laws of nature, and many of their studies leave us with more questions than answers. Moreover, there is a spiritual dimension to all of reality that is beyond scientific analysis. Science can tell us much about the "what" and the "how" of reality, but little about the "why" or about the deeper meanings of reality. Miracles seem to defy the ordinary rules of cause and effect and point to depths of reality that are beyond the reach of science and reason.

Miracles in the Hebrew Scriptures

Jesus' uniqueness as a miracle worker is evident when one considers how rare miracle stories are in the Hebrew Scriptures. In the thousands of years of Jewish history, the only significant accounts of miracles are associated with Moses during the time of the Exodus, with the Elijah and Elisha cycles in the books of Kings, and with a few stories in the book of Daniel.

The stories in the Hebrew Scriptures about natural miracles are, according to most biblical scholars, largely mythical. In the saga of Moses, there are a number of wondrous signs: the burning bush, the plagues sent to the Egyptians, the parting of the Red Sea, the manna in the desert, the pillar of smoke leading the way, and the water coming from a rock. The Joshua stories tell off hailstones coming down on the Amorites, the sun and moon stopping in the heavens to prevent the enemies of the Jews from fleeing at night, and the walls of Jericho miraculously collapsing. The first book of Kings tells of Elijah performing wondrous signs to defeat the enemy, and of his calling down fire to verify his sacrifice to the priests of Baal. The book of Daniel describes a miraculous saving of the faithful from a fiery furnace and a lion's den.

Healing miracles of cures and raisings from the dead are rare in the Hebrew Scriptures. Genesis tells of the healing of Abimelech and his family. Saul is healed of an evil spirit, Elijah restores the widow's son to life (1 Kgs 17) and Elisha performs a similar resuscitation (2 Kgs 4:32–37). There is simply no precedent in the Hebrew Scriptures for the number and kinds of healings performed by Jesus in the gospels. The curing of the deaf, the blind, the diseased, the disabled, and the number of exorcisms so typical of Jesus in his short ministry is unique.

Roman and Greek miracles

Neither is there a strong miracle tradition among the Romans. Tacitus and Suetonius recount stories of wondrous events, but these are generally concerned with portents, omens, and dreams. Accounts of cures are rare, such as the report by Tacitus that the Emperor Vespasian was able to perform cures of the blind and the crippled.

The Greeks, on the other hand, are more familiar with healings. Throughout the Mediterranean world there were shrines to the Greek god Asclepius, who was associated with healings from the time of Homer (eighth century BCE) to the time of Constantine (fourth century CE). The city of Epidaurus was the Lourdes of the ancient world, and many accounts of healings at that shrine have survived. These healings, however, were not attributed to human healers, but to the god Asclepius.

Some scholars have tried to compare the "divine man" Apollonius (d. 100 CE) to Jesus. Apollonius, a contemporary of Paul the apostle, was widely known as a holy man and miracle worker. His cures, which were quite limited in number, seem to have been done through natural therapy and special insight and were seen as displays of Apollonius' divinity. None of these elements appears in the miracles stories of Jesus.

Other ancient documents give examples of wonders such as individuals walking on water and raising the dead, but these are simply isolated events, and are not associated with any message or mission of one individual, as they are in the gospels.

There does not seem to be strong evidence that the gospel writers borrowed from the Greek miracle stories in order to portray Jesus as a charismatic healer. It is possible, however, that the gospel writers at times used Greek literary models for telling their miracle stories. For the most part, the gospel miracle stories seem to be told in the context of the Jewish belief in the healing power of Yahweh, rather than in the framework of Greek mythology or magic. The gospel miracle stories reflect the early Christian conviction that the saving power of God was experienced in both the life of the earthly Jesus and in the continuing work of Christ.

Apocryphal miracles

The apocryphal gospels, which offer valuable material from the so-called Gnostic Christian communities, have their own miracle stories. Some of these stories resemble the miracle stories in the canonical gospels, while others come from the magical tradition. In the gospel of Thomas the boy Jesus shapes some clay pigeons on the Sabbath, and then claps his hands and the birds come to life and fly away. In another story, some of Jesus' playmates spoil the pools of water that he is making, so in revenge he denounces them and causes one of them to fall down dead. In the Acts of Peter, the daughter of Peter is cured of an infirmity to prevent her from seducing the neighborhood lads. And Peter competes with Simon the Magician in stories wherein a dog is made to talk, a broken statue of Caesar is restored, and a fish hanging in the market is brought back to life. For the most part, the miracle stories in these "gospels" do not have the same tone or balance as do those in the canonical gospels.

Other wonder workers of the time

Throughout his lifetime, Jesus most likely would have encountered healers and wonder workers of one kind or another either passing through his village or working in nearby cities. There were the midwives who specialized in assisting women with the often dangerous procedure of childbirth. There were the local healers in the villages, who knew much about the use of herbs and potions for dealing with physical ailments and diseases. Wandering physicians, some with special Greek training, made their living attending the Roman legions. These healers were experts in diagnosis and the care of wounds, and could perform amputations.

Jesus would have most likely encountered magicians and wizards in his travels. These individuals generally worked in secret, and claimed to possess mysterious knowledge and power. They used magical formulas, incantations, and secret potions made from strange substances like garlic or goat's urine. These magicians often claimed to have access to divine power, as well as the ability to manipulate divine spirits, even evil spirits to achieve their ends. Magicians often got their results by overpowering the will of the person on whom they were working their magic. So-called "black magicians" could be hired to put a curse on an enemy. Others could be hired to perform exorcisms of evil spirits.

There were other self-proclaimed wonder workers, who gathered followers and promised to work mighty deeds for them. One such was Theudas, who promised his followers that if they marched with him to the Jordan he would make the waters part like a second Moses. An Egyptian prophet promised his disciples that if they marched with him around the walls of Jerusalem, he would cause the walls to fall. Others took their followers out to the desert, telling them to await the final apocalypse. Often such individuals were perceived by the Romans as troublemakers, and were summarily arrested and executed.

The uniqueness of Jesus' miracles

There are some similarities between Jesus and the other wonder workers of his time. At times, Jesus seems to be secretive, telling those he healed to tell no one. This secrecy, however, seems to have been enjoined to prevent the populace from misconstruing his mission and looking to him for political and military leadership. More frequently Jesus cures in the open, in public, at times surrounded by enormous crowds, and uses his miracles to teach about God's power and rule.

Jesus on occasion also used formulas. Two of them still survive in Aramaic, the language Jesus spoke. He said; "*Talitha qumi*" (girl arise), when he brought a child back to life, and "*Ephphatha*" (be opened) when he cured the deaf-mute (Mk 5:21ff, 7:31ff). Sometimes Jesus used spittle to touch the eyes or the tongue of the person being healed. And he used gestures such as putting fingers in the ears of a deaf person, or laying his hands on the one to be healed. Yet there is nothing ostensibly magical about any of this. They are simply the words and gestures of a healer. Generally, Jesus' cures are brought about with a simple prayer for the power of God to shine forth.

Nor did Jesus promise his followers any great portents such as parting the waters or destroying walls. As for the endtime, he admitted that he did not know when it was to come. His miracles were not done to draw crowds or solicit followers. They were for the most part simply acts of compassion and love, offered to those most in need.

Unlike some of the "divine men" of the time, Jesus makes no claim of divinity or superpowers for himself. His miracles all point to the sovereign power of God over evil. Nor does Jesus attempt to control, manipulate, or enchant the person healed. All he asks of those who come to him is an openness to God's power. Jesus resists those who require "signs," and with little fanfare he freely serves as an instrument of divine creative power. Jesus was without a doubt unique among his peers in his manner of working wondrous deeds.

The historicity of miracles

An important question about the gospel miracles always is: "Did they really happen?" At face value, the miracles seem to be rather far-fetched and quite beyond normal human experience. Is it possible that during this special time of history when Jesus lived all these very extraordinary events actually took place? Or could it be that these are simply mythical stories used by the gospel writers to show that Jesus had divine powers? As mentioned earlier, many biblical scholars stand somewhere in the middle of these two positions, holding that there is some historical basis for many of the healing and exorcism stories. Fewer hold that the natural miracles (walking on water and calming storms) have any historical basis.

Perhaps the most convincing argument for the historicity of miracle stories is the central role they play in the gospels themselves. Mark's gospel, the earliest, devotes nearly one-half of his account of Jesus' public ministry to the miraculous. About one-fifth of the literary units in the synoptics allude to miracles of healing and exorcism, and a significant portion of the Johannine gospel is concerned with miraculous "signs." Much of this material is in the early strata of the gospel sources and is even linked to the earliest "sayings of Jesus." Without the miracle stories, the synoptic gospels simply would not hold together as probative testimonies of the significance of Jesus' words and deeds. Miracle stories are just too integral to the gospel message to be pure myth. The memories of Jesus as miracle worker and of the great crowd response to his wondrous deeds are far too central to the gospel message to simply be symbolic. Moreover, since miracles are attested to by all the gospels, and are congruous with the character of the historical Jesus as portrayed in the gospel, we may reasonably conclude that they have some historical foundation. It is also indicative that even hostile Jewish sources do not deny that Jesus worked wondrous deeds. Josephus, the Jewish historian, remarks that Jesus was known for his "startling deeds," and the Talmud, while not denying Jesus' wondrous acts, writes him off as a sorcerer.

One can accept that there is a historical basis for the miracle stories, and still recognize that these stories have been reworked, edited, theologized, and at times created. From this perspective, the miracle stories are not eyewitness accounts of what happened; rather, they are "faith accounts," written primarily to proclaim the faith of the early communities in the risen Lord.

The main issue for the communities that produced these gospel stories, then, was not "what happened," but rather the meaning of these events of Jesus' life in the light of resurrection faith. The "what happened?" is our modern question. It is a question that arises from our post-Enlightenment concern for the facts and analysis. The ancient world had little access to the facts of the past and was not therefore concerned with such pictorial accounts. For them, the past was always wrapped in myth and story.

For the Jew of Jesus' time, the religious past was only relevant if it could be brought to bear on the present. The great event of the Exodus was considered to be historical, but it was carried forth each Passover in the form of a growing myth as it encountered the current situation. Likewise, the early Christians looked back on the memories of Jesus as a miracle worker and reinterpreted these memories in the light of their present beliefs and struggles. There are many layers in a miracle story, including the original memory of what happened (which can never be clearly recovered), along with the many strata of meaning and interpretation that the story gained in the telling.

In discussing the historicity of gospel miracles, it is important to distinguish between miracle events and miracle stories. There seems to be little doubt that wondrous events occurred during Jesus' life. Otherwise, the later gospel stories seem to have little purpose or meaning. At the same time, we have no way of ascertaining what exactly happened when these events took place. The stories have become too stylized and filled with religious insights for us to be able to peel all that away and recover the original event. Therefore, we can assume that extraordinary events surrounded the mission of Jesus. As to what actually happened we are left to speculate.

As mentioned earlier, the historical basis for Jesus' healing miracles and exorcisms is widely accepted by biblical scholars. At the same time, many scholars are convinced that the miracle stories are more theological than they are factual. What we seem to have in the formulation of the gospel miracle tradition is an author or community taking "the kinds of things" that Jesus did, and using them as a basis for creating a miracle story. These stories then proclaim Jesus to be an instrument of God's power. There is a development here. Jesus did wondrous deeds to teach about the nature of God, and the later communities developed stories around these deeds to teach about Jesus, their Christ.

Do miracles prove anything?

Traditionalists have often viewed the gospel miracles as proof of Jesus' divinity. Those who do not make the distinction between the Jesus of history and the Christ of faith assume that Jesus walked about Galilee as the Christ, performing miracles to demonstrate that he was indeed divine. As we saw earlier, Jesus neither claimed to be divine, nor used miracles to prove such claims. When he did perform miracles he did so through the power of God, whom he believed had sent him. In John's gospel, Jesus says: "I can do nothing on my own....the very works that I am doing, testify on my behalf that the Father has sent me" (Jn 5:30, 36).

The gospel language about miracles generally avoids any notion that these deeds were performed as demonstrations or displays. The gospels avoid the Greek word for miracle (*thauma*), a word used in pagan literature for sensational acts. The word commonly used in the synoptic gospels for miracles is "*dynameis*" (the root of our word for "dynamic" and "dynamite"). This word refers to acts of power, specifically acts of God's power. The gospel of John uses the words "*erga*" (works) or "*semeia*" (signs) to refer to miracles, events that demonstrate God's work through Jesus and which point to his divine identity.

Jesus' rejection of sensational acts is made evident in the gospels. When challenged by the Pharisees to show a sign of God's approval, he sighed deeply and said: "Why does this generation ask for a sign? Truly I tell you, no sign will be given to this generation" (Mk 8:12). Jesus especially refuses signs to those hostile to his message. In the temptation stories, Jesus refuses to perform such stunts as changing stones into bread or jumping safely from great heights. On one occasion Jesus even shows testiness when sincerely asked by a government official to heal his son. Jesus says: "Unless you see signs and wonders, you will not believe" (Jn 4:48). Only the persistence of the man's faith moves Jesus to perform a healing. Jesus' mission was not carried out to prove anything, but rather to reveal the presence and power of the living God. His wondrous deeds demonstrated that all of God's children, especially outcasts, had access to divine power. Such wondrous deeds would be shown only to those who in faith were open to God's power through Jesus.

Another indication that the gospel miracles were not performed as proofs is the fact that they are largely omitted in the letters of Paul and in other New Testament Scriptures. It thus seems to have been acceptable to spread the good news of the Lord without any reference to the gospel miracles. Clearly for Paul, the resurrection stands as the event that validates Jesus' mission, and not the wondrous deeds that he did during his life.

Finally, the diversity of reactions to Jesus' gospel miracles demonstrates that such deeds did not serve as proofs for the observers. In fact, many persons reacted negatively to Jesus' miracles. Some, even his own family members, thought he had lost his senses, while others thought it quite presumptuous that a simple Galilean should do such deeds. Some thought that Jesus was doing the work of Satan. Others were simply filled with wonder and nothing else, while others were moved to faith. No doubt many of those who were cured became Jesus' loyal disciples, but it does not appear that people viewed such wonders as proof that he was divine. As we have seen, only John's gospel, written some sixty years after the death of Jesus, associates miracles with his divinity.

Miracles and faith

Deep within the gospel miracle stories we can hear the early Christian communities struggling with questions concerning faith. As the stories are told, faith is usually needed before a miracle can take place. At times, it is the faith of the person seeking a healing. In the curious story of the woman who had hemorrhaged for many years, she desperately reaches out to touch the cloak of Jesus. Mark says that Jesus was aware that "power had gone forth from him," and after inquiring who touched his cloak, he told the woman: "Your faith has made you well" (Mk 5:25–34). In the case of the leper wanting cleansing, it is his simple faith that elicits the cure. He says to Jesus: "If you choose, you can make me clean" (Mk 1: 40).

On another occasion it is the faith of the supplicant's closest friends that seems to be crucial in the healing. In the story of the cure of the paralyzed man, his four friends are resourceful enough to carry him to the roof and lower him through the ceiling for healing. Luke says that when Jesus saw their faith, he forgave the man's sins and then went on to restore him to wholeness (Lk 5:18–26).

On still other occasions, it is faith on the part of the healer that is required. Matthew tells a story about Jesus' disciples not being able to cure a boy of epilepsy. Jesus is frustrated with his followers and tells them that they could not cure the boy "because of your little faith." Jesus tells them that with faith in God "nothing will be impossible for you" (Mt 17:20).

This faith that is so integral to miracles seems to be an openness to the power of God in one's life or in the life of another. Without such faith, both healer and the one to be healed can block the healing energy. Apparently, such openness is not self-achieved. It is pure gift, and the only contribution an individual can make is one of response and receptivity. Such faith is God-given grace and is a part of the miracle itself. Even Jesus stood in amazement at such faith when the centurion answered Jesus' offer to come and cure his servant with "Lord, I am not worthy for you to come under my roof; but only say the word and my servant will be healed." Jesus remarked: "Truly I tell you, in no one in Israel have I found such faith," and then in accord with that faith, Jesus healed the servant (Mt 8:10–13). Mark makes the astounding remark that even Jesus himself could work very few miracles in Nazareth because of the lack of faith there (Mk 6:5–6).

Karl Rahner has pointed out that faith in miracles presupposes the willingness to enter into the depths of one's existence and an openness to the element of wonder. He has said that today's materialist is too often locked into a one-dimensional reality and is thus unaware of the spiritual and mystical dimensions of life. Miracles have to do with these latter dimensions, and require a willingness to go beyond the observable and the measurable to the transcendent depths of reality.

Resurrection faith

We know that the miracle stories were not composed orally or in writing until after Jesus was raised from the dead. The early Christians saw this resurrection as the supreme miracle. From then on, they believed that Jesus was the Christ, and they now retold all that he said and did in light of their new Easter faith. Stories that originally required a faith in God's power were now told to reveal the power of Jesus as messiah and Son of God. Wondrous deeds that proclaimed the healing power of the creator were then proclaimed to be acts of the Christ. This transition is most apparent in the miracles of John's gospel.

Here miracles are presented as signs (*semeia*) that Jesus is the Christ. Jesus is revealed in his glory at Cana, as the "resurrection" at the raising of Lazarus, and as "the light of the world" in the healing of the blind man.

Miracles teach

It would seem that the main purpose of the miracle stories is to teach about the power of God and the power of Jesus as the Christ. Miracles complement the teachings of Jesus, demonstrating that he both speaks and acts in the name of God. The gospels make it clear that Jesus far surpasses Moses in miracles as he establishes a new covenant and gives a new law. The synoptic gospels use miracles to work alongside the parables and demonstrate the saving power of the kingdom. As people witness these events, they stand in amazement and learn how God's power defeats Satan's work in sickness, death, demonic possession, and even in destructive forces of nature. They see in Jesus' work the realization of Hebrew prophecies that God's dominion will one day be fulfilled in one who is to come. They learn that physical healing goes hand in hand with spiritual conversion. Here again in the synoptic gospels we learn more of the faith in the communities in Antioch and Rome than we do about what happened in the life of Jesus.

John's gospel uses miracle stories to teach in a unique fashion. Here the emphasis is on how Jesus is in continuity and indeed surpasses Moses in working signs for God's people. Jesus' miracles are prophetic signs that God works among people of faith. Miracles teach that Jesus is indeed the "way, the truth and the life." They are symbols that illuminate the identity of Jesus.

Each of the four gospels comes from a different Christian community and thus reflects varying beliefs and interpretations around miracles. In the following we will look at the richness of approaches to miracles in the four canonical gospels.

Miracles in Mark

Most of the synoptic miracle stories are preserved in the gospel of Mark. The other synoptic writers give variations of these and add some stories of their own. The gospel of Mark, which was written around 70 CE, possibly in Rome, begins in Galilee with a portrait of Jesus as teacher and miracle worker. In the early sections, this gospel is preoccupied with miracle stories, each preparing the reader for discipleship. Jesus himself has already been revealed at his baptism as the beloved Son of God, and has begun to select his followers. As Jesus approaches the synagogue to teach, he is approached by a man possessed by an unclean spirit, a spirit that recog-

nizes Jesus as the holy one of God. Jesus silences the spirit and cast
of the man. Mark says that those standing around are amazed at this
teaching with authority." The teaching, of course, is that Jesus has come
defeat the powers of evil. To be his disciple one must be on the side of the
God of goodness and wholeness. The very next story is the homely account
of the curing of Peter's mother-in-law in Capernaum, the center of Jesus'
new ministry. Through this story disciples are called to follow her example
and get up and serve others.

Throughout the following chapters a pattern emerges. Mark has Jesus
teach, work a miracle, and then teach again. It is as though each of these
miracle stories complements the teaching as well as demonstrates that the
power of God is genuinely in the parables and teaching of Jesus. Through
these stories the disciple also learns what he or she can expect of the Master.
He is a man of prayer who communes with God in deserted places. Jesus is
moved to pity the begging leper and cures him. He is stirred by the faith of
the paralytic's friend and forgives and heals him. He dines with sinners and
outcasts, freely putting the law of loving healing over the law of the Sabbath.
Jesus conquers evil and defiantly stands up to those who wrongly claim that
he casts out devils through the power of Satan. The first quarter of Mark's
gospel ends with the calming of the storm. We will never know what amazing event happened that night, but we do learn from the story surrounding
it that faith in Jesus enables the disciple to survive even the most tempestu-
ous events of life.

Mark opens the second quarter of his gospel with the exorcism of many
devils from the Gerasene. Once again, the story teaches that Jesus has come
to defeat the power of sin and evil. That miracle is followed by the story of
the hemorrhaging woman, a story of desperation and faith in the power of
Jesus to save. Next is the touching story of the resuscitation of Jairus'
daughter, a tale of Jesus' compassion and the giving of new life.

Those miracles are followed by more teaching on how disciples must be
free of possessions, and how they must go apart into desert places to meet
with their God.

The next miracle in Mark is the feeding of the five thousand, a story that
again underscores the deep compassion of Jesus, as well as the abundance
available to his disciples. That is followed by Jesus walking on water, a story
that teaches that Jesus represents the power of the Creator and continually

calls his disciples to be fearless and courageous. The series ends with Jesus going from town to town, healing as he goes.

Mark continues with his teaching-miracle pattern. Jesus teaches the Scribes and Pharisees what true uncleanness is and rebukes their empty legalism. Then follows the curing of the Syro-phoenician's daughter of an unclean spirit. The woman is a persistent Gentile, who unmasks Jesus' own prejudices and moves him to open his mission beyond Judaism. This story was no doubt of great importance to the many Gentiles entering the new Jesus movement. It is followed by the story of the healing of the deaf-mute, another feeding story and the healing of the blind man at Bethsaida. All explore Jesus' central theme about a healing and nurturing God meeting the needs of the people.

At the halfway point, Mark begins to get to his central point; the disciple will have to take up the cross and follow the crucified Jesus. The passion of Jesus is predicted, and Jesus is transfigured and once again recognized by God as the beloved Son. This is juxtaposed against the curing of a possessed boy, another lesson in faith. Jesus tells the father of the boy: "All things can be done for the one who believes." The father cries out a line that has echoed down through the centuries: "I believe; help my unbelief!"(Mk 9:23–24). Here and in the other exorcisms, it is demonstrated that God defeats the power of Satan.

Once again the passion is predicted and Jesus tells his disciples that they are to be "last," the servants of all. He teaches them that to receive little children is to receive him, and that sin against such little ones deserves great punishment. Jesus continues to teach about divorce, the value of children, and the dangers of riches and ambition among his disciples. The passion is predicted for a third time and then the striking story of the healing of blind Bartimeus is told, once again reiterating how it is faith that saves the disciple.

In the final six chapters Mark gets to the climax of his gospel: the cross that all must share. The miracles are over, and Jesus heads to Jerusalem for his passion and death. Jesus enters the city triumphantly, cleanses the Temple, continues to teach, gives his great commandment of love, condemns hypocrisy, and predicts the coming of the last days. Then the last events of his death are recounted, followed by the amazing news to the women at the grave: "He has risen." The final miracle, the ultimate work of God's power, triumphs over Satan, sin, and death.

Miracles in Matthew

The author of Matthew's gospel includes most of the miracles of Mark and adds some from other sources. This gospel presents a leaner version of the miracles, editing out many of the details and focusing directly on the person of Jesus. Here Jesus heals with a simple touch or word. Though the miracles still remain significant in this gospel, more attention is given to the development of the teaching of Jesus.

Matthew's gospel was likely written for both Jewish and Gentile audiences in Antioch. At times, the author seems to reach out to the Jewish Christians by linking the miracles with prophecies from the Hebrew Scriptures. The gospel begins with the miracle of the virginal conception of Jesus and presents this as the fulfillment of a prophecy in Isaiah that a virgin will bring forth a son. Jesus is portrayed as the new Moses, saved from a slaughtering despot, and called out of Egypt in a new exodus, as prophesied in Isaiah and Jeremiah.

The adult Jesus moves to Capernaum, calls some of his first disciples and begins his mission of teaching and "curing every disease and every sickness among the people" (Mt 4:23). The master teacher then begins his "sermon on the mount," an extended synopsis of his message. When Jesus comes down from the mountain as the new Moses, he begins a series of ten miracles that eclipse the power of the original Moses. Jesus first cures a leper, instructs him to be secretive lest his mission be misconstrued, and to offer the gift to the priest that Moses commanded. While healing outside the Temple and the priestly system, Jesus is still respectful of it.

Back in Capernaum, Jesus cures the centurion's servant, and once again the emphasis is on faith, as the kingdom is extended to the Gentiles (a theme that Matthew earlier deals with in the story of the magi). Jesus then cures Peter's mother-in-law and continues his teaching, interspersed with miracles, which again fulfill Isaiah's prophecy: "He took our infirmities..." (Mt 8:17).

The familiar theme of faith in the power of God is stressed in most of Matthew's miracle stories. The crowd's reaction is described at one point: "they were filled with awe, and they glorified God, who had given such authority to human beings" (Mt 9:8). Matthew alters some of Mark's miracle stories along the way. For instance, after Jesus walks on the water, Matthew has Peter try to join him, only to founder and then be saved by

Jesus. Peter is chided for his lack of faith and then proclaims the full post-resurrection faith of the Antioch community: "Truly you are the Son of God" (Mt 14:33).

As Jesus crosses over into the land of Genesaret, the crowds swell and the sick are healed by merely touching the tassel of his cloak. Clearly, the power of God radiates from this teacher-healer! Near the towns of Tyre and Sidon, Jesus encounters the Canaanite woman and the scope of his mission is challenged. At first, Jesus limits his work "to the lost sheep of the house of Israel" (Mt 15:24). But he then goes on to cure the woman's daughter, a sign that ultimately his mission would serve both Jew and Gentile; indeed it is for all nations.

The people of Galilee glorify God because the prophecy has been fulfilled wherein the dumb speak, the lame walk, and the blind see. Yet, as in Mark, Jesus refuses to give signs from heaven in order to pass the test of the Jewish leaders. He confronts those leaders for not being able to read the signs of the times and abruptly leaves them with a fierce statement: "An evil and adulterous generation asks for a sign, but no sign shall be given to it except the sign of Jonah" (Mt 16:4).

In chapter 16, Matthew's gospel begins the predictions of the central events of the death and resurrection of Jesus and develops a theology of the cross. The teaching of Jesus intensifies and the miracles fade into the background. Just before Jesus' entry into Jerusalem, Matthew inserts the story of the two blind men who persist over the shouts of angry crowds and cry for the mercy of Jesus. Jesus is moved with compassion, restores their sight, and they follow him. Again a miracle story teaches about the need for a persistent faith in Jesus in order to be saved.

Matthew continues with his strong portrait of Jesus as teacher. The great commandment of love is given, as well as dire predictions of the endtimes. In the famous "final judgment" scene, those who inherit the kingdom are those who bring relief and healing to the hungry, the thirsty, the homeless, naked, sick, and imprisoned. As prophesied in the Hebrew Scriptures, these are the benefactors of Jesus' miracles and the ones to whom the Christian mission of mercy is primarily directed.

The passion and death of Jesus are then described in detail, followed by the greatest miracle of all, the resurrection. Matthew develops the story at the tomb, telling how the women encounter Jesus, embrace his feet and worship him. The eleven then meet Jesus on a mountain in Galilee, where they worship him and receive the commission to baptize and make disciples of all nations. Here we are shown the faith of the early Christian communities in Jesus as the Christ, and their determination to carry on with his mission to the world.

Miracles in Luke

The author of Luke was a master of the Greek language and wrote both a gospel and the Acts of the Apostles. Luke is a great storyteller, creating such magnificent scenes as the annunciation, the visitation, and the birth of Jesus, as well as developing the unforgettable parables of the good Samaritan and the prodigal son. When dealing with miracles, Luke inexplicably omits six of the Markan stories, includes new ones from other sources, and leaves his own signature by using medical terms of the time.

In Luke's gospel Jesus begins his mission in Nazareth by identifying with the preaching and healing mission of Isaiah, where good news is proclaimed to the poor, captives are released, the blind are given sight, and the oppressed are liberated. His neighbors are amazed but question how all this can be the work of the lowly son of Joseph. Jesus says: "Doubtless you will quote to me this proverb, 'Doctor, cure yourself!' And you will say, 'Do here also in your hometown the things that we have heard you did at Capernaum'" (Lk 4:23). Then Jesus laments that prophets are not accepted in their own country and identifies with Elijah and Elisha who could do little healing in their own areas. The villagers are outraged at this and lead Jesus off to a hillside to throw him off. But Jesus simply passes through them and goes to Capernaum, where he is able to cure a demoniac and Peter's mother-in-law. Again, Jesus' miraculous power is connected with that of the prophets, and the connection between faith and miracles is strongly delineated. Clearly, Jesus' miracles are shown to be a stumbling block for nonbelievers.

Luke at times uses miracles as a means of attracting disciples. Before Jesus calls Simon Peter, he fills the boats with a miraculous catch. Simon is intimidated, but Jesus tells him not to be afraid and promises that from now on he will catch people. Simon, James, and John leave their boats and follow Jesus. Two more miracles follow, the curing of a leper and a paralytic, causing the people to glorify God. Soon after this Jesus called Levi the tax collector. Jesus' reputation for eating and drinking with sinners begins, and he explains: "Those who are well have no need of a physician, but those who are sick; I have come to call not the righteous but sinners to repentance" (Lk 5:31–32).

Another great disciple, Mary of Magdala, is called after having been cured of evil spirits and infirmities (there is no indication that she was ever a prostitute). Mary would play a central role in Jesus' ministry, death, and resurrection, and eventually would come to be known as "the apostle to the apostles." She stands as an outstanding symbol of the central role played by women in the Jesus movement.

The cure of the man with the withered hand is used to teach the Pharisees that the law of love is higher than the Sabbath law. After that Jesus prays through the night on a mountain and then calls the Twelve. He then begins his sermon on the plain, and Luke uniquely links the message and miracles when he writes that people had come "to hear him and to be healed of their diseases" (Lk 6:18). As the crowds reach out to touch him and be healed from the power that goes forth from him, Jesus preaches on the blessedness of the poor, the hungry, the sad, and predicts woe to the rich, the comfortable, and the sated. He advocates love of enemy, nonviolence, non-judgment, and generous giving. Later, Jesus enters Capernuam and heals the slave of a Roman centurion, again stressing the openness of his mission and the need for faith. Luke follows that miracle with one he adds, the raising of the son of the widow of Naim. This is a touching story that assures the early communities that a compassionate Jesus is with them in their sufferings and losses. In the story, the miracle moves the people to glorify God, recognize that a great prophet is among them, and believe that God "has looked favorably on his people" (Lk 7:16).

Miracles at times function as evidence of Jesus' prophetic calling. Luke juxtaposes Jesus' prophetic career with that of Elijah, who also raised a widow's son, and like Jesus ultimately ascended to the heavens. And like Elisha, Jesus works a miracle for a military leader and has power to cure leprosy. Unlike Elijah and Elisha, however, Jesus does not call fire or vengeance down upon his enemies.

The earlier theme of Jesus being in the tradition of Isaiah appears again when two disciples of the Baptist come to ask Jesus if he is the one who is to come. At that very hour, Jesus performed many cures and exorcisms, and then told John's disciples: "Go and tell John what you have seen and heard: the blind receive their sight, the lame walk, the lepers are cleansed, the deaf hear, the dead are raised, the poor have good news brought to them" (Lk 7:22–23). The miracles here are offered as validation for Jesus and his mission. Another miracle unique to Luke is that of the cleansing of the ten lepers. Only one, a foreigner (Samaritan), returns to give thanks. Jesus seems to be disgruntled with the lack of gratitude, and praises the man for his faith. The kingdom of God is revealed as open beyond the traditional boundaries of Judaism.

Finally, Luke's miracles are often victories over the powers of evil. Satan at times seems to prowl behind the scenes of Luke's gospel, causing a woman to be stooped for eighteen years, crying out from a demoniac in the synagogue, evincing unusual strength in a naked man who lived in the tombs of Gerasa, moving Judas to betray the Master, and sifting Peter like chaff. Jesus is portrayed as one who has the power to overcome the powers of evil and usher in the rule of the good God.

Luke's theme of the compassion and nonviolence of Jesus comes through again in the scene in the garden of Gethsemane. This is the only gospel where the soldier's ear, which has been cut off by one of the disciples, is healed. The miracle is prelude to Luke's account of the forgiveness of Jesus, which is exemplified by Jesus' words from the cross: "Father, forgive them; for they do not know what they are doing" (Lk 23:34).

Of course the ultimate miracle for Luke is the resurrection. Luke tells the unique stories about the disciples meeting the risen Lord on the road to Emmaus, about Jesus appearing to the disciples gathered in Jerusalem, and the ascension into heaven at Bethany. All these stories present Jesus as the risen and glorified Son of God and Savior.

Miracles in John

The gospel of John is the last to be written (c. 90 CE) and is quite distinctive in its theology of Jesus. From the outset, Jesus is the Word of God made flesh, the Christ, the messiah, the Son of God. The author of this gospel carefully reduces the number of miracle stories and omits the wonder and awe on the part of the people, possibly to avoid any confusion of Jesus with Greek wonder workers. The miracle stories here are extremely well-developed and are often focused on revealing the true identity of Jesus.

The Greeks words *erga* (works) and *semeia* (signs) are used for miracles in John's gospel. Here Jesus seems to heal with his own authority and relies on few rituals or words. Often the miracle stories in this gospel, with their use of water, wine, and bread, seem to point to the later sacramental life of the early churches.

The prologue identifies Jesus as the Word, the co-Creator, the light, the only-begotten Son of God. John the Baptist has already witnessed to the belief that Jesus is the Son of God, and the disciples follow Jesus as the Messiah. The first sign occurs at a wedding feast at Cana. This story reveals the decisive role that Jesus' Jewish mother played in his mission. (She ignores his protests and tells the attendants to do as he says.) Effortlessly, Jesus directs the stewards to fill the jars with water and serve the wine. There is no ritual, no words, and the action is clearly unlike any pagan miracle. The gospel says that the action manifested Jesus' glory and led his disciples to believe in him The event serves as a clear sign that Jesus' identity and mission are from God.

The next miracle, the curing of the royal official's son, is also set in Cana. At first Jesus appears annoyed by the request to come to Capernaum and heal the boy. He complains that the man will not believe unless he sees signs and wonders. The official sidesteps the debate about his faith and stays focused on what he wants—a cure before the child dies. Jesus simply says: "Go, your son will live" (Jn 4:50). Jesus never even sees the boy, and when the official returns home he finds his son cured. The man and his whole household accept the sign and believe. In this story one can hear the community of the beloved disciple celebrating Jesus as the source of life in their families and churches.

In the next story, Jesus heals a man who has been lying ill for many years and has been unable to get to the waters at Bethsaida. (There is possible reference here to early baptism.) Jesus simply says: "Stand up, take your mat and walk" (Jn 5:8–9). Next, a debate ensues and Jesus is persecuted for healing on the Sabbath and for working miracles without the approval of the Temple priests. When Jesus equates his work to that of the Father, his enemies become eager to kill him for making himself equal to God. Here again are reflected the debates over Jesus' identity and authority in the early communities. Immediately after, Jesus says: "anyone who hears my word and believes him who sent me has eternal life" (Jn 5:24). Jesus is to be the center of faith and authority for his followers.

Another sign is given when crowds follow Jesus to Capernaum after a miraculous feeding. Jesus chides them for seeking him because of the food and not because of the "signs." When they ask him how they can perform the works of God, Jesus answers that the true work of God is to believe in him. His sign goes beyond Moses' manna in the desert, in that Jesus himself is "the bread of life" (Jn 6:35). What follows is John's discourse on the eucharist. (This gospel has no eucharist at the last supper.) Disputes follow and some even leave the faith, another indication of the serious divisions in the early churches over the eucharist.

The cure of the man born blind addresses the perennial question of the relationship between sin and suffering. Jesus is revealed as the "light of the world," who does the works of the one who sent him (Jn 9:4–5). The conflict over Jesus' identity in the early communities is reflected here. In this story the Pharisees argue that Jesus is a sinner and not from God, in contrast to the cured man who believes that Jesus is a prophet and from God. The healed man, like the early Christians, is turned out from the synagogue for his belief in Jesus. In the end, Jesus comes to him, reveals that he is the Son of God, and is worshiped by the man. The holistic link between physical curing and spiritual healing is explored in this story.

The last miracle story in John is that of the raising of Lazarus. It is an extensive story that wrestles with questions about sickness and death. Jesus, at the risk of being stoned, goes to Bethany and reveals himself to Martha as the "resurrection and the life." She in turn professes her faith that Jesus is "the Messiah, the Son of God, the one coming into the world" (Jn 11:25–27). The authentically human Jesus is deeply moved and weeps over the death of his friend. When Martha protests that the body is decayed, Jesus says that faith will enable her to behold the glory of God. He then gives thanks to the Father and prays that his followers might believe that he has been sent by God. The final sign occurs as Lazarus is called forth from the tomb. The miracle is a turning point. Many Jews come to believe in Jesus. Others go off to report him to the Pharisees, and the plan is put in motion for Jesus' execution. For the Jesus movement, the matter is clear: Jesus will triumph over death and give that same power to his followers. The restoration of Lazarus to physical life becomes a sign of Jesus' power to give eternal life to everyone.

The ultimate miracle of resurrection is described in great detail by John.

The risen Lord is revealed to the disciple Mary Magdalene, who goes and tells the others what she has seen. Then John describes the poignant scene where the Lord comes to the frightened disciples to say "Peace be with you," and grant the powers of forgiveness to the community (Jn 20: 21–23). The story of "doubting Thomas" is unique to this gospel and explores questions of faith. Thomas ultimately recognizes Jesus to be "My Lord and my God." Jesus then describes the kind of faith needed in all later communities: "Blessed are those who have not seen, and yet have come to believe" (Jn 20:29). Ultimately, faith must be a leap without signs and wonders.

The gospel closes with a final post-resurrection miracle. Jesus helps his disciples with a miraculous catch and then cooks breakfast for them on the shore. None of the disciples any longer have to ask Jesus who he is. He has been fully revealed in resurrection. The gospel closes by saying that there were many other things that Jesus did, but that the world would not be able to contain the books that could be written about them.

Summary

Jesus of Nazareth was indeed an instrument of God's healing and forgiving power. With his healing touch he brought divine healing and forgiveness to the sick, the disabled, and those caught in the clutches of sin. Against the background of other wonder workers of his time, Jesus uniquely demonstrated how the openness of human faith can be linked with divine power. The many miracle stories in the gospels, while based on historical events, go beyond those events and reveal the power of God working in the Christ to show forth the presence of the kingdom of mercy and love.

Questions for reflection and discussion

1. Recall and discuss some incident in your life that you might consider to be a "miracle."
2. What were the unique characteristics of Jesus' miracles?
3. What role does faith play in the gospel miracles?
4. Dramatize several miracle stories in groups and discuss the meaning of these miracles.
5. In John's gospel the miracles are "signs." To what do these signs point?

Sources

Cavadini, John C., ed. *Miracles in Jewish and Christian Antiquity: Imaging Truth.* Notre Dame, IN: University of Notre Dame Press, 1999.

Hendrickx, Herman. *Miracle Stories of the Synoptic Gospels.* San Francisco: Harper & Row, 1987.

Kee, Harold Clark. *Medicine, Miracle, and Magic in New Testament Times.* New York: Cambridge University Press, 1986.

Latourelle, Rene. *The Miracles of Jesus and the Theology of Miracles.* Translated by Matthew J. O'Connell. New York: Paulist Press, 1988.

Meier, John P. *A Marginal Jew: Rethinking the Historical Jesus.* 3 vols. New York: Doubleday, 1991-2001.

Otto, David. *The Miracles of Jesus.* Nashville: Abingdon Press, 2000.

Remus, Harold. *Jesus as Healer.* New York: Cambridge University Press, 1997.

Richards, H. J. *The First Easter: What Really Happened?* Mystic, CT: Twenty-Third Publications, 1985.

Woodward, Kenneth L. *The Book of Miracles: The Meaning of the Miracle Stories in Christianity, Judaism, Buddhism, Hinduism, Islam.* New York: Simon & Schuster, 2000.

CHAPTER FIVE

The Birth Stories

The centerpiece of the earliest gospel message was the death and resurrection of Jesus, and gradually this developed into a written gospel narrative. Only with time did the gospel writers begin to concern themselves with the meaning of Jesus' birth. The first gospel, Mark, has no birth story, but begins with Jesus' baptism. Matthew and Luke alone present nativity stories, and both offer quite different accounts and interpretations. The last gospel written, that of John, offers a theological reflection on the Word becoming Flesh.

Little if anything is known about Jesus' actual birth. Scholars agree that most, if not all, of the details given in the two gospel birth stories are theological reflections on the faith meaning of the event of Jesus coming into the world. They are meditations, often drawn from material in the Hebrew Scriptures, on Jesus as he was grasped by the early Christian communities. They are not so much concerned with the past, as with the present beliefs of the early disciples, beliefs that they wish to proclaim to the world so that more people might be drawn to the faith.

In part, interest in writing about the birth stories seems to have arisen from a desire to establish Jesus as a real historical figure, a real human being who was born like everyone else. Against charges that Jesus was illegitimate, it was explained that this birth was from God, from a mother who was blessed and pure. For new Jewish converts, the birth was linked with Old Testament prophecies and with Hebrew expectations of the messiah, and Jesus' mission is connected with figures like Abraham, David, and Moses. For Gentile and poor converts, stories of pagan figures from the east and shepherds were included. For all, Jesus was proclaimed to be the savior and Son of God by angelic messengers who are symbolic in Jewish literature of God's presence.

For the most part, the historicity of these stories is sketchy, especially since sources do not seem to be available. Joseph's early disappearance from the gospel story eliminates him as a source, and it is unlikely that Mary would have provided such conflicting details. It would seem, then, that neither Matthew nor Luke is concerned with presenting the facts of Jesus' birth. Rather, they focus on why Jesus was born and on his true identity. Using symbols such as the star, angels, the magi, shepherds, a manger, and ruthless despots, the gospel writers reveal that this birth was a defining moment in history, the coming of the divine into the world.

As we said earlier, in the gospels the memories of Jesus' life are seen through the filter of resurrection faith, a faith that is now deeply embedded in the Christian communities forty to sixty years after the death of Jesus. It is the Spirit of the risen Lord that colors all the gospel stories, including these accounts of his birth. As the great biblical scholar, Raymond Brown once observed, each of these gospel stories serves as a "miniature gospel," summarizing faith in the person and message of Jesus. Now let us take a look at these two stories.

Similarities

There are some commonalities between these two nativity stories, perhaps indicating that the authors are at least in part drawing from the same sources. In both, the parents of Jesus are named as Mary and Joseph, with Joseph being of Davidic descent. Both stories include an angelic annunciation, conception through the Holy Spirit, the intended naming of Jesus, and his designated role of savior. In addition, both stories place the birth in Bethlehem during the rule of Herod the Great, and point out that Jesus was raised in Nazareth.

Differences

There are also many contrasting elements in the two birth stories. Matthew's genealogy differs considerably from that of Luke. Matthew begins with a family tree that traces Joseph's lineage back to Abraham. Luke, on the other hand, places the genealogy after Jesus' baptism, and goes back all the way to Adam. Matthew's story focuses more on Joseph, while Luke pays more attention to Mary. Matthew's account suggests that Jesus is born in Joseph's house in Bethlehem after the couple has been married. Then, after a visit from the magi, the couple flees to Egypt to protect the child's life, and then they settle in Nazareth. In Luke, the engaged couple has to travel from Nazareth to Bethlehem for a census. Here Jesus is born in a manger, and then, after a visit from shepherds, the family returns to Nazareth.

The use of Hebrew Scriptures

It would seem that the authors of these stories drew from a variety of sources: oral and written stories, but most especially from the only Scriptures then available—the Hebrew Scriptures. Prophetic passages from Micah, Isaiah, Hosea, and Jeremiah are linked with the birth, and the figures in the stories are paralleled with people like Abraham, Sarah, Moses, Samson, and Samuel.

Matthew's birth story

Matthew's gospel most likely came from a Gentile-Jewish community in Syria around the year 80. By this time, Jerusalem, the Temple, and classical Judaism had been destroyed, and Jews and Christians were separate and alienated. This gospel seems to have been written for catechetical purposes and appeals to both Jewish and Gentile converts. Matthew's nativity story is an exotic tale of dreams, angels, and mysterious Gentile astrologers from the East. It has all the marks of a myth, and significantly its details never come up during Jesus' public life as an adult.

In this birth story, Jesus is depicted as a descendant of Abraham, the great Jewish patriarch and father of both Jew and Gentile. Jesus is a son of David and Abraham, the new Moses, a final king and lawgiver. For the early Christians, who wrote this good news, Jesus' birth marks the coming of the Son of God, the messiah for whom the Jewish nation had long been waiting.

The author begins with a reconstructed genealogy that traces Joseph's lineage back through many generations, to such great figures as Solomon, David, Jacob, Isaac, and finally Abraham. Jesus' gene pool includes saints as well as sinners, Jew and Gentile, signaling his continuity with other significant figures in Jewish history, his true humanity, and his universal power of salvation. Jesus' birth is proclaimed to be the fulfillment of Hebrew expectations, the climax of human history.

Matthew's story features Joseph, a young carpenter whose parents had arranged a betrothal and marriage with a maiden named Mary, who would have been around thirteen years old. According to custom, the couple would have been in the stage of waiting a year before Joseph took Mary to his home as his wife. In the meantime, Mary became pregnant, a situation in which it had to be determined whether the girl was seduced, raped, or had committed adultery, all grounds for immediate divorce. No matter what the outcome, Mary would have suffered public disgrace, so the observant young carpenter mercifully decides to quietly divorce Mary, most likely on lesser charges than infidelity. As Joseph prepares to obtain the writ of divorce, the angel of the Lord appears to him in a dream and informs him that the child has been conceived through the Holy Spirit. The Spirit in the Hebrew Scriptures is the source of creation and life; it now produces the beginning of a new creation in Jesus.

This is the only birth story that explicitly refers to a virginal conception. Whether or not this is historical is difficult to ascertain. While there are some parallels in the birth stories of other great heroes, this story is unique in that a god does not impregnate the woman as in the pagan myths. Some have proposed that the story of a virginal conception was invented to counteract the charge that Mary had been impregnated by a Roman soldier named Pandera. This disparaging legend, however, came much later than the gospels and was used to discredit Jesus.

The Christian tradition has always held strongly to the tradition that Mary was miraculously impregnated by the power of the Spirit. Belief in the virginal conception appears in the early creeds and has been strong in Christian traditions, although it has never been defined as dogma. Some exegetes maintain that the virginal conception is primarily a proclamation of the divine origin and nature of Jesus Christ. Whatever one's conclusion about the factuality of the virginal conception, the import of the passage seems to be fundamentally one of faith.

Joseph is told to name the child Jesus (Joshua) because he will save his people from their sins. Joseph, whose character seems to have been patterned after the figure of Joseph in Genesis, has received a message from God (symbolized in the figure of the angel). Included in the divine message is the prophecy of Isaiah to his people, who are about to be overcome by the Assyrians, that a new king would one day be born from a young maiden. This person would lead his people to freedom. Joseph awakens, marries Mary, and their first-born son is born in the husband's home in Bethlehem. Normally, Mary and Joseph would have had other children as well, and the new testament does refer to the brothers and sisters of Jesus. Jesus' brother James is described in Acts as the leader of the Jerusalem community.

Bethlehem is a town five miles south of Jerusalem, and is highly symbolic, for it was the birthplace of David as well as the site where he was anointed King by Samuel. Whether or not Jesus was actually born there is difficult to ascertain. Many scholars think that Jesus was in fact born in Nazareth, the village where he was raised and by which he came to be identified (Jesus the Nazarean).

The Magi

Matthew tells us that around the time of Jesus' birth, a group of magi arrived in Jerusalem seeking the newborn King of the Jews.

The term "magi" may refer to Zoroastrian priests from Persia, but more broadly could mean that these men were people from the occult arts: astronomers, fortune tellers or even magicians. (They are neither designated as being three in number nor referred to as kings.) This exotic group seems to be the stuff of myth, and, as we shall see, their presence in the birth story is richly symbolic.

The magi have seen the child's rising star and have come to pay him homage. (There was a common belief in ancient times that a new star appeared at the birth of a great figure, and there are Roman accounts of stars, conjunctions of planets, and comets marking special events.)

The magi's search for "the new king" alarmed the present king, Herod. In the account, which parallels the tale of Pharaoh and Moses, Herod calls in his scholars and is told of the prophecy of Micah that a great ruler of Israel would be born in Bethlehem. Herod tells the magi to seek out the child and to report his whereabouts so that he can pay homage to him. The magi joyfully follow the star to the child, enter the house, and pay homage to the baby. (Here the early Christians describe the joy of being disciples and worshippers of the Son of God.) The magi then offer exotic gifts of gold (appropriate for a king), frankincense (used for worship), and myrrh (an embalming spice that presages Jesus' death). The passage bears echoes of Isaiah 60, where kings enter a new dawn of Israel bearing gifts of gold and incense. Then, warned in a dream not to return to Herod, the magi depart for home.

The parallels with Pharaoh and Moses continue as Herod searches for the child to kill him. Joseph the dreamer is warned to flee with his family, and like his namesake, Joseph of the Hebrew Scriptures, is forced into exile in Egypt. The "new Moses" remains in exile until he can come forth in a new exodus.

Like the Pharaoh of old, Herod massacres many infants in an attempt to eliminate the newborn "king." The event is then linked with Jeremiah's account of Rachel weeping for her children. Once Herod dies, the angel of the Lord again appears to Joseph in a dream and tells him to return to the land of Israel. The new exodus takes place as the new Moses sets out for the promised land of Israel. Joseph is again warned in a dream of Herod's son, Archelaus, who rules in Judea, and is told to go north and establish the family home in Nazareth of Galilee.

The myth of the magi also tells us about the early Jesus movement. Their interest in the infant Jesus strongly speaks of the irony that exists in the early communities. Jesus now has more appeal to Gentiles than to his own Jewish people. At the same time, these pagans who learn of God from nature (the star) must listen to the Hebrew prophetic tradition (the teachings of the chief priests and scribes) to learn of the messiah. The forced exodus of the family to save the child places the shadow of the cross over the cradle, and the slaughter of the innocents by Herod points to a later Herod (Antipas), who supported both the crucifixion as well as the persecution of Jewish Christians by Jewish leaders at the time when the gospels were written. Here Jesus is the authentic King, the new David, indeed the messiah for whom the Jews had been waiting. His reign will be one of love and peace, in contrast to the tyrannical and brutal domination of the Herodian family. Jesus represents a kingdom of love and peace.

In this episode we discover that Jesus' birth is an extraordinary divine event, one that had been long anticipated in the Hebrew consciousness. This child is a new shepherd King from David's lineage, who has come to supercede Moses and act as the savior of his people. The virginal conception, the message from an angel, and the prophecies serve to convey the clear message that this birth is from God, who has sent a redeemer to his people.

Luke's story

The gospel of Luke seems to have been written around the year 80 CE, possibly in the community at Antioch. The audience here appears to be predominantly Gentile, for it stresses the mission to the Gentiles as part of God's plan and the work of the Holy Spirit. The scope of the gospels seems to be global in that the context is established within the Roman imperial reigns of Augustus and Tiberius.

This story focuses on Mary rather than Joseph. The feminine emphasis is found throughout the gospel, which includes accounts about Mary Magdalene, Joanna, and Suzanna being among the disciples, and the touching stories of the woman at Simon's dinner, Jairus' daughter, Jesus' friendship with Martha and Mary, and the women who first witness the resurrection. This emphasis seems to suggest that women played important pastoral roles in the Lukan community.

Luke's nativity story links Abraham and Sarah (through the parallel experience of Elizabeth and Zechariah) to the story of Jesus' birth. The Holy Spirit is portrayed as continually acting from the ancient Hebrew times to the time of Jesus. Jesus is celebrated as the messiah, the son of David and son of God; and his birth incorporates what may be magnificent hymns from early Christian liturgy: the *magnificat, benedictus, gloria in excelsis,* and *nunc dimittis.*

Luke begins his nativity story with the annunciation of the birth of Jesus' mentor and precursor, John the Baptist. In a story that echoes that of Abraham and Sarah, the parents of John, Elizabeth and Zechariah, are both too advanced in age to have children. The link with Abraham is perhaps for the benefit of Gentile Christians, since he was known as the father of all nations. Zechariah, a priest of the Temple, is about to offer incense, when the angel of the Lord announces to him that his wife will bear a son. The boy is to be named John, and he will be filled with the Holy Spirit and, like Elijah, will turn many of Israel toward their God, and will prepare the people for the Lord Jesus. Both John and Jesus are thus inserted into the Hebrew prophetic tradition.

Then Zechariah is struck dumb for his lack of faith, perhaps symbolic of the later rejection of the gospel and Jesus Christ by the Jewish priesthood. The context of priestly worship in the Temple places the historical Jesus, as well as those who later converted from Judaism to Christianity, within the context of traditional Judaism. Once again Gabriel, the angel of the Lord from the book of Daniel, represents the presence of God in the event.

The annunciation story for the Baptist is then followed with a parallel story of the same angel, Gabriel, coming to a virgin Mary who has been betrothed to Joseph. The angel announces that Mary will conceive a son and call him Jesus. Here, the annunciation is made in Nazareth, rather than in Bethlehem, as it appears in Matthew's story. This child will be the Son of the most high, will rule over the throne of David and the house of Jacob and the kingdom forever. The feisty young maiden challenges the angel as to how this can be since she has not yet had sexual relations. The angel answers that the Holy Spirit will come to her and the power of the most high will overshadow her. She will give birth to a child who will be holy, indeed the Son of God. In complete faith, the young maiden accepts what has been asked of her.

Once again the conception event is used by the early Christian church as an occasion to profess its faith in Jesus the Christ, the Son of God, as well as to model this faith on that of a woman who is called upon to play such an active role in the incarnation itself. Here the virginal conception is not explicit, and the important belief professed here by the early Christians is that the conception of Jesus was an extraordinary work of God's Spirit.

Next the story tells of Mary's visit to Elizabeth. On her arrival Elizabeth cries out concerning the blessedness of Mary and the baby she is carrying. Even the baby in Elizabeth's womb jumps for joy. These details reflect the exhilaration and joy that the early believers experienced when they heard the good news of Jesus.

At that point in the tale, echoing the Canticle of Hannah (1 Sam 2:1–10), Mary proclaims the greatness of God who has done this great thing for her.

She extols God's mercy, as well as the divine power that will disperse the arrogant and throw the powerful from their thrones. God will lift up the lowly, fill the hungry, and send the rich away empty. God keeps his promises to Abraham and his descendants.

In this canticle, the early Christians celebrate the prophetic ministry of Jesus and summarize his earthly mission. Jesus has come to reveal the blessedness of the poor and the outcast, and to confront oppressive and corrupt leaders. He was prepared for his mission by his mother, who in the story grasps its significance from the beginning.

Elizabeth bears a son and insists that he be called John. Her leadership and power again signals the influence of women in the later community. Zechariah regains his speech, is filled with the Spirit, and speaks prophetically, proclaiming that his son will be a prophet who will go before the Lord to make ready the way of the redeemer and deliverer. His canticle is most likely another example of a liturgical hymn from the Antioch community.

The description of John bears echoes of Samuel and Samson, who were also Nazarites. The story, with its parallel annunciation, clearly says to the later followers of the Baptist that there should be no rivalry between John and Jesus, and that indeed John was sent to prepare the way for Jesus. The early communities affirm that, although Jesus was mentored by John and submitted to his baptism, John must play a role subordinate to Jesus. John's followers, who still existed when this gospel was written, are called to follow Jesus as the savior.

The birth of Jesus

Luke's nativity story is set in the context of Roman oppression, whence comes an outrageous decree from the Emperor Augustus to have a worldwide census. Such a census does not reflect the historical procedures of the Romans, but rather it serves as a symbol of the oppression under which Jesus was born and would ultimately die.

Early Christian compliance with Roman rule is perhaps indicated by how Joseph and his pregnant betrothed travel for many days by caravan from Nazareth to Bethlehem to avoid Roman reprisals. As mentioned earlier, the designation of Bethlehem as his birthplace is largely symbolic, identifying Jesus with David, who was also born there.

The young maiden gives birth to her first-born, wraps him in cloth, and lays him in a manger. The fact that there is no room in the town for Jesus and the birth occurs in a manger might well point to the simplicity and humility of his origins, as well as to the rejection he experienced in his life. The tender care and protection that the baby receives from his parents in these difficult circumstances points to the special dignity given by Christians to Jesus' birth.

Nearby shepherds receive from an angel the "good news" for the whole people. Here the story seems to indicate that the gospel has been given directly from God and is for Jew and Gentile alike. The gospel proclaims to the world that Jesus is the savior, the messiah, the Lord. The fact that the message is given first to shepherds might symbolize that lowly outcasts have been given preference in Jesus' mission. The shepherds also carry the symbolic meaning of Jesus being the new David, the good shepherd. A great army of angels, singing the divine praises, stands for the fullness of the presence of God. The shepherds then go and find the baby of whom the Lord had spoken. They amaze those present with their tale and give the mother Mary much to ponder in her heart. The shepherds then go back praising God for all that they saw and heard. Eight days later the Jewish baby was circumcised and named Jesus.

Once again, the story indicates how the last become first, and how the little ones are chosen to both spread and receive the Christian gospel. Moreover, the gospel of Jesus is declared to be inclusive, a joyous invitation to anyone who is willing to receive it. It is a message to be pondered carefully, as Mary did.

There is a striking contrast in the story between the Emperor Augustus, whose peace is sustained through fear and repression, and the Prince of Peace, who rules his kingdom through love, mercy, and justice. Here we see implied the tension that the nonviolent Christians face, being part of an Empire that is oppressive and violent.

The early followers, just as Mary and Joseph in the story, have no other choice but to comply with Roman demands. But the promise is given to them that ultimately the mighty will be removed from their thrones. The meek and humble peacemakers will ultimately inherit the earth.

John's birth story

The gospel of John is the last written, around 90 CE. This gospel has no nativity narrative, but instead celebrates the meaning of Jesus' birth in a magnificent prologue that blends liturgical hymn, gospel story, and theological reflection. The prologue has been called the "overture" to the gospel in that it introduces the themes ahead. Word, life, light, darkness, the coming of Jesus, his rejection, his acceptance by those who become the children of God, and the coming of a new creation will be the gospel themes.

The gospel opens with the words of Genesis "in the beginning," indicating that Jesus is a new creation from the hand of the original Creator. The central image is that of the Word or "Logos." For the Jews, the Word was the means through which God was active in history, the mode through which God exercised divine presence and power. It was through the Word that God created, acted as a prophetic agent, and served as a source of wisdom. In Proverbs (8) the Word or Wisdom becomes personified as Lady Wisdom, who accompanies God in creation.

For the Greeks, the Word held a different meaning. The Word was not so much a means for functioning as it was a principle of order and rationality. The Word was the link between God and rational creatures, a notion that often led to a dualism in Western thought.

The gospel is presented as the new Word, the good news of God's salvation in Jesus Christ. Once again the Word becomes personified and Jesus becomes the speaker of wisdom in preaching and miracles. Jesus is professed as the Word made flesh, the gospel incarnate. In John, the Word was with God from the beginning, indicating the pre-existence of Jesus Christ. The Word indeed was God, acknowledging that Jesus Christ is truly divine, a common theme in the gospel of John. Although Christ is one with the Creator, the Word and God retain their uniqueness. It is through the Word that all things came into existence. Just as God brought light and life into existence through a word, now Jesus Christ brings light and life into the world. Jesus is now recognized by the early churches as the light of the world and source of eternal life. Jesus, through his intimacy with God, now brings forth the words and deeds of God.

Just as the original creator overcame darkness with light, now the Word overcomes the darkness of sin and death. In John's gospel, Jesus comes as the godly king reigning over a kingdom of love and service. For John, that is the meaning of Jesus' birth, the commencement of this new creation and kingdom.

Interjected into the hymn is the story of John the Baptist. As mentioned earlier, followers of John still existed in the early church. Paul encounters some of them in Ephesus (Acts 19:7). For those followers, it is made clear that John is not the light, but rather was called to prepare for the coming of the light of the world, Jesus Christ. John is to speak for the one who will come after him, for one greater than he, one who existed before John was ever born.

Jesus is declared to be the center of salvation. He enlightens every person who comes into the world, an indication of the universal call to salvation. John's gospel uses the word *cosmos* (world) with its wide range of meanings. At times the world merely stands for creation, the context of God's salvation. At other times, the world refers to reality that has turned from God. In Jesus' prayer at the last supper, he both prays that the world might believe that God has sent him, and at the same time declares that neither he nor his disciples are "of the world" (Jn 17:16).

Again we go from hymn to story, as it is told how Jesus was rejected. Just as Yahweh "pitched his tent" among his people in the desert, the Word came to the world that was made through him and to his own people and was not recognized. The God who at one time dwelt in temple and tabernacle, now dwells in Jesus Christ, and he has been rejected by the chosen people themselves. In the year 90 CE the sting still smarts that Jesus came as a Jew to his own people and was rejected by them.

According to John's gospel, salvation belongs to those who receive the Word and believe in his name. To those he gives the power of becoming children of God. Salvation is a rebirth. It is not "of blood." (The ancients thought that conception came about by a mingling of male seed and female blood.) It is not of the flesh or of anything that humans can do to earn it. It is pure grace, pure gift freely offered by Jesus who has its fullness. The climax of this magnificent hymn to the human-divine nature of Jesus Christ is in the passage: "And the Word became flesh and lived among us, and we have seen his glory, the glory as of a father's only son, full of grace and truth" (1:14).

The early believers celebrated the fullness of grace that they had been given through Christ. As God gave the law through Moses, God gives grace and truth through Jesus Christ. He is the only Son, the same as God, and has made God known. First, the gift of the law was given by Moses, and now the law is perfected in the gift of truth through Christ. He is the perfection of all god's gifts; he is the light and life. Only the Son has seen God and is now the full revelation of God.

Summary

Although we have little factual knowledge about the birth of Jesus of Nazareth, three gospel stories tell us a great deal about what this birth meant to the early Christian communities. The event is celebrated in the context of Jewish history as the coming of the new King of the Jews, the messiah, Son of God and savior. The birth is proclaimed as God's advent to the lowly ones of the earth. This is the nativity of God's incarnation in one who will suffer, die, and be raised as the savior of the world.

Questions for reflection and discussion

1. What historical facts do we know about the birth of Jesus?
2. Compare and contrast the birth story in Matthew's gospel with the one in Luke.
3. Discuss the possible meaning of such elements as the manger, the magi, the star, shepherds, and angels.
4. What specific post-resurrection beliefs are in the nativity stories?
5. What is unique about the birth story in John's gospel?

Sources

Brown, Raymond E. *The Birth of the Messiah: A Commentary on the Infancy Narratives in the Gospels of Matthew and Luke.* New updated ed. New York: Doubleday, 1993.

Garland, David E. *Reading Matthew: A Literary and Theological Commentary on the First Gospel.* New York: Crossroad, 1993.

Horsley, Richard A. *The Liberation of Christmas: The Infancy Narratives in Social Context.* New York: Crossroad, 1989.

Moloney, Francis J. *The Gospel of John.* Collegeville, MN.: Liturgical Press, 1998.

Richards, H. J. *The First Christmas: What Really Happened?* Mystic, CT.: Twenty-Third Publications, 1986.

CHAPTER SIX

The Passion Stories

We have seen how the birth stories celebrate a private and hidden event in mythical fashion. In contrast, the passion stories focus on a very public event, and thus tend to be more historical in character. This is in part evidenced by the fact that throughout all the stories there is a consistently uniform sequence of events. Underneath the stories there seems to be solid memories of an event in a garden, betrayal by Judas, denial by Peter, some sort of trial or hearing before Jewish and Roman leaders, the journey toward Calvary, and the crucifixion between two criminals.

This is not to say that the passion stories are to be viewed as historical narrative. Rather, all four passion stories seem to transform early memories of these tragic events into dramatic "plays," tragedies if you will, that explore the meaning of Jesus' death. Each gospel story consists of "scenes" that present different approaches to Jesus' suffering and death. The gospel writers use literary techniques, images, even "props, " to dramatize the theological meaning of Jesus' passion. At the same time, they link the events of Jesus' suffering to experiences that the early Christian communities are having at the time. As we shall see, we often learn as much about the time when the stories were written (forty to sixty years later) as we do about the actual events being discussed.

The early followers of Jesus seem to have been embarrassed by the crucifixion. After all, they now acclaimed Jesus to be the risen Christ, the Son of God, the savior-messiah. Amidst all the various expectations of a messiah by the Jews, there was little notion of one who would suffer, much less be crucified. And yet, the disciples had to acknowledge that their master had been condemned and executed as a common criminal. He had died in disgrace, naked on a cross outside the city of Jerusalem. For this reason, Jesus was seldom portrayed on a cross for centuries after the event. It would take years of reflection before the disciples could come to terms with such a death and be able to explain its meaning in the context of faith.

The four gospel accounts of Jesus' passion set out to develop theologies of Jesus' suffering and death, and then link these theologies to their current experience of the early church. Using memories of the events, early pre-gospel traditions, parallel material from the Hebrew Scriptures, as well as original creations, the gospel writers created four extraordinary faith accounts of the passion and death of Jesus. Along the way, the gospels pursue two themes: Jesus was innocent, and both Jewish and Roman authorities conspired to execute him. Here we will extensively explore the earliest gospel account (Mark), and then indicate the unique contributions to the tradition by the other three gospel writers.

Mark's gospel

In Mark, the earliest of the gospels (c. 70 CE), the action begins as the last supper concludes with a hymn and then a short walk by Jesus and his followers through the city gates to the Mount of Olives. In "going out" of the city, Jesus separates himself from the city, perhaps a symbol of the subsequent break of his followers with Judaism. The site carries memories of David weeping and praying in this same area after he was betrayed by Absalom. It is also the site where Jesus earlier spoke of the coming end-times, to which the crucifixion later would be compared. Jesus is disturbed with his disciples from the outset, convinced that they will desert him when he is attacked. At the same time, he predicts that he will rise from the dead and come to them in Galilee. (This links Jesus' death with his ministry in Galilee.) Then Jesus is portrayed as a prophet and contrasted with the false prophets who brought about his death, as well as with those who misled the people during the early Christian days. Mention of the resurrection indicates that the Easter event now represents a victory over the cross for the gospel writer and his community.

Answering Jesus' predictions, Peter loudly proclaims that he will never desert Jesus, but Jesus rebukes Peter with the prediction that he will deny him three times. (Jesus' foreknowledge of his resurrection and Peter's denial seems to be a post-resurrection perspective on Jesus' divinity.) Peter, the leader of the disciples, vehemently protests that he is willing to go to the death for Jesus, and the others join in with the same resolve. Mark portrays Jesus here as tense, doubtful of his own followers, and seemingly resigned to his fate. The play prepares us for Mark's key theme that Jesus died abandoned and desolate. This theme might also reflect the early Christian converts' realization of how challenging and indeed dangerous it was to follow Jesus. The gospel writer here also reflects on the Jewish notion that all of these happenings are part of a divine plan. The gospel community is wrestling with the age-old question: "Why do bad things happen to good people?"

In the next scene the group comes to a place called Gethsemane, where Jesus tells his disciples to sit and pray. Then, in a gesture reminiscent of the transfiguration, Jesus takes Peter, James, and John and continues on. Jesus confides in them that he is deeply grieved that he could die, and then tells them to remain and stay awake. Now the writer cuts Jesus off from everyone. Alone, Jesus throws himself on the ground and prays the words of what might well have been an early Christian hymn: "Abba, Father, for you all things are possible; remove this cup from me; yet, not what I want, but what you want" (Mk 14:36). The scene is a powerful dramatization of Jesus' humanity, of his longing to be saved from the ordeal that appears to be inevitable. Though he fears death and the darkness of Sheol, God's plan must be fulfilled! One is reminded of a parallel in Hebrews, where Jesus cries out loudly with tears and is heard because of his role in the cause of salvation (Heb 5:7–10). This prayer also may well come from early Christian liturgy.

Unlike the Greek heroes, such as Socrates, or the Jewish martyrs in Maccabees, who faced death nobly, Jesus writhes in agony on the ground, like the stricken victims of the Hebrew Psalms. Using "Abba" for God is a very intimate and personal term, and, as used here, is unique to Jesus. It demonstrates his closeness to God; yet at the same time he is subject to providence. The prayer also echoes the "Our Father." Jesus had earlier asked his disciples if they could "drink the cup," and at the supper he had identified the cup with his own blood (Mk 10:39; 14:24). As for what God "wills," traditionally that has been interpreted as being the crucifixion. Another view might be that Abba wanted his son to continue his mission, even if it inevitably meant execution at the hands of his enemies.

Jesus next returns, presumably to his three closest companions, and rebukes Peter for sleeping. Again he tells him to be alert for "the time of trial" and pray. (The "time of trial" seems to allude to the endtime as well as the upcoming tragedy.) The passion is put on the same level as the endtime and must have seemed like that to the disciples who experienced it. Their world with Jesus was coming to a horrible end. Then Jesus utters the oft-quoted lines: "the spirit indeed is willing but the flesh is weak"(14:38). This is often interpreted in terms of the Greek dualism between matter and spirit. In fact, the Hebrews were much more holistic about reality. For them the flesh was the perishable, earthy dimension of reality, the weak side of humanity through which the powers of evil worked. The flesh was the place in one's self wherein one can turn from God. The spirit, on the other hand, was where one remained faithful to the Creator. Here Jesus demonstrated his own participation in and understanding of human weakness. Again, this provides consolation for those in the early communities who struggled with their faith and with fears of martyrdom.

Once more, Jesus goes to pray the same petition, and then returns to find the disciples sleeping. Mark partially excuses them by saying that their eyes were heavy, but in fact they have no answer for Jesus. A third time Jesus prays and again finds them asleep. Jesus seems agitated and says "Enough." He recognizes that they have not been alert enough to watch and warn him. He has been betrayed into the hands of sinners, and Judas already approaches. Jesus is portrayed as completely vulnerable: not warned by his closest followers, betrayed by one of his own, and about to be arrested by the leaders of his own people. Perhaps the later tragic separation between the Way and Jesus' own Judaism is reflected here. The details of the garden story also show us the importance to the Markan community (possibly in Rome) of prayer, watchfulness, and loyalty at a time when they suffered betrayal and persecution from their own people, perhaps even from their own families.

The action begins to build as a crowd with swords and clubs approach, led by chief priests, scribes and elders. The struggle begins between Jesus' nonviolent and loving ways and the violence of those among the Jews who reject him and his teachings. (This is the same quandary faced by those being martyred in the Markan community. Does Jesus represent a God of vengeance or a God of peace?) The irony becomes even more obvious when a kiss, the very sign of love and affection in the community, is used by Judas to betray Jesus to his enemies.

One of Jesus' followers decides to reject the nonviolent ways of Jesus and cuts off the ear of the high priest's slave. Jesus challenges his opponents for coming after him violently as though he were a bandit, pointing out that when he was teaching in the Temple they did not arrest him. Jesus seems to be identifying himself with the best of Judaism (the Temple). This puts him in continuity with the hopes of the Hebrew Scriptures and points out how his mission had been to renew Judaism. Mark begins to develop the theme of the innocence of Jesus and the injustice of the arrest. He underscores the sinfulness of those persecuting innocent advocates of love, an important theme for early members of the Jesus movement.

Once again Mark dramatizes how deserted and alone Jesus appears at that moment. He stands cut off and abandoned, as a young man in a linen cloth becomes so frightened that he runs off naked, almost comically leaving his garment in the hands of those who attempt to grab him. This is an excellent dramatic touch by the author, perhaps pointing to the timidity or even cowardice of some of the disciples in the early communities. This might even stand as a symbol of those who cast off their baptismal robes and deny Christ in the early days of the church.

Next Jesus is taken to the Jewish leaders. Peter follows behind and sits with guards to warm himself by the fire. (This serves as a preface to Peter's betrayal, an incident so embarrassing for Peter and the early communities as to argue for its historicity.) The council hearing seems to be designed by the gospel writer to make it clear that Jesus was an innocent man, who was put to death unjustly. False witnesses are lined up, each with conflicting testimonies. Jesus stands silently before his accusers, portrayed as the "suffering servant" of the Hebrew Scriptures. Bypassing all these lies, the high priest asks Jesus why he is silent and then curiously asks him as the defendant of "what" he is being charged. Frustrated at Jesus' silence, the high priest challenges Jesus straight out "Are you the messiah?" Jesus answers simply "I am," a phrase that parallels "Yahweh," the name used for God.

This might well reflect the "one God" debate among early Christians and the Jews. Jesus then refers to himself as the Son of Man, a Hebrew title that Jesus often used of himself, and which refers to a person who is a servant of God and who manifests God's power. At that the high priest tears his clothes (an ancient symbolic gesture of extreme anger or grief), and claims that Jesus has committed blasphemy and deserves death. Jesus is spit upon, blindfolded, and beaten. Of course, the informed Jewish-Christian audience listening to this play would have quickly realized that it is not blasphemy to claim to be the messiah. Jewish law describes blasphemy as cursing the name of Yahweh. (This charge of blasphemy is perhaps the very charge made against early Christians for their homage to Jesus.) Once again Jesus has been convicted on false testimony and erroneous charges! The entire procedure seems to fly in the face of standard Sanhedrin procedure.

Jesus stands here as a victim of his own people, just as were many members of his early communities. The issue of his messianic identity seems to have been a later debate between Christians and Jews inserted into the actual event of Jesus' passion. During the time of Jesus, there was actually little messianic expectation in Jerusalem. It is true that some Jews hoped for a new king who would restore the glory of the nation, and groups like the Essenes seemed to anticipate an imminent endtime. But Jesus hardly fit the profile for these expectations. Therefore, it is doubtful whether Jesus was charged with claiming to be the messiah, especially since he never seems to have actually made such claims. The recognition of Jesus as messiah seems to have occurred after the resurrection.

The next scene is a touching bit of history. Peter, leader among the apostles, denies Jesus three times: twice intimidated by a servant girl and once by mere bystanders. When he remembers the Lord's prediction, Peter breaks down and cries. This is a story that no doubt strengthened the belief of the early community in the availability of forgiveness for even the most heinous sin. It no doubt gave comfort to those who, under pressure from their Roman or Jewish persecutors, did in fact deny loyalty to Jesus.

In the next scene it is morning and the whole council decides to bind Jesus and hand him over to the imperial Roman prefect, Pontius Pilate. Although it would seem that the Sanhedrin at that time had the authority to execute, generally they would have had to seek the approval of the Roman authority. The Jewish authorities realized that this was Passover, and that such an execution would cause turmoil. Better that the Romans be brought in, especially since they had the authority to execute by the horrendous means of crucifixion.

Jesus is brought bound before Pilate, who asks him a question about an accusation not previously mentioned: "Are you king of the Jews?" It is likely that this was the actual historical charge raised by the Jews. Even though it never comes up in the life of Jesus, the Jews knew that its political implications would disturb both Pilate and Herod. Jesus is evasive with "You say so." Then the chief priest makes many unspecified charges, and when Pilate asks Jesus how he answers, he says nothing. Again, Mark continues to portray Jesus as alone, unjustly charged, and resigned to the fact that, no matter what he says, he stands condemned to die. He has felt his enemies' hatred all along and now it has grown to the point where they will destroy him. Jesus' battle with Satan has come to its climax, and, though Jesus now stands vulnerable, the gospel writer knows that ultimately Jesus will be victorious in his resurrection and exaltation.

The next scene opens with information that a prisoner of choice can be released for the feast. It is pointed out that a man named Barabbas was in prison for being a rebel and murderer. When Pilate asks the people if they want "the King of the Jews" released, the chief priests stir the people to ask for the release of Barabbas. When Pilate asks what is to be done with Jesus, they cry out "crucify him." Pilate asks why, since Jesus has done no evil, but he is shouted down. Bowing to the wishes of the mob, he releases Barabbas, has Jesus flogged, and hands him over to be crucified.

The historicity of the release of a prisoner and the existence of Barabbas is extremely problematic. The release of a violent terrorist is quite unlikely, and at best, a prisoner at the time of Passover could receive a lessened sentence. The name "Barabbas" is highly symbolic (son of Abba) who now stands in stark contrast to the true son of Abba. The dramatic impact of the scene is more important, and points to the reality that, again, the violent and evil are chosen over the nonviolent and innocent—often the choice in the kingdom of this world. This was commonly the experience of the early martyred Christians of gospel times. Yet the communities held steadfast to the belief that Jesus indeed conquered evil in a nonviolent manner in his life, death, and resurrection.

In the next scene Jesus is led by the soldiers to the palace courtyard, where he is dressed in purple, crowned with thorns, beaten, spat upon, and mocked. The "King of the Jews" motif is carried forth here, and the mockery is particularly shameful in light of the early Christian realization about Jesus' true kingship. Jesus is then dressed again in his own clothes and led off to be crucified. On the way to Golgotha (skull-shaped hill), Simon of Cyrene is recruited to carry the cross, a stark indication of the condition of Jesus. Jesus refuses the drugged wine and is crucified, as his garments are divided and wagered over (a reference to a passage in Ps 22:18). This incident underscores the humanity of Jesus, his utter exhaustion from abuse, and his determination to consciously endure this sacrifice rather than abandon his mission.

Then the scene of crucifixion is described. The time is noted: nine o'clock in the morning. Jesus hangs between two bandits; a sign over his head reads "King of the Jews." He is mocked and ridiculed by passersby and the Jewish leaders. At noon darkness envelopes the land and lasts until three o'clock. Jesus cries out: "My God, my God, why have you forsaken me?" (Those standing by think he is invoking Elijah.) Jesus lets out a loud cry and dies.

The scene of Jesus' death is highly symbolic. Jesus hangs among the outcasts who were central in his ministry. For the gospel writer, the Master truly is the King of the Jews, in spite of the derision intended by the sign over his head. The darkness over the earth perhaps symbolizes both the chaos before creation and the endtime. Jesus dies a truly human death, apparently abandoned by all, and feeling as though he might even be forsaken by God. Psalm 22, which Jesus prays, is one that would be recited by someone faithful to God who ultimately is saved by God. Mark portrays Jesus as the light of the world who overcomes chaos and darkness. The ridicule, apparent chaos, suffering, and death depict the same dreadful context in which the early disciples often found themselves. Nevertheless, their faith remains steadfast in Jesus Christ, the light of the world, who has triumphed over chaos and evil and who now promises them eternal life.

After Jesus dies, the Temple curtain is torn in two. A Roman centurion says: "Truly, this is God's Son!" Standing at a distance are Mary Magdalene, Mary the mother of James, Salome, and many other women disciples. In the evening, Joseph of Arimathea, a member of the council asked Pilate for the body, wrapped it in linen, laid it in a rock tomb, and rolled a stone against the door—all under the watchful eye of Mary Magdalene and Mary the mother of James.

So much in this scene after Jesus' death symbolizes aspects of the early church: the divisions in the Temple over Jesus and the casting out of his followers, persecution and death, the conversion of Gentiles, including highly placed Romans, the conversion of Jewish officials, and the central role of women in the community. The close monitoring of Jesus' burial is addressed to those who denied the resurrection and charged that Jesus' body was either misplaced or stolen.

Matthew's drama

The author of Matthew's version of the passion and death of Jesus borrows heavily from Mark's gospel. Thus we will not repeat the entire drama, but will only mention some of the unique dramatic elements in Matthew, which seem to come either from the author himself or from other, earlier sources.

In the scene in Gethsemane, when one of those with Jesus cuts off the ear of the high priest's servant, Jesus tells him to put away his sword: "for all who take the sword will perish by the sword" (Mt 26:52). This emphasizes the nonviolent aspect of Jesus' message. Jesus also reminds his attackers that should the Father wish, he could be saved by legions of angels (a Hebrew symbol of God's power). Jesus does not endorse the idea of a warrior God. The Master then challenges his attackers for not having arrested him when he taught in the Temple, and points out that all this takes place so that the Scriptures of the prophets might be fulfilled. Jesus' death is put into the context of messianic expectations.

In Matthew's gospel, Jesus is brought before Caiaphas, who has gathered scribes and elders at his house. They look for false testimony, and finding none, they charge Jesus with saying that he can rebuild the Temple in three days if they destroy it. When Jesus does not answer, the high priest challenges Jesus to say whether he is the messiah, the Son of God. Jesus is more evasive than he was in Mark's gospel, saying only: "You have said so" (26:64). This might go back to the actual historical event, where Jesus never claimed to be messiah. As we have seen, the issues of Jesus' claims to be the messiah and the Son of God are obviously more reflective of later debates between Jews and Christians. Next, Matthew's gospel has Jesus speak in terms of the endtime where the Son of Man will come on the clouds of heaven. For this, Jesus is falsely condemned for blasphemy, his death is decided upon, and he is led away to Pilate. The theme of Jesus' innocence and unjust conviction is once again dramatized.

Matthew also develops the scene where Pilate washes his hands to indicate that he is innocent of the blood of this just man. This dramatic detail shifts the blame for Jesus' execution to the Jewish leaders, and then Matthew reiterates this by having the people say: "His blood be on us and on our children" (27:25). Tragically, this has been interpreted as the "blood curse" upon the Jewish people through the ages. In fact, it is nothing more than an acceptance of responsibility on the part of those individuals involved in the crucifixion event. While it reflects the animosity that existed between early Christians and the Jewish community, it has no relevance to any time after that and can certainly not justify anti-Semitism. Unfortunately, there has been a strong Catholic tradition in writers such as Origen, Augustine, John Chrysostom, Thomas Aquinas and Martin Luther, of holding the Jewish people responsible for Jesus' death. The Second Vatican Council clearly contradicted this tradition and firmly stated that Jews today cannot be in any way blamed for Jesus' crucifixion.

Matthew also adds the scene where Judas repents, returns the thirty pieces of silver to the elders, and admits to betraying innocent blood. When Judas is ignored, he casts the coins down in the Temple, and goes out and hangs himself. The chief priests buy a potter's field with the silver. There is another version of the incident in Acts 1:16ff where Judas' insides burst open. The early Christian writer, Papias, adds another version, wherein Judas, after being crushed by a wagon, dies of a horrible disease. Whatever the story, there can be little doubt that Judas came to a horrible end.

The Judas tradition stands in contrast to Petrine tradition on the availability of forgiveness to the repentant. In the case of Judas, the community reflects on how tragic it is to despair over infidelity to Jesus when forgiveness is always available. The story of the thirty pieces of silver reiterates Jesus' teaching that one cannot serve two masters, God and money, and warns the early communities against selling out their faith for material rewards.

This gospel also adds the elements of an earthquake and the opening of graves and raising the dead, both symbols of the apocalyptic endtime. The crucifixion is placed on the same plane as the apocalyptic end, to which it must have seemed comparable to those who witnessed Jesus' passion. At this point in the story, there is a curious leap ahead to the time after Jesus' resurrection when these saints enter Jerusalem and appear to men. This adds another eschatological dimension to both the death and resurrection of Jesus. In Matthew the centurion is joined by all those who are keeping watch and stricken with fear, and together they say: "Truly this man was God's Son" (Mt 27:54). This perhaps is an attempt to reflect the broader diversity of people who recognize Jesus' identity after the resurrection and in the ensuing years of the early church.

The author of Matthew offers more details about Joseph of Arimathea, noting that he was a disciple of Jesus and that he wrapped the body and put it in his own tomb. Once again, such details serve to dispel the rumors that Jesus' body had been stolen or misplaced. In the same vein, Matthew also adds the scene where the Jewish leaders remind Pilate of Jesus' predictions to rise, and ask to have a guard posted to prevent his followers from stealing the body. Historically, Pilate might well have been willing to comply, since the violation of tombs was at that time considered to be a serious offense. Pilate tells the Jewish leaders to take care of the matter themselves, so they seal the tomb and post a guard. This story serves to further rule out duplicity on the part of the disciples concerning Jesus' resurrection.

Luke's drama

While the Mark/Matthew tradition explores the theme of abandonment and despair, the author of Luke's gospel develops the themes of loyalty, solidarity, and forgiveness. In the Gethsemane scene, Jesus solemnly kneels in prayer and is strengthened by an angel (again symbolic of the power of God). At the same time, Luke does not diminish Jesus' anguish, adding the detail of his sweating blood. Jesus does not have to tell his followers to watch because he knows he can trust them to keep an eye out for him. Here Jesus prays only once, and when he returns to his followers, they are sleeping "out of sorrow," and not out of abandonment. There is no need for Jesus to be frustrated or impatient with the disciples here. The purpose of these details is to strengthen the early Christians who have been loyal and faithful, and to encourage them to continue in fidelity.

In Luke, Jesus speaks directly to Judas with the touching line: "Judas, do you betray the Son of man with a kiss?" Jesus refers to himself as the righteous servant of God, who will be persecuted and yet vindicated by God. In this drama, when the disciple cuts off the servant's ear, Jesus not only puts a stop to the violence, he touches the man's ear and heals it. This action more emphatically dramatizes Jesus' commitment to nonviolence, and it accents his teaching on the forgiveness of enemies. As Jesus is arrested, he speaks of the hour of his enemies and the power of darkness, another indication of Jesus' struggle to overcome Satan.

Luke describes only one session before the Jewish council, and it is in the morning. When Jesus is asked if he is the messiah, he is evasive, saying: "If I tell you, you will not believe" (Lk 22:67). This possibly refers to the later unwillingness of many Jews to join the Jesus movement. When asked if he is the Son of God, Jesus again does not give a direct answer, but simply says: "You say that I am" (22:70). The Son of God debate about Jesus, of course, arose later between Jews and Christians, after the resurrection. Based on these vague answers, the Jewish leaders unjustly claim that they have sufficient evidence to charge Jesus, who once again is portrayed as clearly innocent.

Then the scene shifts, as Jesus is taken to Pilate and charged with matters unrelated to the previous interview: he is said to have perverted the nation and to have forbade the paying of taxes to the emperor. Then Jesus' accusers add a charge to which Jesus had not ever confessed—that he claimed to be the messiah and a king. Even Pilate can see that these charges are groundless, and so the Jewish leaders, without hesitation, conjure up another accusation on the spot—that Jesus incited the people through his teachings. Here the author of Luke goes even beyond Mark and Matthew to dramatize that the Jewish authorities convicted an innocent man and made a mockery of Jewish law in doing so.

The author of Luke also adds the scene where Pilate sends Jesus to Herod. This further develops the point that in Pilate's eyes Jesus is innocent. Herod held authority over Jesus as a Galilean. (Jesus' place of ministry is here re-established as a context for his crucifixion.) Herod says he is glad to see this Jesus of whom he has heard so much and he anticipates seeing some magic. (This reputation of Jesus is reflected in later rabbinic documents, which state that Jesus was convicted of sorcery.) Herod questions Jesus, but gets no cooperation from the prisoner, and then orders his soldiers to ridicule him. They put a "kingly" robe on Jesus and send him back to Pilate. Then Luke provides a curious detail, which is obviously a metaphor for the divine power of peace and forgiveness in Jesus' kingdom: Herod and Pilate become friends! Pilate then calls together the Jewish leaders and informs them that neither he nor Herod find Jesus worthy of death. He says he will chastise Jesus and release him. Luke's gospel further fortifies the early Christian conviction that Jesus was convicted unjustly by the Jewish authorities. As said before, the utter innocence of Jesus better enables the early communities to accept the gruesome fact that their Lord was ignominiously crucified.

These scenes once again reflect the animosity that existed between the early Christian and Jewish communities over Jesus. At the same time, they indicate that the early Christians acknowledged that they could not afford to alienate the Romans who dominated them. Especially after the destruction of Jerusalem, the Romans and not the Jews were the main threat to these communities. Perhaps it was this concern that led the gospel writers to soften Pilate's responsibility for the crucifixion and, contrary to actual history, portray him to be a fair, albeit weak, leader.

The author of Luke pursues his theme of loyalty and fidelity by having Jesus proceeding to Calvary, followed by a great number of people including many women who weep for him. Jesus calls them "daughters of Jerusalem," and tells them not to weep for him but for themselves and their children. Once again Jesus alludes to the endtime, when people will pray for the mountains to fall upon them. This again links the passion with the eschaton and also seems to refer to the eventual destruction of Jerusalem, which many Christians at the time believed was God's punishment for the execution of Jesus. The scene also dramatizes the unique phenomenon wherein Jesus had women followers, who often showed more commitment and courage than the men.

Luke's scene on Calvary is filled with forgiveness. Jesus' first words from the cross are: "Father, forgive them; for they do not know what they are doing" (23:34). (Early copyists were inclined to leave this line out of Luke because it was so unbelievable.) This demonstrates that Jesus came to bring forgiveness and not judgment. Then in the midst of mockery and ridicule from the crowd, as well as from one criminal next to Jesus, the thief on the other side declares Jesus innocent and asks to be remembered when he comes into his kingdom. Here Luke's gospel demonstrates that Jesus came to save sinners and outcasts when Jesus says: "Truly I tell you, today you will be with me in Paradise" (24: 43). This scene is the climax of Luke's treatment of the theme of forgiveness, and it demonstrates how salvation is available to the community through the crucified and risen Lord.

Jesus' death is strikingly different here from the Markan tradition. From the darkness comes a cry of commitment: "Father, into your hands I commend my Spirit" (Mk 23:46). Jesus is purposeful and intimate with the Father. In contrast to the Markan tradition, the centurion in this story praises God and proclaims Jesus' innocence. Instead of abandoning Jesus, the crowds return home beating their breasts, and Jesus' followers and the women stand at a distance and watch. The "watching" again adds an eschatological dimension to the event.

John's play

The Johannine passion story is unique, stressing the themes of the divinity and majesty of Jesus. Jesus is not abandoned, submissive, or resigned. Rather, he undergoes the ordeal of the passion and death with power and regal bearing. After long and highly theological discourses at the supper, Jesus leads his disciples into a garden in the Kidron valley. In this gospel, there is no falling on the ground, or prayers asking that suffering be taken away if possible. The disciples do not sleep and there is no kiss of betrayal by Judas.

Judas immediately shows up in the garden, leading soldiers, police, and Jewish leaders, all with lanterns, torches, and weapons. Jesus is described as having divine foreknowledge of what is going to happen to him. He makes the first move, asking the arresting party of both Jews and Romans for whom they are looking. When the group says "Jesus of Nazareth," he identifies himself and they all step back and fall to the ground overcome by his power. Jesus is forced to ask them again for whom they are searching, and again he identifies himself. This time he says that if they are looking for him, they should let his followers go. Clearly Jesus has complete control here, and must fulfill his mission, while at the same time he nobly protects his followers.

Peter is named as the one who with bravado draws his sword and cuts off the ear of the servant. Jesus tells him to put away his sword, so that Jesus might drink the cup that the Father has given him. He makes it clear that his kingdom is not one of power or violence. Jesus is in a decisive position and fully prepared to accept his destiny. One hears in this drama the early Christian faith in Jesus being present to protect them when they too are threatened with violence, as well as their faith in being part of the divine plan. Jesus is the Christ who is their savior.

In this play, there is no trial. Jesus is simply brought before Annas for questioning about his disciples and his teaching. Jesus is portrayed as confrontational, pointing out that he had spoken openly in synagogue and in public, and that Annas should ask those who have heard him speak. A guard thinks Jesus is being insolent and strikes him. Jesus then proceeds to take on the guard, challenging him to say that he is wrong, and he protests the injustice of the blow. (Traditionally, one was expected to be humble and submissive before the Jewish authorities, but Jesus is portrayed as being quite bold.)

Annas has had enough, and sends Jesus to his son-in-law, Caiaphas. The animosity between the chief priests and Jesus in these scenes seems to be symbolic of the later conflicts between the Johannine community and the synagogues. Without a trial or further questioning, Caiaphas takes Jesus to Pilate's headquarters. A vague exchange ensues, once again stressing the blamelessness of Jesus and the miscarriage of justice in his execution. Pilate inquires about the charge, finds nothing specific, and then tells the Jews to deal with the matter themselves. The Jews maintain that they do not have the authority to put Jesus to death. Historically, the Jews seemed to have authority to stone to death, but not to crucify. In all cases of capital punishment, the approval of Rome was required.

In the next scene Jesus faces Pilate, and when the prefect asks the suspect where he is from, Jesus refuses to answer. Pilate angrily points out that he has the power to execute him, and Jesus counters that Pilate would have no authority unless it came from above. Early Christian belief in the primacy of the divine authority over the authority of Rome is reflected here. Clearly the early Christians believed that Jesus Christ's kingdom was of God, and they did not consider themselves subject to Roman authority. The kingdom of God was incompatible with the kingdom of Caesar.

Pilate appears to be on the spot and clearly wants to release Jesus, but the Jews say that this would threaten his loyalty to the emperor, since Jesus has claimed to be a king. (This is the first mention of any charge against Jesus and seems to come as an afterthought.) Next Pilate brings Jesus outside and declares "Here is your King!" (Jn 19:14). When Pilate hears the cries of "Crucify him!" he asks if he should crucify their king. The Jews answer that they have no king but Caesar, and Pilate hands Jesus over to be crucified at noon (a highly symbolic time, for this is the hour when the Passover lambs are slaughtered in the Temple). This scene dramatizes the extent to which the Jewish leaders were willing to go to condemn Jesus. They would even pretend to accept the authority of their Roman oppressors over Yahweh in order to bring about the death of Jesus. Once again the later hostility between the Johannine community and the Jews is reflected in this scene.

Now begins John's version of the crucifixion. Note that there are no jeering mobs, and Jesus is able to carry his cross on his own. He is crucified with "two others"(not designated here as criminals), and over his head hangs the sign that reads "Jesus of Nazareth; the King of the Jews," written in Hebrew, Latin, and Greek. This scene seems to confirm that historically the charge against Jesus was that he claimed to be King of the Jews. (The dramatic touch of the sign in different languages points to the later belief that Jesus was truly the new messianic king, and that Christians were commissioned to witness to this belief to all nations.) The chief priests protest that the sign should read that he said that he was king of the Jews, but Pilate insists that the sign remain as is. The soldiers divide Jesus' garments, but spare his seamless tunic and gamble for it. Jesus' utter detachment and human vulnerability are here dramatically revealed.

In this play, there is a highly representative community under the cross: Jesus' mother, Mary; Mary, the wife of Cleophas; Mary Magdalene; and the beloved disciple. Jesus gives his mother and the beloved disciple to each other. This dramatizes the special place held by Mary and women disciples in the Johannine community. As though reigning from the cross, Jesus gives his mother and the beloved disciple to each other. (This seems to symbolize the shaping of the first Christian community.) Jesus then cries out in thirst, takes some bitter wine, and then dies, completing his mission with the words "It is finished" (19:30). The divine Jesus does not so much submit to some divine plan, but determines the completion of his own mission.

Jesus had condemned the extreme legalism in his own religion. To highlight this, the author describes a scene filled with irony and hypocrisy. The Jews, engaged in a horrendous act of cruel injustice, are concerned with the law that no corpses be left on the cross on the Sabbath. They ask Pilate to have the legs of the victims broken and their bodies taken away, but the soldiers see that Jesus is dead and put a spear in his side. (This answers later charges that Jesus really did not die on the cross, and that he was "revived" rather than raised.) Blood and water come out from Jesus' side, which some commentators think might have sacramental symbolism (eucharist and baptism). Such symbolism is common in the gospel of John.

As in earlier versions, Joseph of Arimathea, who here is specifically designated as a disciple of Jesus, asks for the body. Nicodemus, a ruling Pharisee who earlier had come to Jesus for instruction under the cover of darkness, enters the picture. Nicodemus brings a hundred pounds of spices and helps bury Jesus in a new tomb in a garden. Joseph and Nicodemus might symbolize the later conversion of Jewish leaders such as Paul, which created an even deeper chasm between Christians and Jews. The enormous amount of spices suggest that Jesus is given the royal burial appropriate for a person who truly is the King of the Jews. The newness of the tomb further rules out any later confusion as to the burial site.

Why was Jesus killed?

It has never been clear why the young Jesus, a peasant workman from Nazareth, who spent several years preaching a gospel of love and healing the afflicted, was crucified. What had he done to deserve being beaten, hauled through the streets as a criminal, and hung naked on a cross until he could no longer catch his breath? Whom had he offended? What motivated his enemies to convict him on patently false charges and execute him by the cruelest means?

Scholars have offered a wide range of answers to the question why Jesus was killed. Bultmann and some of his followers maintain that Jesus was killed by the Romans who mistook him for a rebel. This view reduces the whole matter to an accident, disconnects Jesus' death from his life and ministry, eliminates any intentionality on Jesus' part, and robs the death of any significant meaning.

Fundamentalist scholars take the gospel accounts at face value, and, by harmonizing the gospels, assume that they have arrived at historical reality. This approach, of course, fails to explain the obvious differences in the gospel accounts, rejects any biblical criticism of the texts, and generally loses sight of the rich theological layers in these stories.

A few scholars hold that Jesus was in fact sympathetic toward the Zealot movement, and was thus arrested and executed as a seditionist. This position by-passes Jesus' teaching on nonviolence. It also ignores the important fact that Jesus' followers were not arrested with him, which would have been the case had he been a rebel leader. Neither does this view acknowledge that Jesus' early followers rejected violence and did not take part in the insurrections in the early decades of the first century, or of those in the 60s and 70s CE.

Other scholars challenge the basic historicity of the Jewish responsibility for Jesus' death. They claim that the gospels were written with a bias against the Jewish people, which ultimately led to persecution of the Jews and even to the holocaust. They maintain that no Jews were responsible for Jesus' death, and that the blame for his death must be laid at the door of the Romans. This approach seems to ignore the memories of Jesus' "dangerous" sayings that were aimed at reforming his own religion and challenging Roman oppression. Jesus vehemently opposed the abuse of power, whether it be by his own religious leaders or by the occupying forces of the Emperor. In addition, this position ignores the collusion that existed among the Roman authorities and the Roman-appointed Jewish leaders. Any attack on the abusive authorities of his time would have been regarded as hostile by both Jews and Romans.

Finally, there seems to be a valid link between the hostile attitude toward the Jews in the gospels and later persecutions by the Jews. The gospel writers were dealing with memories of hostilities that Jesus had with individual Jews of his time. They are also reacting to the rejection and persecution that some Christians had received from their Jewish enemies. The conflict was a localized one and it was over religious matters. Only later were these conflicts falsely used to politically persecute Jews in general, and then to racially devalue their humanity and attempt to annihilate them in the holocaust.

Jesus' death was the culmination of his life and his message. Execution came to this young man because of what he stood for and because of his relentless refusal to back off from his prophetic positions even under the threat of death. But what was it in his life and teachings that brought such hatred toward him and moved both Jewish and Roman leaders to want him to be eliminated?

As we have seen, the central reality in Jesus' teaching was about the Kingdom of God, and like many of the prophets before him he believed that this meant the reign of love, justice, and forgiveness in the world. Jesus uniquely taught that the kingdom was the experience of the creative and liberating care of Abba, the dear parent God of all. For Jesus, Abba's blessedness was extended in a special way to those traditionally seen as outcasts and sinners—prostitutes, the disabled, the possessed, the poor, and those suffering oppression. Jesus championed all of those who were dispossessed and proclaimed that a new and magnificent kingdom was breaking into the world that would recognize the dignity of all children of God. This new creation would challenge the security and luxury of the corrupt leadership in both religion and state, and would ultimately bring about their downfall.

Jesus taught that the immediate breaking in of this kingdom called for a radical conversion. It required a turning away from old biases and legalism, a rejection of domination by leaders, an end to the hypocritical abuse of the rights of others, and a cessation of violence. To illustrate such conversion, Jesus gathered a community of followers who would love each other in the same manner as he loved them. They would be friends, equal partners, humble servants who lived simply and with love toward all their neighbors. They would spread this good news of freedom for the children of God and call others to follow.

Jesus

It should be clear why such a person with a message like this would make enemies. Jesus was no doubt a serious threat to those who took away the self-esteem of others and dominated them through fear, superstition, and oppression. Not only was Jesus condemning the oppressors, but at the same time he was empowering those on the bottom. Jesus had said: "So if the Son frees you, then you will be truly free." Most certainly the call to freedom and dignity is always threatening to those who control the lives of others! This is indeed a call to revolution, a nonviolent revolution in the heart. This is a call to a subversion that is ultimately more effective than that of the terrorist, for it unleashes the insurmountable force of love.

But it was more than the message that brought Jesus' downfall. It was his own personal life, a life which forcefully reached out to others, especially those in the alleys and side roads of poverty and disability. It was his power to heal, forgive, and drive out evil. It was his startling teaching set forth with his own authority. It was his courageous stand against the hypocrites and charlatans of his time. Never before had one with such love and tenderness been present in the land.

These are some of the reasons why those religious leaders who lived sumptuously off the fears, superstitions, and ignorance of their people would hate Jesus. He clearly challenged the contradiction between their lifestyle and their religious commitment. He openly exposed their corruption, abuse of power, and cruelty. And, in addition, he proclaimed the nobodies of his society to be more blessed than their own leaders.

As for the Romans, their interests were in maintaining their rule of subjugation, and they did not tolerate resistance. They were not so concerned with religious matters, except where they involved disturbance of the people. Anyone with a message that affirmed the rights of the downtrodden and stirred them to resist oppression would be immediately suspect. And any person who challenged the Jews whom they appointed to lead the people would be considered dangerous. Jesus qualifies as subversive on all counts.

Jesus' actions most likely played a part in his tragic end. His wondrous deeds of healing and forgiving demonstrated that either the power of God or the power of Satan worked through him. His enemies had to choose. If they acknowledged that the power of God worked through Jesus, they would have to accept him and his message. They chose to convince themselves that Jesus represented evil. Besides miracles, Jesus offered equality and dignity to women, children, sinners, and outcasts of all kinds. No doubt such actions would have been offensive to many of his religious leaders.

In the end, there were some key actions that led to his ultimate execution. First, he proceeded into Jerusalem on a humble donkey, accepting recognition as a king of peace and justice from those receiving him. No doubt this alarmed both the Jewish and Roman authorities in Jerusalem.

Secondly, he trashed the Temple commercial area, visibly challenging the corruption and materialism of the Roman-appointed Temple leadership. This seemingly was the straw that broke the camel's back. This young upstart rustic from Galilee had to go!

Crucifixion

Death on a cross was the most horrible form of execution in the ancient world. It was such an unspeakable punishment that we find very little mention of it by ancient authors. Actually, the most detailed description of crucifixion comes from the Christian gospels. The details in these gospel descriptions have been verified by excavations of ancient cemeteries, where skeletal remains reveal the brutal details of this practice. Crucifixion had been used by the Hebrews up until the time of the Roman occupation. After that, the Romans reserved the right for such executions, but never allowed such a horrible execution to be carried out on its own citizens.

Crucifixion was designed to humiliate, torture, and kill in a manner that would satisfy every desire for vengeance. It was a method of execution designed to appeal to the blood lust of soldiers and spectators, and to serve as a deterrent against rebellion. The sight of rows of men writhing in agony as they were being picked apart by birds of prey and wild dogs was intended to quiet any thoughts of resistance to the empire.

Flogging or scourging the victim was an integral part of Roman crucifixion. This brutal beating debilitated the condemned person so that no resistance to hanging on a cross was possible. The process of killing began with this flogging. First, the prisoner was stripped of his clothing, and then his hands were stretched out and bound to the top of a post that was upright in the ground. This position exposed the back, buttocks and legs for the whipping. The instrument used was a short whip with a number of braided thongs that contained small iron balls and sharp pieces of animal bone. Two muscular soldiers on either side of the victim would flog the victim alternately, and the iron balls and pieces of bone inflicted deep contusions and cuts. Eventually the blows tore through the skin to the muscles, causing severe pain, loss of blood, and usually shock.

After the scourging, the victim was cut down, a hundred-pound crossbeam was placed along his shoulders, and the arduous march to the place of execution began. Some soldiers roughly prodded the victim along, while one carried a sign bearing the victim's name and crime for all to see. John's gospel tells us that Jesus' sign read: "Jesus of Nazareth, King of the Jews."

Once the group arrived at the place of execution outside the city, the crossbeam was placed on the ground and the prisoner was thrown down on it face up and nailed to it through the forearms with six-inch nails. Soldiers would the lift up the crossbeam with the nailed victim and fix it to the upright beam that was permanently in the ground. The discovery of a crucifixion victim in an ancient boneyard has revealed that the victim's feet were placed one over the other and the large nail was then driven from the front of the feet through the heel bones. In order to prolong the agony, a crude seat was provided on the upright beam, on which the victim could rest between gasps for breath.

Studies by medical teams have revealed that death on a cross was one of slow asphyxiation. The hanging position severely restricted breathing, causing the victim to rise up and strain to get air in the lungs. As the person pulled himself up by his nailed forearms to catch a breath, he would experience excruciating pain from the severed nerves in his hands and feet. Eventually, he would become too weakened to continue the process and would collapse and die. Before removing the body from the cross, the legs of the prisoner would usually be broken to insure that he could no longer rise to catch a breath. At times, a spear would be pushed through the heart to insure death.

Summary

The passion and death of Jesus at first brought confusion, humiliation, even despair to his followers. Only after the resurrection did they begin to understand the true meaning of his life and death. The gospel writers have given us four plays wherein we find the early communities reflections on the meaning of Jesus' suffering and death. Resurrection faith had moved them to see these horrible events as saving events, acts of love and forgiveness from the Son of their God. Next we will look at the resurrection event that made such faith possible.

Questions for reflection and discussion

1. Why are the passion stories thought to have more of the historical in them than the birth stories?

2. Compare and contrast the personality of Jesus in the four passion stories.

3. Discuss the different accounts of what Jesus says as he dies.

4. What are the dramatic and theological reasons for using natural images such as darkness or an earthquake in these stories?

5. Why do you think Jesus was crucified?

Sources:

Brown, Raymond E. *The Death of the Messiah: From Gethsemane to the Grave: A Commentary on the Passion Narratives in the Four Gospels.* 2 vols. New York: Doubleday, 1994.

Grassi, Joseph A. *Rediscovering the Impact of Jesus' Death: Clues from the Gospel Audiences.* Kansas City: Sheed & Ward, 1987.

Senior, Donald. *The Passion of Jesus in the Gospel of John.* Collegeville, MN.: Liturgical Press, 1991.

————. *The Passion of Jesus in the Gospel of Luke.* Collegeville, MN: Liturgical Press, 1992.

————. *The Passion of Jesus in the Gospel of Mark.* Wilmington, DE: Michael Glazier, 1984.

————. *The Passion of Jesus in the Gospel of Matthew.* Wilmington, DE: Michael Glazier, 1985.

Sloyan, Gerard. *Jesus on Trial: The Development of the Passion Narratives and Their Historical and Ecumenical Implications.* Edited, with an introduction, by John Reumann. Philadelphia: Fortress Press, 1973.

CHAPTER SEVEN

Raised from the Dead

The earliest account of the resurrection that we have is from Paul the apostle and dates from the 50s. Paul recounts to the church in Corinth the gospel message that he learned upon his conversion in the 40s: "that Christ died for our sins in accordance with the scriptures, and that he was buried, and that he was raised on the third day in accordance with the scriptures" (1 Cor 15:3–4). Paul then reports appearances to Peter, the twelve, more than five hundred people at once, James, and all the apostles. Last of all, Paul describes the appearance that he experienced, which was the basis for his mission to the Gentiles. (Acts offers three accounts of this encounter with the risen Lord.)

For Paul, the resurrection was not so much an event to describe, as it was a belief to be proclaimed. It was the basis for faith in the resurrection of the dead. He says: "If Christ has not been raised, your faith is futile and you are still in your sins" (1 Cor 15:17). Through the resurrection, Paul became identified with the risen Lord, sharing in Christ's life, death, and resurrection. He wrote to the Galatians: "and it is no longer I who live, but it is

Christ who lives in me. And the life I now live in the flesh I live by faith in the Son of God, who loved me and gave himself for me" (Gal 2:20–21).

The gospel stories take a different approach to the resurrection in that they are less theological and more concerned with interpreting the nature of the resurrection experiences through stories. The earliest account is in Mark's gospel and it takes up only eight verses of chapter 16. (The other endings of Mark's gospel were inserted at a later time.)

Mark's account

The author of Mark sets the scene very early Sunday morning, when three women disciples, Mary Magdalene, Mary, the mother of James, and Salome bring spices to the tomb to anoint Jesus' body. They were concerned about whether they would be able to roll away the stone away from the tomb, but discover on their arrival that the tomb is open.

The scene is set at dawn, symbolizing a new day, a new creation, the raising of the light of the world. It is significant that women disciples are the ones with the courage to come to the tomb. Once again the key role of Jesus' women disciples is underlined, and they stand in contrast to their male counterparts who hide, betray, and deny Jesus in the passion stories. This might well reflect the situation in the early communities.

The women entered the tomb and were alarmed to see a young man in a white robe. He told them not to fear, and announced that the crucified Jesus of Nazareth had been raised from the dead. The young man in the white robe seems to symbolize a heavenly figure who brings the word of God. This resurrection event is an act of God and must be announced as such. The young man then told the women to tell the disciples and Peter that Jesus is going ahead to Galilee to meet them as he told them. The promise to appear in Galilee links the resurrection with the center of Jesus' saving ministry in the northern province. The women went out and fled in terror and amazement and said nothing to anyone.

It is evident from the story that the first reaction to news of the resurrection was not so much faith as amazement and fear. No doubt this also reflects the fear that early church members had in preaching this good news abroad. From the time of the resurrection to the day in which the gospels were written (and even today), disciples tend to be silent about this wondrous event. In confessing the risen Lord, one risks derision or at least skepticism. Yet the fact is that somehow the good news of God's power seems to get out in spite of human fears. Note that in the story the good news comes through the word and not through sight or touch.

Here also the point is made that the empty tomb is not proof of Jesus' resurrection. The resurrection is a work of God that requires faith for acceptance. There simply is no proof in such matters. Yet it is made clear here that the one raised is indeed the same person as Jesus of Nazareth.

Matthew

The author of Matthew develops his drama in four scenes. Again, using Mark as his main source, he sets the scene at dawn, but reports a different number of women present. At the tomb, they experience an earthquake and watch as an angel who shines like lightning and snow rolls back the stone, striking terror into the guards. The angel announces that Jesus has been raised. With the earthquake, Matthew lends an eschatological dimension to the event, just as he did at Calvary. And more dramatically than Mark, he shows that this is an act of God with the symbol of an angel surrounded by biblical light symbols of lightning and snow. By noting the presence of the guards he once again answers the charge that the apostles had stolen the body. His account also puts to rest a story going around that the gardener had moved the body. As in Mark, the women are told that Jesus has been raised and that they are to tell the disciples that he will see them in Galilee.

At this point, Matthew seems to go to another source. In this scene the women leave the site filled with both happiness and fear and run to tell the disciples. On the way, the women actually meet Jesus, kneel before him, grasp his feet, and worship him. Then they proceed to bring the good news to the community. Clearly the zeal of the early communities is reflected here, as well as the central role played by women disciples. Post-resurrection faith in the divinity of Jesus and its place in the early liturgy are also indicated here.

The scene now shifts to the Sanhedrin. The guards tell the priests what they have seen, and the elders determine to pay the guards to say that Jesus' disciples have stolen his body while the guards slept. Once again this account refutes the rumor that Jesus' body had been stolen. Apparently such stories were still going around when this gospel was written fifty years after the death of Jesus.

In Matthew's final scene, the eleven are back in Galilee, the place where Jesus carried out his ministry. Here they see Jesus and worship him. The "seeing" is most likely a seeing in faith, and the worship reflects post-resurrection faith in Jesus' divinity. Still, it is pointed out, some have doubts. This reflects also the situation in the early communities. Next, Jesus solemnly commissions his followers. Calling on the divine authority given him, Jesus tells them to go and teach all nations, to baptize, and to teach all that he has commanded them. Then he gives a solemn promise: "And remember, I am with you always, to the end of the age" (Mt 27:20).

This episode embodies the essential faith of the early communities. The resurrection has revealed to them the divinity of Jesus Christ, and they have been called to share this good news with everyone. They can do this confidently knowing that the risen Lord is with them as they face incredulity and persecution.

Luke's gospel

The author of Luke's gospel develops a small drama with three interlocking scenes that creatively dramatize the nature and meaning of the resurrection appearances. In the first scene, Luke seems to be working out of Mark. The setting once again is dawn, although a slightly different group of women come along. In the tomb, they encounter two men dressed in dazzling clothes who terrify them. Again, the men symbolize a message of God's power, which can indeed generate both awe and fear. The men ask them why they are looking for the living among the dead, and then announce that Jesus is not here, that he has risen. The women are reminded how the Lord said in Galilee that he would be handed over to sinners and crucified, and would rise on the third day. They remember and go to tell the eleven and all the rest; but given the position of women at the time, they are not believed. Peter runs to the tomb to see for himself, stoops to look in and, upon seeing only linen clothes, goes home amazed.

Again we are reminded by the gospel writer that Jesus' words were not understood in his lifetime, and remained mysterious to many even after the resurrection. We see epitomized in the early disciples the same doubts, amazement, and gradual coming to faith in the risen Lord that occurred in the early church. And we can note the inclination of male disciples to resist the authority Jesus gave to his women followers.

In the second scene, two of Jesus' disciples are returning to their lives in Emmaus, near Jerusalem. As they rush home, they talk about the crucifixion and the events that happened several days before in Jerusalem. Symbolic here is the dispersal of Jesus' followers in fear and confusion after the crucifixion. Possibly implied here also are the desertions of some early Christians when threatened with persecution, and also the separation of the "Way" from the Temple, and ultimately from Jerusalem after its destruction.

While the disciples talk, Jesus joins them, but they did not recognize him. As we shall see, this non-recognition of the risen Lord by his own disciples is a recurring device in the stories. It serves to teach that the risen Jesus has been transformed into a new state of existence.

Jesus next asks his disciples about their conversation. Cleopas, one of the disciples, replies that he was amazed that the stranger is ignorant of the events that had happened. Jesus asks: "What things?" The men rather impatiently report how Jesus of Nazareth, a prophet mighty in word and deed, was handed over by the chief priests and leaders to be crucified. They admit that they had hoped Jesus would redeem Israel. This section dramatizes the hopes and dreams in Jesus as prophet, and how these hopes were shattered by his death. The historical situation of Jesus being handed over is marked here also, and is identified with the risen Lord, who now walks unrecognized with his disciples.

The disciples report that some women from their group went to the tomb that morning, did not find the body and exclaimed that angels had said Jesus was alive. Others went to the tomb, found it empty, but did not see Jesus. Again, we have evidence of how long it took the original disciples to believe that Jesus was risen, even though it had been announced as an act of God. We see also that the empty tomb did not convince them, and that there was a need on the part of the disciples to somehow "see."

The gospel "playwright" then has Jesus rebuke the disciples for being foolish and slow to believe the prophets. He observes that it was necessary that the messiah should suffer all this and then enter into glory. He follows this with a lesson in typology. This section indicates how the early communities came to see Jesus as the fulfillment of the Hebrew messianic hope, and eventually situate his death in the providential plan of God. Years of reflection and prayer enabled them to integrate the life and death of Jesus into their Jewish messianic tradition.

As the group approaches Emmaus, the disciples ask Jesus to stay with them. Jesus agrees to stay, and while at table he takes bread, blesses it, breaks it, and gives it to them. The disciples recognize Jesus, and he then vanishes. The two men comment on how their hearts burned on the road with him, and when he spoke of the Scriptures.

These incidents seem to point to the table ministry of Jesus and to the early Christian recognition of the risen Lord in the eucharist. The disappearance of Jesus again indicates that he has been raised to a new mode of existence and is no longer limited by temporal or spatial restrictions. In addition, the Scriptures are now seen by the early communities as the living word where Christ can be encountered.

In the next scene, the Emmaus disciples have returned to Jerusalem, where they find the eleven and the others discussing how the Lord has risen and has appeared to Simon. The two men report what happened on the road and how they recognized Jesus in the breaking of the bread. The gradual dawning of faith in the resurrection, both among the original disciples and in the early church, is again sketched out in this section of the gospel

While the group of disciples talk, Jesus suddenly stands in their midst and says, "Peace be with you." The disciples are startled and terrified, thinking this is a ghost. Jesus asks them why they are afraid and doubtful. He then shows them his hands and feet and invites them to touch him. The disciples are joyful, and yet still experience disbelief and wonder. To allay their doubts, Jesus asks for a piece of fish and eats it.

This episode continues to explore the meaning of the appearances. The transformation of Jesus is indicated by the suddenness of his coming into their midst. Jesus' benediction reveals the unconditional mercy and forgiveness available to his followers. The many emotions surrounding the acceptance of his resurrection are reiterated: fear, doubt, joy, wonder. Luke adds the physical details of having Jesus show his hands and feet and eat fish in order to assure his readers that the risen Lord is real, even though now transformed. This ultrarealism is perhaps intended to counteract an early view that Jesus had come to his disciples as a ghost.

Next Jesus reminds his disciples of his earlier teachings and reiterates how everything in Moses and the prophets must be fulfilled. He opens their minds to the Scriptures, which reveal that the messiah was to suffer, die, and rise from the dead. Luke describes Jesus as the new Moses, and puts him in continuity with the Hebrew tradition and its messianic hopes. Resurrection validates Jesus as the Christ, the messiah and savior. It also enables the disciples to better understand Jesus' teachings during his public life.

Then Jesus commissions his disciples. He tells them that repentance and forgiveness of sins is to be proclaimed to all nations and that they are to be the witnesses. He urges them to stay in the city until they are clothed with power. Then he leads them to Bethany, blesses them, and is carried into heaven. They worship him, return joyfully to Jerusalem, and continually bless God in the Temple.

The ascension brings the resurrection appearances to a close and marks the beginning of the power of God's Spirit in the commissioned disciples. Repentance and the availability of forgiveness are to be central to the gospel message, and it is to be spread all over the world. The disciples can now worship Jesus as the Son of God and yet still continue their following of the Jewish faith.

John

The author of John's gospel seems to be working from sources different from the synoptics. He opens the first scene of his drama early Sunday while it is still dark. The fact that there is darkness rather than dawn might be symbolic of the confusion and doubt that the death of Jesus brought into the lives of his followers. Mary Magdalene comes to the tomb alone, and, finding the stone removed, runs to tell Simon and the beloved disciple that someone has taken the body of the Lord. Peter and the beloved disciple run to the tomb. As they arrive, each in turn finds only burial cloths in the tomb. The beloved disciple enters the tomb, sees, and believes, even though, it is pointed out, neither he nor Peter yet know that the resurrection has been foretold in Scripture. The point here seems to be that resurrection faith came only in stages to the early followers of Jesus, only after much searching of the Scriptures. Again, the ambiguity of the empty tomb is noted, evidence that even among the disciples the absence of the body from the tomb was problematic.

In the next scene, Mary weeps outside the tomb, and then peers in and sees two angels in white sitting on either end of where Jesus had been. When the angels ask Mary why she weeps, she explains that the Lord has been taken and is missing. She then turns and sees Jesus but she does not recognize him. The scene reflects the grief and confusion of Jesus' disciples after his death. Again, the non-recognition of Jesus points to the transformation that he underwent by this act of God's power.

Jesus asks Mary why she is crying, and Mary, thinking he is the gardener, pleads with him that if Jesus has been carried away he should tell her where he is so she can recover the body. Here is another case where non-recognition demonstrates the transformation of Jesus. This incident seems also to refer to an early rumor that a gardener had moved the body to another grave.

Jesus utters her name (the Hebrew sign of her true identity), and Mary recognizes him. This seems to teach that recognition of the risen Lord in faith comes from the initiative of God and represents a unique personal covenant with God. Then Jesus tells her not to hold on to him because he has not yet ascended. He charges her to tell the brothers that he is ascending to God the Father. Mary runs to tell the disciples that she has seen the Lord (a post-resurrection title of Jesus) and reports to them what he said. These elements seem to indicate that the risen Jesus is no longer physically accessible because he has been exalted. The charge to Mary indicates that the resurrection is now the good news that should be spread to others through the word.

In the next scene, it is Sunday evening and the disciples are in a house behind locked doors for fear of the Jews. Jesus comes and says: "Peace be with you." Then Jesus shows them his hands and side. The disciples are happy to see Jesus, and he wishes them peace again and sends them forth as he has been sent. Again, Jesus' appearance through locked doors dramatizes his new transformed state. His resurrection overcomes fear, brings peace to the soul, and moves followers to spread the message. The physicality of Jesus' hands and feet symbolize that in the appearances Jesus is real, yet markedly different.

Jesus then breathes on them and says: "Receive the Holy Spirit. If you forgive the sins of any, they are forgiven them: if you retain the sins of any, they are retained" (Jn 20:22–23). The breath of new life is given in the "new creation," recalling Genesis. The Johannine community, from which this gospel comes, realized that Jesus' mission, which is to be carried forth by them, is one of forgiveness. The saving power of the resurrection is professed!

To set up the next scene, the author of John has the disciples tell Thomas, who missed it all, that they have seen the Lord. He refuses to believe until he can see and touch the marks on the hands and put his hand into Jesus' side. This might well point to the tendency of early non-believers to want physical proof of the resurrection.

The next scene is set a week later, and Thomas is now with the disciples in the house with the doors shut. Suddenly, Jesus appears and says "Peace be with you"—another reiteration of the new state of Jesus, and of how peace is the center of the kingdom. Jesus invites Thomas to place his finger and see his hands, and to put his hand in his side. He asks Thomas to stop doubting and believe. Thomas replies: "My Lord and my God." Jesus points out that Thomas has seen and believed, and then stresses that they are blessed who have not seen and have believed. This stands as a key profession of the resurrection faith of the Johannine community in the divinity of the risen Lord, a faith that is not based on "seeing." The author of this gospel then says that Jesus did many other things, but that "these are written so that you may come to believe that Jesus is the messiah, the Son of God, and that through believing him you may have life." God has raised Jesus to his full identity and has thus pledged life eternal for all.

The final scene has a special charm to it. It is set on the Sea of Galilee (the area of Jesus' ministry), where Peter and some of the other apostles have returned, apparently to resume their former professions as fishermen now that Jesus is gone. After a night of fishing and catching nothing, Jesus (whom they don't recognize) calls from the shore, inquires about their catch and directs them to cast their net on the right side of the boat. This results in an enormous catch. (The story is reminiscent of an earlier fishing miracle story, which is here adapted as an appearance story. One thinks also of Jesus' earlier promise to make them fishers of men.)

Peter recognizes the Lord. Apparently fishing in the nude, Peter, confused, puts on his clothes and jumps into the sea. The others come to shore dragging the net full of fish. When they reach the shore, Jesus has a fire ready. Simon hauls the fish ashore and Jesus invites them to have breakfast. They recognize who Jesus is as he serves them a breakfast of fish and bread.

This folksy, almost comical scene reveals what the Spirit of the Lord can do with weak human beings. It also goes back to Jesus' table ministry and reveals how the early Christians felt the presence of Jesus even in such mundane events as meals. The early communities saw Jesus as their friend. The incident also points to the eucharistic presence of the risen Lord in the early community house churches.

After breakfast, Jesus asks Simon Peter if he loves him more than the others do. Peter says yes and Jesus tells him to feed his sheep. Jesus asks him two more times and Peter answers yes. This seems to be another recognition of the primacy of Peter among the apostles, who share in the mission of feeding others. The dialogue also is a dramatic way to offer Peter the opportunity to make amends three times with words of love for the three times he denied Jesus. The theme of Jesus' unconditional love and forgiveness is further emphasized.

Jesus then tells Peter that when he was young he fastened his own belt, but when he grows old someone else will do this for him and take him where he does not want to go. Then Jesus says: "Follow me." This looks forward to Peter's mission and death, but it may also allude to the early martyrs. To follow Jesus is to take up the cross of suffering and death as a means of salvation. At the same time, the choosing for the mission ultimately comes from the Master himself, who accompanies his disciples.

Some context for resurrection

The uniqueness of Jesus' resurrection is best understood in the context of beliefs in afterlife current in the ancient world. Greek religious thought was deeply influenced by Homer's notions of the survival of the soul after death, with immortality among the stars the reward for the good, and punishment in Hades reserved for the wicked. There are also traditions of the raising of divine figures like Isis, Asclepius, and Adonis. But none of this seemed to apply to ordinary men and women, however, for whom death meant annihilation.

Roman authors speak of emperors being seen borne aloft into the heavens by eagles or chariot. But again, this was hardly relevant to the Roman citizen. Roman cemetery markings reveal little hope in life after death. And pagan critics were known to mock the early Christian belief in resurrection.

The resurrection of the dead was not unfamiliar to the Jews of the first century CE. Both Elijah and Enoch had been whisked off to heaven, the psalmist reflects on union with God after death, and Hebrew writers describe Sheol as a holding place where the dead await final judgment. In the book of Daniel (c. 538 BCE) there is an account of the heavenly exaltation of one "like a human being coming with the clouds of heaven" (Dan 7:13), an image similar to the descriptions of Jesus in the gospels. Daniel also testifies that "Many of those who sleep in the dust of the earth shall awake, some to everlasting life, and some to shame and everlasting contempt" (Dan 12:2). The book of Wisdom describes the souls of the just who have been persecuted as being "in the hand of God" (Wis 3:1–8). Belief in afterlife is even more explicit in the Maccabean period, not long before the time of Jesus (c. 170 BCE). As a young son is tortured and left to die in the presence of his mother, he says to the king persecuting him: "You accursed wretch, you dismiss us from this present life, but the King of the universe will raise us up to an everlasting renewal of life" (2 Macc 7:9).

The Hebrew tradition on afterlife often appears in an apocalyptic context, wherein Jews expressed hope for survival during times of crisis. This included a strong belief that God would intervene to save his people, helping them transcend death and enter into some heavenly state. Creation would be transformed and exalted, and God's people would be ultimately vindicated. All of this, of course, was to be fulfilled in some endtime. In later rabbinic writings, the Mishna Sanhedrin, it is proclaimed that "all Israelites have a share in the world to come." The righteous will enter into paradise and await the future messianic banquet. The wicked, however, will be consigned to Gehenna, a place of fiery torture, where they will await the Great Judgment.

During the time of Jesus, the Pharisees held firmly to a belief in the resurrection of the body at the endtime. The Sadducees, however, were noted for their refusal to believe in such a resurrection. Many of them believed that the wealth and power that they enjoyed in this life was sufficient sign of God's blessing.

All this being said, the resurrection of Jesus, the raising of a single individual immediately after death by an act of God, and the promise of this same resurrection to all who believe in him is unprecedented. The raising, transformation, and exaltation of Jesus are recognized and proclaimed in the New Testament as being profoundly unique. It is the culminating event in Jesus' life, an event that validates his entire life and death.

The resurrection event

The question is often asked, "What really happened in the Easter event?" Here, of course, we do not mean the actual resurrection of Jesus, for not even the gospels attempt to describe the actual raising of Jesus. The focus should be on the nature of the disciples' experience of Jesus as risen.

Early on, those hostile to Christians offered their explanations for the resurrection stories. As mentioned earlier, one of the first attacks charged that the disciples stole the body and made up the stories of the empty tomb and the appearances. Celsus, who wrote one of the most venomous attacks on Christianity in 180 CE, maintained that the "appearances" were mere hallucinations or hysteria on the part of the disciples. Celsus denied the reality of the resurrection; he argued that the disciples had witnessed nothing but a resuscitation, and that if Jesus had truly been raised from the dead everyone would have experienced it. Origen (d. 254), one of the most brilliant of the early Greek fathers, effectively answered the attacks of Celsus.

Attacks on the resurrection have also been made in modern times. H.E.G. Paulus, a nineteenth-century writer, proposed a "swoon theory," which maintains that Jesus was not really dead when taken down from the cross but had in fact been buried alive and revived in the tomb. Jesus then came forth from the tomb and was only thought to have been raised. This theory is based on two unfounded assumptions: that the Romans were careless in their executions, and that the disciples were stupid enough to mistake a beaten and half-dead man for their glorious messiah.

Solely subjective experiences

Some scholars maintain that the resurrection was purely a subjective experience on the part of the disciples. In other words, in the resurrection nothing happened to the dead Jesus. The Easter event, then, was a purely subjective experience, a case of the disciples finally having grasped the significance of Jesus' message and of their decision to continue his mission. The appearance stories then are nothing other than dramatizations that the cause of Jesus lives on, but not Jesus Christ himself.

Objective/subjective

As the appearance stories indicate, not only were the disciples affected by the resurrection, but Jesus himself was transformed and exalted into a new state of existence. The disciples' experience was of the actual Jesus, the same person whom they had known while he was alive, but now in a different mode of existence.

This was not a case of Jesus being "back in town." It was not the resuscitation of a corpse, a raising up of a dead body as in the case of Lazarus and others. It is clear from the gospels that the risen Lord could be experienced only by the faithful. The Pharisees could not stand on the street and debate him again. He could not be again brought before the Sanhedrin or Pilate to be condemned. Jesus could no longer be tortured and killed. There was no way that the disciples could produce material evidence that Jesus was alive again.

As we have seen from the appearance stories, the experiences of the risen Lord were of the real Jesus, and yet he was now different in that he was often unrecognizable and no longer limited by time or space. Paul preaches that Christ's risen body was not flesh and blood, but now an incorruptible spiritual body (1 Cor 15: 42–43). Jesus was now clearly the Christ, the Son of God, and could be worshiped as such. He is the "first-born" of a new creation whereby the entire world has been radically changed and given a new relationship with the creator (Col 1:15–20). Jesus is now the cosmic Christ, and God plans to "gather up all things in him, things in heaven and things on earth" (Eph 1:10). With the raising of Jesus, the cosmos now has a new creative energy within it, driving it toward its fulfillment in God.

It was through the experience of this risen Lord that the original disciples were themselves transformed and moved to begin one of the most significant religious movements in history. By encountering this risen Lord, these disciples were changed from a group of frightened, confused women and men into enthusiastic witnesses for Jesus Christ. They were now willing to risk everything: loss of their Judaic identity, financial insecurity, even death, in order to profess and spread the good news of Jesus' saving life, death, and resurrection.

The pharisee Saul, a formidable opponent of the Jesus movement, hunted down the followers of Jesus in order to have them punished. Suddenly, he was knocked down, blinded, and led to a deep conversion by his encounter with the risen Lord. That conversion culminated in Paul's becoming an authentic apostle and a tireless missionary to the Gentiles.

Was the resurrection historical?

There has been a great deal of debate about the historicity of the resurrection. The notion "history," of course, is ambiguous, especially in dealing with faith events. If we look at history in terms of concrete and recordable events that are witnessed by impartial witnesses, the resurrection does not fit into historical categories. No one seems to have witnessed the actual raising of Jesus from the dead, and only the faithful report encountering him as risen. At the same time, the resurrection occurred "in history," at a certain point in time, involving specific historical figures; and it started a movement that was and still is observable.

Even acknowledging the historical dimensions of the resurrection event, the raising of Jesus and the encounters with him were spiritual happenings that cannot be verified through the usual standards of historical evidence. Jesus never set out to prove by historical evidence that he had risen. He invited his followers to accept it in faith. Neither did the disciples offer concrete proof that Jesus had risen. Instead, they proclaimed that he had been raised and that they had experienced him as such. They invited others to accept the risen Lord as Jesus Christ, their Lord and God.

What did the disciples see?

"Seeing" and "hearing" are part of the gospel descriptions of the appearance. Are we to conclude, then, that the appearances included real sights and sounds? The Greek word commonly used in these stories to denote seeing is *ophthe*. It is the passive form of the verb "to see" and might be translated as "appeared to." The word has a range of meanings, from spiritual encounters with God to actual physical seeing. In the case of the resurrection appearances, the word seems to mean "seeing with the eyes of faith." In other words, these experiences were real for the faithful, and brought new insights into the identity of Jesus. Had these sightings been observable by physical sight, they would have been accessible to disinterested observers. But as we have pointed out, the experiences were only visible to those who accepted Jesus in faith.

Eschatological dimensions

The resurrection is often described as an eschatological event; that is, an event that reveals the endtime that God has planned for all creation. The kingdom of God is announced as near, intensely present, and yet still to come in future fulfillment. The raising of Jesus from the dead discloses the exaltation of Jesus as well as the endtime of divine vindication for those who have suffered unjustly. The resurrection is thus perceived as a unique breaking in of divine power. This event contradicts the apparent failure of Jesus' mission and the brutal reality of martyrdom, and proclaims the saving power of God over life and death. The resurrection ushers in a new age of the reign of God.

Summary

The raising of Jesus from the dead as the Christ is at the very heart of the Christian tradition. It includes vividly real experiences of the Master as risen and glorified on the part of the disciples. This experience went far beyond expectations of afterlife in the Hebrew Scriptures. In an unprecedented event, the young Jesus, who had been executed just days before, was now experienced in faith as alive, present, and transformed into a new kind of existence.

As a result of this experience, frightened, guilty, and confused disciples were gradually transformed and became empowered by the Spirit of the Lord to proclaim the good news to the world. In the resurrection stories we hear of the witness of these first disciples, as they experience in faith the presence of the risen Lord. A "new creation" is initiated, where there is hope for peace and justice in the world and eternal life beyond it.

Questions for reflection and discussion

1. Why is the resurrection so important in the Christian tradition?

2. Discuss the differences between those who consider the resurrection to be only a subjective experience and those who believe it is also objective.

3. What are some of the important things that the resurrection stories teach us about the first experiences of the risen Christ by the disciples?

4. Dramatize several of the resurrection stories in groups and discuss their meaning.

5. In what ways can Christians today experience the risen Christ?

Sources

Bernard, Pierre R. *The Resurrection of the Lord: Mystery of Faith.* Translated by Francis V. Manning. New York: Alba House, 1996.

Brown, Raymond E. *A Risen Christ in Eastertime: Essays on the Gospel Narratives of the Resurrection.* Collegeville, MN: Liturgical Press, 1991.

———. *The Virginal Conception and Bodily Resurrection of Jesus.* New York: Paulist Press, 1973.

Davis, Stephen T., Daniel Kendall, and Gerald O'Collins, eds. *The Resurrection: An Interdisciplinary Symposium on the Resurrection of Jesus.* New York: Oxford University Press, 1997.

O'Collins, Gerald. *Interpreting the Resurrection: Examining the Major Problems in the Stories of Jesus' Resurrection.* New York: Paulist Press, 1988.

———. *Jesus Risen: An Historical, Fundamental, and Systematic Examination of Christ's Resurrection.* New York: Paulist Press, 1987.

———. *The Resurrection of Jesus Christ: Some Contemporary Issues.* Milwaukee: Marquette University Press, 1993.

Osborne, Kenan B. *The Resurrection of Jesus: New Considerations for Its Theological Interpretation.* New York: Paulist Press, 1997.

Perkins, Pheme. *Resurrection: New Testament Witness and Contemporary Reflection.* Garden City, NY: Doubleday, 1984.

CHAPTER EIGHT

Jesus and Women

Past biblical and theological interpretations of Jesus reflect a largely male perspective. More recently, many women have joined the ranks of biblical scholars and theologians, and have given us fresh insights into Jesus' treatment of women and a new understanding of early Christian attitudes toward women disciples. At the same time, women theologians have helped Christians reinterpret their understanding of Jesus in a way that better suits the contexts in which women live today. In this chapter we will review the gospel perspectives on how Jesus related to women against the backdrop of his times. Then we will proceed to an overview of women's views on Christology today.

Women in Jesus' time

It is very possible that Jesus was influenced by the women's movements in the Hellenic and Roman cultures that surrounded him. Jesus no doubt knew women who struggled for freedom and equality, and it is possible that these women, as well as his own mother and his women disciples, helped him develop an enlightened view on the dignity of women. Let us look at some of the trends in these ancient times.

In the Hellenistic period, which had great influence on the time of Jesus, women had acquired extensive rights within the family, as well as in the social and economic spheres. Spartan women participated in the Olympics, and there are records of excellent women athletes in the foot and chariot races just forty years before the time of Jesus. Women also distinguished themselves at that time in music, medicine, arts, crafts, and in the professions. They also were writers and philosophers, and played a priestly role in the Hellenistic cults and mystery religions. Of course, it needs to be noted that these achievements usually were made by the wealthier women of the day.

In contrast, women in the Roman Empire did not enjoy such favored status. The family structure was largely patriarchal, divorce laws favored the men, and there was a double standard with regard to sexual practice. At the same time, some elite Roman women were exceptionally educated and were active in business, politics, literature, art, and medicine. Some women were also given official religious positions, and even served as priests in some of the cults.

Women in the Hebrew Scriptures

In the gospels, Jesus is portrayed as one who tried to reform his own Jewish religion by restoring the best of its traditions. The Hebrew Scriptures, which were a thousand years in the making, reflect a wide variety of attitudes toward women. There are two accounts of the creation of women in the Genesis stories. The earlier Yahwist account tells of woman being created from the side of man, from his own bone and flesh. This account is followed by the story of the first woman, Eve, being led into evil by the serpent, and then in turn persuading Adam to sin. This story has been traditionally interpreted to mean that women are inferior to men and tempt them to evil.

A later Genesis story, composed by priestly writers, tells of how both woman and man were created in the image of God and how both were blessed and commissioned by God. This story, though it relates to a period when notions of women were much more progressive among Jews, has generally received less attention than the "garden story."

Overall, the Hebrew Scriptures show mixed attitudes toward women. Yahweh is often portrayed in masculine imagery: as a warrior defending his people, a father extending love and care to his children, and as a husband displeased with the infidelity of his spouse (the chosen people). On the other hand, there are many instances where God is described as a woman: a seamstress clothing her people, a nurse caring for her children, a midwife bringing forth new life, and a loving mother. During the Babylonian exile, the Hebrews incorporated into their rituals a devotion to the goddess of fertility. Such worship was eventually condemned by the prophets Isaiah and Jeremiah, and the Jewish feminine images of Yahweh were then translated into the Wisdom tradition.

The social structures of Israel were generally patriarchal. Women were often viewed as property and as servants who were expected to be obedient. In spite of this, the great women of the tradition, Sarah and Rebecca, were honored as mothers of Israel. Miriam, the sister of Moses, was described as a prophet and one of the leaders of the exodus. Deborah is portrayed as both prophet and judge who brought God's word and justice to her people. At different times women served as queens of Israel. Most notable was Alexandra, whose rule was marked by peace and prosperity seventy years before Jesus was born. These women, of course, were rare exceptions in a culture where inequality and even oppression were more the norm for women.

Women in Jesus' time

It is difficult to ascertain the lot of Jewish women at the time of Jesus. There were many "Judaisms" going on during his lifetime, and Jesus would have experienced much diversity with regard to the legal, mystical, theological, ritualistic, and prophetic elements of his religion. The Jews of his time would have argued over the role of women in their society and religion, as there was a wide divergence of views on this subject. Jesus most likely took part in such arguments and put forth his own interpretations of the Jewish tradition. His own personal teachings about the dignity of women seem to be the seed for the more fully developed notions we encounter in the gospels.

During the time of Jesus, a woman's identity was generally derived from her role in the family as wife and mother. Women were expected to marry young, and marriages were arranged by the father. Success for women was largely measured by how well they carried out their duties at home. A girl was thought to come of age at twelve-and-a-half. Prior to that, she generally had few rights, and often was not permitted to have personal possessions or to keep payment for work done. Daughters were handed over in marriage for sums of money, and when fathers were desperate, they were allowed to sell their daughters into slavery.

The home was the proper place for women, so they were seldom seen in public. If women did have occasion to go outside, their faces were to be covered and they generally were not to speak with anyone, especially men. Any dealings with another man could be punishable with a writ of divorce from the husband. In the rural areas, with which Jesus was familiar, women were permitted to work in the fields, but never alone with another man. (These customs are still observed in some Arab countries today.)

The strict segregation of women was prescribed for several reasons. First of all, the Jews viewed themselves as a "chosen people," a tribal nation. In order to keep this identity pure and to preserve bloodlines and inheritances, women had to be closely monitored. Women were thought to be weak and seductive, so careful safeguards were introduced to prevent infidelity. At the same time, men enjoyed a greater degree of sexual freedom.

Women were expected to be obedient servants and in return could rightfully expect shelter, food, sexual relations, care when ill, and a decent burial. Mothers could not expect the same respect from the children as could fathers. Husbands were permitted to have multiple wives, although this was not common because of the expense of "purchasing" wives and the risks of having to support them in case of a divorce.

The divorce laws for Jews favored men. Women had few rights in court and could rarely sue for divorce. Opinions varied as to the grounds upon which husbands could issue writs for divorce against their wives. There were two main schools of thought on this at the time of Jesus. Rabbi Shammai allowed a man to divorce his wife for infidelity, while the more liberal Rabbi Hillel permitted men to divorce their wives for a more attractive woman or even if she was a poor cook. Public stigma and the need to financially support the divorced wife seem to have prevented divorce from becoming widespread.

In religious affairs, women generally stayed in the background during the time of Jesus. The sacred sign of the covenant itself, circumcision, was a rite only for males. While mothers were significant in the lives of their children (one had to have a Jewish mother to be considered a Jew), fathers carried out the instruction in the Torah. Women were usually exempt from studying the Torah, and were for the most part forbidden to be official teachers. There were, of course, exceptions. Records tell of a woman named Beruria, whose father and husband were both rabbis. She was a recognized scholar of the Torah and was a respected teacher of the law.

Women did not share the men's obligation to make pilgrimages to Jerusalem for the feasts; and if they did have occasion to visit the Temple, they were confined to the lower Court of Women. Generally, women also remained segregated in the synagogues and were generally forbidden to read at services. Women were never permitted to be priests or to prepare sacrifices in the Temple. The main reason for such discrimination was that women were considered to be "unclean" from menstruation and pregnancy. Leviticus (12:1–8, 15:1–32) taught that issue from sexual organs was one of the causes of ritual impurity. Since women were considered to be "regularly unclean," they were not permitted to function officially in the Jewish religion.

Most of what we know of the religious role of women is filtered through the eyes of male authors. We know little of what really went on in daily life, especially among the common folk. We can assume that many Jewish men held women in respect, and that Jewish women often struggled against the odds to be well-informed and devout Jews. Most likely it was those examples who helped Jesus formulate his progressive views on women in society and religion. Most certainly, Jesus was not anti-Jewish in his views on women, but he was opposed to the rigid and oppressive views toward women that existed in his own religion.

Jesus' perspective

We are well aware that the gospels were written decades after Jesus' death, and that they reflect the lives and theologies about Jesus of later communities. At the same time, these gospels are based on clear memories of Jesus' person and teachings. Looking at these gospels, as well as what we know from other available sources, we can make some educated guesses about Jesus' attitudes toward women.

Jesus grew up in a large Jewish family, and seems to have been respectful of the customs of his religion. Most of his life was spent around Nazareth, where he worked as a craftsman, the trade of his father, Joseph. If Joseph did die early in Jesus' life, as tradition has it, Jesus grew up with his mother, a single parent, whom he likely supported with his work. His mother, Mary, no doubt was a major influence on Jesus' formation during the nearly thirty years that he was at home.

During Jesus' short public life, he challenged the patriarchal system of his time by refusing to view women as property or servants. He insisted that everyone was a child of God, and he revealed a reign of God where people related as brothers, sisters, and friends. In the gospel stories, Jesus is portrayed as regarding women with the same respect and love that he extended to all persons. There is no indication that he talked down to women, or considered them to be inferior or in any way less worthy of human rights and freedom than men. For Jesus, personhood was more important than gender. Jesus treated all persons, young or old, married, single or widowed, healthy or disabled, sinner or saint, accepted or outcast, rich or poor, Jew or Gentile, as sacred creations of God. Women, therefore, received their fundamental identity and meaning from being human persons, and not from their gender or from their roles of wife and mother.

There are a number of stories in the gospels which indicate that Jesus' followers remembered him as someone who challenged the negative attitudes toward women in his day. There is the well-known story of the woman captured for adultery (Jn 8:1–11). Admittedly the story is late (perhaps inserted into the gospel in the third century), but is of a piece with other stories that reveal Jesus' views of women. In the story, the woman is publicly humiliated and threatened with death for her sin of infidelity. (Consistent with the prevailing double standard, no mention is made of the man involved.)

Jesus intervenes in a situation that could have been dangerous for him. Emotions are high and the woman is about to be stoned to death. Jesus bravely turns the tables on the woman's male accusers when he says "Whichever one of you has committed no sin throw the first stone at her." After the would-be executioners slink away, Jesus speaks to the woman with tender respect and compassion, sets her free without judgment or rebuke, and simply tells her to sin no more.

Another well-known example is the story of the woman who comes to Jesus while he is at table among the guests of Simon the Pharisee (Lk 7:36–50). The woman seems to be a prostitute, and the men at the table are offended by the presence of such a sinful outcast. (Jesus would have known that prostitutes then, as today, were generally victims of social conditions, male oppression, and sex-abuse as children.) The woman, who is not even given a name, comes to Jesus in the role of servant and beggar, washing and kissing his feet, and drying them with the flowing locks of her hair. Jesus does not allow her to stay in this traditional subservient female posture. Instead, he speaks of her as one who offers him the hospitality that Simon the host should have offered. Jesus raises her above the men present as a paradigm of love and faith. He does not treat her as an outcast, nor does he show any concern for the taboo against being touched by a woman in public. Not at all embarrassed by his apparent friendship with this woman, Jesus proclaims her wholeness and dignity. From his own Abba experience of a God of tenderness and love, he extends this same regard to her as a member of the human family.

On mothers and children

Jesus further challenges the patriarchal views of his time that give preference to fathers over mothers. He reminds the teachers of his day of God's command to "Honor your father and your mother" (Mt 15:4). Jesus is also portrayed as honoring the dignity of all children, both girls and boys. In Jesus' time, children had few rights, and were shown little regard outside of their own homes and families. Inside the home, girls were not given the same value as boys. Men often said a prayer of thanksgiving that they were not born female, and they rejoiced much more over the birth of a son than a daughter.

On one occasion, Jesus' own disciples display their disregard for children and try to get them out of Jesus' way. Jesus rebukes his followers and asks that all the children, both girls and boys (along with their mothers), be brought to him. He then points out that these children in their innocence and simplicity should be models for gospel living (Mk 10:13–16). Luke includes another story where Jesus takes a child to his side and proclaims: "Whoever receives this child in my name receives me" (Lk 9:48). This stands as a profound statement on the dignity of all children, whether they be female or male.

The "pairing" of gospel stories

Scripture scholars have called attention to how the mention of couples and the "pairing" of gospel stories might be reflective of Jesus' teaching on sexual equality. Luke cites couples, such as Mary and Joseph, Elizabeth and Zechariah, Anna and Simeon, and others to possibly demonstrate women and men in partnership before God. In addition, miracle stories are often paired, as if to proclaim that the power of God worked through Jesus on women and men without partiality. Some examples are Luke's pairing the cures of Peter's mother-in-law and the demoniac; the cure of the woman who had hemorrhaged for twelve years and the Gerasene demoniac; and the raising of the widow's son and the cure of the centurion's servant (Lk 4:31–41; 8:26–48; 7:1–17). In all these stories, Jesus reaches out to both women and men as children of God, revealing the power of a God who heals, enables, and liberates all.

Challenging abuse in divorce

Jesus' stood in opposition to the abuse of the divorce laws of his time, laws that nearly always favored the husband. The text opposing divorce in Mark, and the one where Matthew offers an exception, have remained extremely controversial (Mk 10:1–12; Mt 5:31–32). Whether Jesus was setting an ideal or imposing a law remains unresolved, but most agree that he did oppose the liberal interpretations of both Hillel and Shammai. We saw earlier that both teachers allowed divorce for reasons that favored males. Jesus opts to return to the Torah tradition of a permanent partnership in marriage and opposes the oppression of women in the current application of divorce laws. In addition, Jesus' insistence that lust comes from the male heart seems to be a direct challenge to the traditional notion that women are the seducers (Mt 5:28). Jesus' views on such issues were indeed considered to be dangerous in some scribal quarters, and no doubt brought him some fierce opposition.

Advocate of widows

The gospels also reveal another aspect of Jesus' message: his advocacy of widows, a group victimized by the patriarchal system. Widows were often impoverished and left extremely destitute and hopeless by the deaths of their husbands. They had few rights of inheritance, and their futures usually rested in the hands of other male members of the family. Some widows ended up as beggars, others were driven into prostitution.

Jesus is portrayed in the gospels as a dedicated advocate for widows. In Mark, Jesus attacks the hypocrisy of the teachers of the law for their devotion to prayer while they contributed to the oppression of widows. Jesus observes that the two copper coins that the widow dropped into the Temple treasury are worth more than the large offerings of the rich, because the woman has so little to give (Mk 12:38–44). Luke tells the touching story where Jesus is moved to pity in seeing the widow taking her only son to be buried. He reaches out to her, consoles her, and returns her son and only means of support to her (Lk 7:11–17).

Ignoring the "unclean" taboo

In the gospels Jesus challenges the religious taboos that prohibit the participation by women in the authority and rituals of their religion because of their "uncleanness." Mark's gospel weaves together two stories on this theme. One story begins with Jairus, a Jewish official, who comes to Jesus to plead with him to lay hands upon his sick daughter. As Jesus follows Jairus home, he encounters a woman who is constantly unclean because she has been hemorrhaging for twelve years. She wants to touch Jesus' cloak, hoping to be magically cured, and then slip back into anonymity. Jesus will not allow her to remain anonymous or outcast. Not the least bit concerned about becoming unclean himself by physical contact with such a woman, Jesus calls her forth, praises her faith publicly, heals her, and reveals her human dignity for all to see. Then Jesus proceeds to Jairus' home only to find that the daughter was already dead. Jesus pays no attention to the taboo that forbids touching a dead body. He takes her hand and speaks to her: "Little girl, I tell you to get up." The girl is restored to life; and Jesus, in the midst of all the amazement, orders that she be fed (Mk 5: 21–43).

Jesus called upon the best of his Jewish traditions and reminded his people that all are children of God. He shed new light on values and truths long forgotten by many of the Jewish leaders of the time. Jesus set standards that would continue to dominate the early communities that were to follow. Paul the apostle reflects these standards when he proclaims to the community in Galatia: "There is no longer Jew or Greek, there is no longer slave or free, there is no longer male and female; for all of you are one in Christ Jesus" (Gal 3:28).

The reign of God is for all

As we have seen, the reign of God is a central notion of Jesus' teachings. Jesus preaches a version of this Jewish tradition that is inclusive and which opposes violence and injustice. It is remarkable how often feminine images are associated with the reign of God in the gospel stories. In the story of the wedding feast of Cana, a symbol of the reign of God, the mother of Jesus orchestrates Jesus' first miracle for a couple and their guests (Jn 2:1–12). In Matthew's judgment scene both women and men come together for the days of fulfillment (Mt 25:31–46). And in the parable of the virgins at the wedding feast (again a symbol of men and women joining in the reign of God), the women who act wisely are able to enjoy the celebration (Mt 25:1–13).

The gospels also use "parallel stories" to show that in the Jesus movement both women and men carry forth the mission of Jesus. In the parable of the sower, a man sows the seed of the word of God, while in the parallel story of the yeast a woman spreads the message (Mt 13:1–17, 33). Luke pairs the parable of the good shepherd rejoicing in the finding of the lost sheep with the parable of a woman celebrating the recovery of her lost coin (Lk 15:1–10). It is noteworthy that here the searching woman stands as an image of God seeking those who are lost.

Matthew's gospel reflects the memory of Jesus' unique willingness to use feminine imagery for himself as he weeps over Jerusalem. He says: "How often have I desired to gather your children together as a hen gathers her brood under her wings, and you were not willing!" (Mt 23:37). The passage seems to reflect the memory of Jesus' comfortable use of feminine images for God and the inclusivity of his own ministry.

Although Jesus' mission of reform seems to have been largely directed to his own Jewish people, there are indications in the gospels that Jesus gave his followers precedents for inviting both women and men Gentiles into his movement. A most striking example of this is the story of the Syro-Phoenician woman. As told in Mark, Jesus was in seclusion in a house in Tyre when a Gentile woman sought him out and begged him to cure her daughter. Jesus was not inclined to cooperate, and either in an effort to test her resolve or to brush her off, he at first refuses her request: "Let the children be fed first, for it is not fair to take the children's food and throw it to the dogs" (Mk 7: 27). The woman was not to be intimidated, and smartly responded with what might be feigned humility: She says "Sir, even the dogs under the table eat the children's crumbs." Jesus is caught in his own bias and learns from the woman a lesson in inclusivity. He commends her for her insight and heals her daughter. The woman, whom Matthew calls "a woman of great faith," seems to symbolize the many persistent Gentile women who became leaders and mentors of great faith as the early communities spread beyond Judaism (Mt 15:26–27).

The call of women disciples

Traditionalists have made much of Jesus' choice of only male apostles, even to the point of thereby justifying an all-male hierarchy and priesthood. Biblical scholars see the Twelve as primarily symbolic of the heads of the tribes of Israel, and some scholars propose that such symbolism is actually post-resurrection.

Those who were apostles were certainly key witnesses to the person and teachings of Jesus, but the mission was not theirs alone. Christianity was spread also by other "apostles" beyond the twelve, and by disciples, preachers, prophets, and leaders of both sexes. As a matter of fact, the Twelve, and we have conflicting lists of their names, were not replaced as they died. Judas was replaced by Matthias, but after that the role of the Twelve was allowed to die out. Paul uses the title for himself, by virtue of his experience of the risen Lord, but for that matter the same title could just as easily be given to Mary Magdalene and the other women in the resurrection stories.

The choosing and sending forth of women disciples was without parallel in Jesus' time. It was indeed one of the most radical moves of his career. In doing so, he challenged the patriarchal notion that a woman's identity comes from her role as wife and mother. While Jesus did not attack home or family, he made it clear that ministry to the reign of God took priority over family ties.

This seems to be the point in his statement to his mother at Cana that he alone must decide when his time has come. In the story of the boy Jesus being found in the Temple by his parents, the lad makes it clear that his "Father's business" takes priority over family ties. All three of the synoptic gospels tell the story of Jesus' mother and brothers who, apparently thinking that Jesus has lost his senses, hope to get through the crowds to calm him. Jesus rebukes them with the statement that those who do the will of God are his true relations.

Finally, there is the story of the rich young man, which underscores the seriousness of the demands that Jesus makes on his disciples, even to the point of leaving their families. Jesus' radical call to discipleship allows women to identify themselves in roles other than familial. Women like his mother, Mary, Joanna, Mary Magdalene, Martha, and Mary were able to step out of the patriarchal structures and assume the identity of disciple on an equal par with men. Jesus encouraged women to follow him and live among his group of male disciples, challenging the idea that women were weak and seductive. Jesus also seems to have been personally comfortable being with women both in domestic and public situations, and apparently ignored the taboos of uncleanness.

It is significant that John's story of the woman caught in adultery (Jn 8:1–11) takes place while Jesus is teaching in the Temple. Similarly, Luke's story of the healing of the crippled woman (Lk 13:10–17) is set while Jesus is teaching in a synagogue. There is a subtext in each of these stories that may reflect an interest in the early church in more fully integrating women into the ritual life of the community.

Jesus' encounter with the Samaritan woman at Jacob's well (Jn 4:1–30) is also significant. This highly symbolic story tells of a "renegade Jew" who has been much married and divorced. Cut off from the Temple in Jerusalem and even from her own Samaritan temple in Garizim, she is offered "living water" by Jesus. He promises that she will be able to "worship the Father in spirit and truth" (Jn 4:23). The woman goes back to her village and brings the entire population to Christ. This story illustrates Jesus' religious calling to women, as well as the central role played by women in worship and ministry in the Johannine community.

Leading women disciples

The New Testament provides us with many examples of outstanding women who followed Jesus. In the gospels, women are not called "disciples" (there was, in fact, no ancient Hebrew or Aramaic word for female disciple), but many of them fully qualified for discipleship. Women accompanied Jesus in his mission and were singularly present at key events in his life, including his death and resurrection. These individuals are not only real historical figures; they also symbolize the prominent role that women held in the early Christian communities.

First is Mary, Jesus' mother, whose consent as a young maiden is required before the nativity can take place. Her Magnificat places her in the prophetic tradition of Hannah, the mother of Samuel, a tradition that cries out for justice for the poor. At Cana, Mary orchestrates the first miracle, with all its sacramental symbolism. She stands bravely beneath her Son's cross, in solidarity with Jesus' loving and forgiving gift of self. In John's Calvary scene, she is joined with the beloved disciple to begin the community and continue a partnership of ministry. In the upper room she is part of the pentecostal community as the church is symbolically born in the Spirit.

Mary Magdalene was one of Jesus' closest disciples. Although traditionally thought of as a converted prostitute, there is no justification in the gospels for such a reputation. Mary was instead a woman of means, who underwrote the work of Jesus and the disciples after she had received a miraculous cure. The high level of her ministry is clear from the role she is given at the cross, as well as from her being privileged to be the first witness to the risen Lord. With justification, Mary was known in the early centuries as "the apostle to the apostles."

The gospels also tell of Martha and Mary, two close friends of Jesus. It is Martha who is reminded that domestic roles are not as important as listening to the Word of God. In John's gospel, Martha "serves" at the dinner at Bethany and is a central figure in the resuscitation of her brother, Lazarus. Jesus reveals to her that he is the resurrection and the life, and she in turn professes her faith that he is the messiah and the Son of God. Such stories once again reveal an advanced feminine ministry in the Johannine community, a community apparently founded by a close friend and disciple of Jesus, one who knew well Jesus' openness to women.

Mary of Bethany, Martha's sister, is also a model of early ministry. Breaking with tradition, Jesus came to her house, taught her, and held up her right to be a hearer of the Word. Just before Jesus' death, at what has been called a "miniature last supper," Mary anoints Jesus' feet as if for burial with an abundance of her best perfume and dries them with her hair. Here she becomes a striking symbol for women carrying out early sacramental ministry. Indeed, Jesus is portrayed as following her ritual as he washes the feet of his disciples at the last supper in John's gospel.

Joanna is apparently a woman who felt Jesus' call to leave the luxury of the corrupt court of Herod, where her husband was the minister of finance. She stands as a model for women of success to use their independence to carry out the mission of Jesus. Luke points out that she was one of the original witnesses to the resurrection, as well as one of the women who brought the good news to the apostles.

Finally, we have the women of the Pauline communities. There is Priscilla, who worked closely with Paul. Paul wrote to the Romans that Priscilla and her husband risked their necks for him. She was one of the founders of the community at Corinth, and a key leader of the communities in Rome and Antioch. There was Junia, whom Paul said was distinguished among the apostles. There was Phoebe, a leader in the church at Cenchrae. There were Tryphosa, Julia, and many other women who led churches and acted as early preachers, teachers, and leaders of liturgy. It is clear that those who wish to deny women equality in the ministry today will not find justification for such a position in the New Testament.

Christology and women

Once Christianity acknowledged the legitimacy of a "theology from below," a theology arising from the context of human experience, a diversity of voices was raised. Western women scholars began confronting patriarchal structures and the traditional Christology used to justify oppression. Women scholars who had been bypassed in much of the original black and liberation theology, began to speak for new interpretations of Christology. Then followed the voices of women theologians from Asia and Africa, and most recently from Eastern Europe. All are seeking a Savior who can inspire them in their own struggles for freedom.

Some women theologians have expressed discomfort with the "maleness" of Jesus, since maleness has so often in the past been used to justify oppression. Black women (womanists) point to "slave-holding Christianity," which saw no contradiction in following Christ and at the same time "owning" people and treating them as inferior creatures. They point to whites and blacks as well, who followed a patriarchal Jesus and saw no contradiction in segregation and even in the exclusion of women in their own churches. They point to the many black women today who are caught in a male-designed welfare system that renders them powerless.

Latina women (*mujeristas*) point to the image of Christ the King that was used by the conquistadores to subject whole peoples to genocide and servitude. They also observe that the image of Jesus as "liberator," proposed by male theologians, usually ignored *machismo*. This male force in their culture allowed men to abuse women, desert them, and subject them to inhumane working conditions. Other theologians from Latin America object to the "metaphysical Christ" of the early councils. They complain that this Christology is based on Hellenic philosophy where women were seen as inferior, and therefore requires that salvation can only come about if a male God becomes a male savior.

Feminist theologians deal with the maleness of Jesus in a number of ways. Some choose to leave Christianity, concluding that it is a religion that is too locked into a male and patriarchal Christology to be applicable to women. They see the Church as irrevocably committed to a patriarchal system that denigrates women, and encumbered by a clerical system that demands obedience from women while at the same time excluding them.

Other women scholars choose to stress Jesus' humanity rather than his maleness, and thus interpret the incarnation as God's embodiment in humanity, indeed in all of materiality. From this perspective, Jesus represents the wholeness to which all women and men, as well as the earth, are called. Some Latina theologians are not so much put off by the fact that Jesus was male. They are drawn to the historical Jesus, who, as a male, raised up women in his own life, and who now liberates all of God's children from oppression.

The Christology proposed by women more often emphasizes the Christ of faith than the historical Jesus. For many theologians, this Christ is not the metaphysical Christ of the early councils, who is unintelligible to the women of today, most especially to African and Asian women. More appealing and relevant is the risen Christ, who, in resurrection, transcends sexuality. This glorified Christ is seen to be in solidarity with women in whatever context they are oppressed, and empowers them in their particular struggles for liberation. This Christ can be seen in the faces of women of all colors and backgrounds, who suffer degradation, poverty, and subjugation under neo-colonial policies. He stands in solidarity with women who experience abuse within their own indigenous religions, and even within their own families.

The Christian notion of redemptive suffering is widely challenged by women theologians. They observe that too often the belief that Jesus saved us from our sins through suffering has been used to persuade women that they should stoically and patiently accept their own suffering as God's will. In this traditional view, Jesus is the New Adam, the Son of God, the man for others, who saved mankind from the sin of Eve. Here women are often viewed as weak seductresses, who lead men astray. Women therefore should stay in the background, stand by their men, and allow men to lead them and save them from their weakness and sins. They should be taught to bear the sins of others as Jesus did, and to allow themselves to be sacrificed as victims of domestic violence or unjust labor practices.

Many women theologians believe, rather, that suffering, both for Jesus and others, comes from evil people and systems and not from God's will. Therefore, women should be made more aware of the social, economic, political, and religious evils that suppress them. Women should be encouraged to reject and resist such oppression, rather than patiently endure it. They should see Jesus as a fellow sufferer who took the side of outcasts, and who was crucified for his condemnation of oppression.

Christ in this view is one who suffers with the women who are victims, whether they be abused wives or daughters, the homeless bag lady in an inner city, the abandoned mother of nine in a barrio, or a girl forced into prostitution in a tourist town. Christ walks with the underpaid factory worker, the lesbian, the woman with AIDS. He accompanies the mother searching for clean water and food for her children in a remote area of Korea, the disappeared girl, tortured and killed in Latin America, the madres protesting the cruelty of repressive governments. He is seen in the face of a disabled girl in an orphanage, or an elderly crippled woman in a nursing home. This is not so much the image of Jesus as the "the suffering servant," an image that can often lead women to further distress and depression. Instead, many women seek a Jesus who affirms them, strengthens them, and gives them courage to set limits, sort out their priorities, and resist abuse. This Jesus Christ saves in suffering and from suffering, rather than through suffering.

Some point out that Christ's mission should not be restricted to women who are victims or outcasts. There is also the need for a Christology that speaks to women who live comfortably and who have good opportunities for education and work. Too little theological work has been done to speak for the woman who has a good marriage, but feels overwhelmed by the responsibilities of homemaking and mothering. Who is Christ for working mothers or for professional single women? Who is Christ for those who work in the military, the corporate world, or the fields of law, medicine, sports, education, and other areas? These women also need a Jesus Christ that offers them wholeness, and who calls them to generous service of others less fortunate.

Women theologians often develop a theology of incarnation that includes the female body. They point out that the life-giving, feeding, and nurturing dimensions of women's bodies have often been neglected or even denigrated in Christology. Once again, they look for an understanding of incarnation as the embodiment of God in the human body, both male and female, which gives new dignity to both. This requires a reclaiming of feminine metaphors for God in Scripture (nurse, mid-wife, mother) and the realization that Jesus embodies the human in its fullness. This is the earthy Jesus who healed bodies with his touch, and who challenged the sexual taboos of his time. This theology looks to a sensuous Christ, who makes women proud of their bodies and confident of their beauty, and who gives them power to demand respect and dignity. This is a Christ who is intuitive, comfortable with relating and intimacy, and who can be discovered in new ways in the feminine experience.

Some women theologians have gone beyond attacking sexism and patriarchy as the only culprits in their oppression. They point to the ethnic superiority that has led to the slaughter of women in the holocaust, in ethnic cleansing and genocide. Women scholars today expose racism's responsibility for the enslavement, segregation, and degradation of women. They document the worldwide impoverishment of women in particular. And the voices of women are heard who carry multiple stigmas: they are not only women, but also of color and poor at the same time. A Christ is called for who can be seen in the faces of all such women, and who can support and inspire them to overcome the multiple forces that suppress them.

Women theologians have reclaimed the prophetic image of Jesus. This Jesus proclaims the poor and outcast blessed, condemns those that lay heavy burdens on their backs, and frees them from whatever imprisons them. Women, whether they are "imprisoned" by the stifling routine of the suburbs, the squalor of the barrios, the environmentally degraded villages of Eastern Europe, or the isolated villages in the African bush look to a Jesus who is a strengthening presence in their midst. Women have accepted Jesus' prophetic interpretation of the kingdom of God as the reign of God's mercy and power over the dominating and unjust powers of institutions. They have experienced "woman power" and "woman church" as they dialogue, organize, and struggle to gain respect and dignity in their cultures and religions.

A number of women theologians have reclaimed the Wisdom or Sophia tradition from the Hebrew Scriptures and the gospels. Elisabeth Schüssler Fiorenza depicts Jesus as the prophet of Sophia, who initiated a movement of itinerant healers and teachers. The disciples left their patriarchal families and lived as a community of brothers and sisters, a discipleship of equals. Their mission was to spread the creative, relational, and joyful message of Sophia.

In the Hebrew Scriptures, Sophia is the divine Lady who mediates between God and the creation. She comes into the world to bring caring and salvation, to conquer evil, and to reveal the interconnectedness of all things. In the gospel of Matthew, Jesus is portrayed as a child of Wisdom, and John identifies Jesus with the Word of God who comes to heal and save. Unfortunately, the feminine image of Wisdom was from the time of Jewish writer Philo made into the male Logos, and the feminine dimension of God was suppressed. Now the authentic Wisdom tradition is being reclaimed by women theologians. In addition, a newly emerging "Spirit" theology of Jesus Christ is being developed by women theologians. This Spirit theology emphasizes Jesus' risen transcendence over race, gender, and sex, and reveals his availability to all.

Interreligious dialogue is helping women incorporate images from their native religions into their understanding of the Christ. The tribal religions of Africa describe Jesus as midwife, entering into the suffering of women to bring new life into the world. Hinduism provides images of the goddesses and the cosmic power of the feminine for Christology. Korean women view Jesus as the shaman, the mediator with the spirit world who exorcises and heals, and incorporates the belief in the Goddess Kuan Yiu, who personifies relatedness, community, and wisdom into Christology. Some Native Americans associate Christ with the Corn Mother, who provides food from her own body and sacrifices herself for her children. Many Latina women have returned to their indigenous religions and have brought a new depth of spirituality to liberation theology with their beliefs in cosmic energy and the sacredness of the earth.

Women theologians and biblical scholars have begun to reread the Christian Scriptures and doctrines through feminine eyes and through the feminine experience in many diverse parts of the world, and have come to new interpretations of the tradition. To the issue of gender, they have added the perspectives of race, culture, class, interfaith differences, and sexual preference. Some have moved into a post-modern Christology, where both history and the personal are relativized, where there is no center or constant. This is a defused Christology with no boundaries or absolutes. Others have chosen to work more carefully and seek to find common ground with the tradition, hold the center, and be true to the process of doctrinal development. These women theologians hope to develop new interpretations of the tradition that will be shared by a discipleship of equals in a Church that is renewed.

Summary

Jesus was unique in the way he ignored the taboos and unjust laws of his time with regard to women. He treated women with dignity and respect and, in an unprecedented decision, chose women for his own disciples.

Many gospel stories reflect memories of Jesus befriending, teaching and healing women, as well as sharing his mission with them. At the same time, these stories proclaim the significant roles that women disciples played in the early communities. Today women around the world are developing new reflections on Jesus, which will help the churches liberate women and extend to them an equal role in ministry.

Questions for reflection and discussion

1. Discuss the cycle of women's equality in history. At what stage is that cycle today?
2. In what ways was Jesus unique for his time in his attitude toward women?
3. Dramatize several stories about Jesus and women and discuss what relevance these stories might have for the role of women in the church today.
4. Discuss the portraits of Mary, Jesus' mother, Mary Magdalene, and the Samaritan woman that appear in the gospels. What do these stories tell us about the role of women in the early church?
5. Do you agree with the belief that Jesus' choice of women as disciples opens the way for the ordination of women today?

Sources

Brock, Rita Nakashima. *Journeys by Heart: A Christology of Erotic Power.* New York: Crossroad, 1988.

Douglas, Kelly Brown. *The Black Christ.* Maryknoll, NY: Orbis, 1994.

Eigo, Francis A., ed. *Discipleship of Equals: Towards a Christian Feminist Spirituality.* Villanova, PA: Villanova University Press, 1988.

Fabella, Virginia, and Sun Ai Lee Park, eds. *We Dare to Dream: Doing Theology as Asian Women.* Maryknoll, NY: Orbis Books, 1990.

Hopkins, Julie M. *Towards a Feminist Christology: Jesus of Nazareth, European Women and the Christological Crisis.* Kampen: Pharos Publishing House, 1994.

Isherwood, Lisa. *Introducing Feminist Christologies.* Cleveland: Pilgrim Press, 2002.

Moltmann-Wendel, Elisabeth. *The Women Around Jesus.* Translated by John Bowden. New York: Crossroad, 1982.

Schüssler Fiorenza, Elisabeth. *In Memory of Her: A Feminist Theological Reconstruction of Christian Origins.* 10th anniv. ed. New York: Crossroad, 1994.

———. *Jesus and the Politics of Interpretation.* New York: Continuum, 2000.

———. *Jesus: Miriam's Child, Sophia's Prophet: Critical Issues in Feminist Christology.* New York: Continuum, 1994.

Soelle, Dorothee and Luise Schottroff. *Jesus of Nazareth.* Trans. by John Bowden. Louisville, KY: Westminster John Knox Press, 2002.

Stevens, Maryanne, ed. *Reconstructing the Christ Symbol: Essays in Feminist Christology.* New York: Paulist Press, 1993.

Tamez, Elsa, ed. *Through Her Eyes: Women's Theology from Latin America.* Maryknoll, N.Y.: Orbis, 1989.

Tetlow, Elisabeth Meier. *Women and Ministry in the New Testament: Called to Serve.* Lanham, Md.: University Press of America, 1985.

Weaver, Jace, ed. *Native American Religious Identity: Unforgotten Gods.* Maryknoll, N.Y.: Orbis Books, 1998.

Witherington, Ben, III. *Women in the Ministry of Jesus: A Study of Jesus' Attitudes to Women and Their Roles as Reflected in His Earthly Life.* New York: Cambridge University Press, 1984.

CHAPTER NINE

Christology and the Environment

Christology has always had to keep pace with the times in order to continue Jesus' mission of salvation through each era. During the earlier centuries it was necessary to clarify both the humanity and divinity of Jesus. In the modern era, Christians have had to integrate their beliefs in Christ with the discoveries of evolutionary biology and astrophysics. During the struggles over slavery in the South and oppression in Central America, a new Christology of liberation was born.

Today we are in the midst of an environmental crisis, where pollution threatens the quality of our water and air, depletion of the ozone layer endangers living plants and human health, and a "greenhouse effect" endangers the balance of weather patterns. Toxic chemicals, nuclear waste, and garbage degrade many areas. The rapid destruction of the rain forests is having adverse global repercussion; over-fishing and desertification threaten the food supply. This process of degradation advances at an alarming pace. Facing this crisis, theologians reflect on links between the study of Jesus Christ and concerns for the health of the planet. In the following pages we will attempt to relate the historical Jesus, the incarnation, salvation, and the resurrection to environmental concerns.

The historical Jesus

It would be an anachronism to portray Jesus of Nazareth as an environmentalist or to pursue such questions as "What would Jesus drive?" Although he must have had concerns about the devastation that had been inflicted on the land of Israel by plundering conquerors, Jesus did not face the magnitude of global destruction that we have today.

The gospels portray Jesus as a man of the earth, a Jew devoted to the Hebrew tradition that the earth is the Lord's and has been given to his people as a good gift. Jesus is depicted as a person deeply aware of the presence of a loving and caring God in the people and the world around him. He grew up among people who prayed: "The heavens are telling the glory of God; and the firmament proclaims his handiwork" (Ps 19:1).

Jesus of Nazareth spent most of his life in a rural area known for its natural beauty. For approximately eighteen years of his life he worked with his hands, building things out of natural wood and stone. His later teachings reflect his appreciation for his Abba's creation. Jesus uses fruit, mustard seeds, salt, the sun, lightning, rain, fish, sheep, and other natural images to demonstrate the presence and power of the reign of God.

In the Sermon on the Mount, as recounted in Matthew's gospel, Jesus points to both wildflowers and birds as examples of how God's love and care are extended to creation. He proclaims the same covenant that God extended to "every living creature that is with you" after the great flood (Gen 9:10). Abba's embrace of his creation extends from the tiniest sparrow to all the children of God. As we have seen in our discussion of the parables, Jesus demonstrates a sacramental sensitivity to the revelation of God's saving power as discovered in sown seeds, harvests, vineyards, and flocks of sheep. It is a mindset most useful for those interested in protecting the earth.

Jesus teaches that God provides daily bread and resources for all. In his miraculous feedings and catches of fish, he demonstrates the abundance of these gifts. Jesus warns that deprivation is brought about by those who selfishly protect their riches and store up treasures. His own simple lifestyle proclaims the lesson, "Take less and give more!"

The natural miracles, such as the walking on the water and the calming of the storm, are symbolic of God's power over creation. In the Near East the sea was a common symbol for the powers of evil and chaos, and it is clear from these stories that the Creator can overcome these powers. For those experiencing a sense of helplessness in the face of so much environmental devastation and who wish to somehow be empowered to make a difference, this is a useful reminder.

The healing miracles, as we have seen earlier, demonstrate God's desire for healing and wholeness. These stories teach that much physical and moral wrong results from human ignorance or evil, and should not be ascribed to a vindictive creator. In the gospels, we meet a God who moves powerfully against all that subverts creation. We encounter a God who intends that the resources of creation be healed, sustained, and shared.

The incarnation

The Christian doctrine of the incarnation teaches that God has entered creation as a human being. John's gospel proclaims: "And the Word became flesh, and lived among us" (Jn 1:14). This means that the Logos, which for the Hebrews was the creative principle in Yahweh, actually became part of creation itself. John goes on to say that this Logos, which was always with God, and through whom all creation came about, became one with the material world.

Traditional theology has been greatly influenced by Thomas Aquinas (d. 1274), who taught that the incarnation came as a result of the Fall and in order to save humankind from sin. Contemporary theology often prefers to take its lead from John Duns Scotus (d. 1308), who proposed that the incarnation was in God's plan from the beginning and represents a climactic stage of creation. In this view the divine goal for creation was to be fulfilled in the birth of Jesus and would then move toward an ongoing re-creation of all reality through Christ. In this vision, Christ is the creative force behind a new creation, which is taking place now and which will come to fulfillment in the endtime. Humans and indeed all creatures are somehow called to play unique roles in the creation of a "new heaven and a new earth" (Rev 21:1).

A new dignity for materiality

The incarnation brought a new dignity to the material world. God entered the very fibers of creation in a unique way and became present to and part of the universe, the earth, and all that is in it. The coming of Jesus Christ is the acme of the creative process, the revelation of where matter has been heading from the very beginning as it evolved toward spirit. The person of Christ reveals how completely God has communicated Self to creation and embraced it in all its dimensions. God is revealed as the center of creation drawing all things toward fulfillment in the divine.

This perspective on material things challenges the dualism that has been so commonly part of the Christian tradition. Early on the Docetists rejected the value of matter and held that Jesus only "appeared" to be human, that he wore his humanity as a kind of cloak. The Gnostics viewed matter as evil and were repelled by the thought that God could become united with the physical. The early councils denounced these views and defined that in Jesus Christ God did indeed enter the material and physical world of the human. Yet Christianity continued to have a disdain for the physical and the material world. As a result, the Church has often avoided involvement in the worldly affairs of politics, science, and economics. Only in modern times has the social teaching of the Church come to recognize the integral relationship between the material and the spiritual and thus move to be active against injustice and oppression in the world.

In the contemporary secular era, dualism had taken on new forms. Materialism and consumerism separate the spiritual from "the real world," and assign value in terms of profit and usefulness. Material things are simply to be used up and discarded.

Many believe that this separation of the material from the spiritual, of religion and life, is a factor in the environmental crisis. Without spiritual values, industry and business have no reason to sustain the material world. Conversely, lacking interest in the material world, religion can do little in the struggle for the integrity of nature and its resources.

Some theologians have helped us understand the need to integrate the material and the spiritual. The visionary work of Pierre Teilhard de Chardin (d. 1955) has helped us to better realize the link between the material and the spiritual, the "withinness" in all things, and the drive of the material toward the spiritual. Teilhard's vision came both from his lifelong study of rocks and fossils and his passionate love for Jesus Christ. He sensed God radiating from matter and could sense the presence of Christ when he studied it.

For Teilhard, matter is blessed, and through faith we can see Christ as the heart of the world. Jesus Christ is the center of all things, and continues to be revealed through matter. Christ is hidden in the forces that give increase to the earth and move it toward fulfillment. Teilhard experienced the earth as the body of Christ, was enchanted with the charm of earth, and reached out to be embraced by the earth. He was convinced that humans had a responsibility to build the earth rather than debase it. Teilhard's vision can offer us a new respect for the earth and motivate us to prevent its neglect and devastation.

The theology of Karl Rahner has also helped us understand that matter is oriented toward spirit and that it develops toward spirit by virtue of its inner being and potential. Rahner maintained that matter and spirit have a common history and find their ultimate source in the same Creator. He saw creation as a whole, with one Creator bringing forth one system of being, and acting as the ongoing creative force that sustains, empowers, and draws all toward fulfillment. Thus the world has from the beginning been "graced" with the life of God.

For Rahner, Christ is the perfect union of the material and the spiritual. His person and life reveal how completely God has communicated Self to creation in all its dimensions. In Christ, God comes to creation and continues to be present to the universe. The incarnation radically affirms that God is the heart of all of creation.

This perspective offers us a new appreciation of nature and all its resources, and provides a new level of motivation for sustaining our earth.

The incarnation and the human

The incarnation serves not only to reveal the pristine dignity of one human individual, Jesus Christ but also to bring a new dignity to human life in general. Here God enters the cellular, the genetic, the DNA of humankind, and reveals the ultimate meaning of humanity. (The ancient Eastern theologians often said that God became human so that humans could become God.) In Jesus Christ we see humanity at its best, fully and perfectly expressing divinity. The incarnation proclaims that God is not isolated somewhere as a "sky God," but is intimately present to the world. The God of Jesus Christ has been involved in creating from the beginning, and will remain so until the end of time.

The incarnation gives new meaning to the Hebrew belief that humans are made in the image and likeness of God. Jesus becomes a role model for living a human life. Like all humans, Jesus experienced a physical life with all its appetites, pleasures, and limitations. He enjoyed food, drink and was known for his active table ministry with people of all kinds. He knew joy, pain, laughter, loneliness, love, and rejection. Jesus lived his life with extraordinary generosity, love, and compassion. He carried out his God-given mission, first as a craftsman, then as a teacher and healer with dedication and courage. He underwent the horrors of the crucifixion with forgiveness and an unrelenting determination to stay the course. Jesus was the perfect combination of the human with the divine, and as such is the apex of the creative and evolutionary process.

As a human person, Jesus Christ leads us to see the dignity of all humans, especially those on the periphery of society. His humble friendship with the "least of the brethren" moves his followers to be concerned about those who live under the worst conditions, lacking decent housing, adequate food, clean water, and healthy air. This must give pause to the people of the United States, who comprise only five percent of the world's population yet use sixty percent of the world's resources. America spends hundreds of billions of dollars on armaments, while tens of thousands die each day of hunger worldwide. Jesus' mission of saving should move his disciples to be actively involved in providing for others and confronting the political and economic systems that oppress them.

The theology of the Word

As mentioned earlier in our discussion of the early doctrines on Christ, the theology of the Word has been central in the Christian tradition of the incarnation. It is an image taken from linguistics wherein our words are viewed as symbols of our thoughts and feelings. For the Jews, the Word

(Logos) was the creative expression of God, the way God was active in history as a creative, prophetic, and saving power. The notion of Logos also appears in Greek philosophy to designate the rational and ordering principle in God. When the notion is used by the early Fathers to explain the incarnation, it is often a blend of both Jewish and Greek thought.

The early theologians taught that it was the Logos that ultimately entered into the creative process as the person of Jesus Christ. The ancient Logos theology uniquely links creation with the incarnation. This theology highlights the connectedness of all created things by showing that all reality is an expression of God. Such connectedness is essential to an environmental perspective. The coming of Jesus is then a creative event that brings a newness to the earth. Since the Word and the world are now more uniquely one, the world must be reverenced and treasured. That is why the American bishops urge that their people recognize "the web of life," and dedicate themselves to living in harmony with nature. That is the reason why the mountain churches of Appalachia urge their people to preserve traditional values by which they live freely and simply, close to land and kin.

Irenaeus' approach to Word theology and incarnation has had a significant influence on theology today. For Irenaeus, there was a continuity between matter and spirit. He also maintained that creation, incarnation, and redemption were all part of one continuous process. It was his position that the Logos is indeed the creative aspect of God, the means whereby God externally communicates the divine self. God lovingly shared Self in creation and even more dramatically in the incarnation. For Irenaeus, the incarnation of the Word is the climax of creation, for it sums up or "recapitulates" what God intended from the beginning: the union of the divine with the human. From this perspective, Jesus Christ is a new creation for humanity, a bold statement of what God meant for humanity from the very beginning. In this magnificent and worldly theology of Irenaeus, God's saving plan is to "gather up all things in him [Christ], things in heaven and things on earth" (Eph 1:10).

This incarnational theology reconnects the human with all creation and integrates creation, incarnation, and redemption. Creation has been transformed by the coming of Jesus Christ, and the benefits of redemption are shared by all of creation. This vision of the world is clearly needed for ecology today. If the plan of God is to be one with creation, to save the world and bring it to fruition, then abuse of creation must be seen as evil. By the same token, those who reverence the Creator are called to expose all exploitation and destruction of God's creation. That is why so many oppose such dangerous projects as the Three Gorges damming of the Yangtze River in China. This means the destruction of thirteen cities, 140 towns and 1,353 villages, the relocation of over a million people, and unlimited problems for the environment.

Wisdom theology

The Hebrew notion of Logos seems to be linked with the rich Wisdom tradition. Denis Edwards has done pioneering work in exploring this tradition and connecting it with the environment. He has observed that Wisdom for the Hebrews was intimately connected with God's work of creation. The Wisdom literature focuses on the interrelationships among human beings, the rest of creation, and God. Wisdom dwelt with the natural things of creation, and from all this people can learn of God's self-revelation.

Wisdom was understood by the Hebrews as a feminine figure who was present before creation and who stands at the Creator's side, joining the human with the divine. She delights in creation, and she stands as a friend, teacher, and lover to human beings, revealing to them the mysteries of God and creation. Indeed, she stands as a reflection of the feminine dimension of the divine.

Jesus as the Wisdom of God

The Christian Scriptures connect Jesus Christ with the Wisdom tradition. When Jesus invites his followers to take up his yoke, he echoes a similar invitation in the Book of Sirach. Similarly, John's passage on the Word becoming flesh and entering the world is paralleled in both Wisdom and Sirach. The author of the Letter to the Hebrews, in describing the Son as the radiance of God's glory, also seems to be using Wisdom literature. And Paul draws from this tradition when he describes Christ as "the power of God and the wisdom of God" (1 Cor 1:24–25). To the Colossians, Paul writes lyrically about Jesus, calling him the "image of the invisible God," and "the firstborn of all creation." He proclaims that all things were created through and for Christ, who reconciles all things with God (Col 1:15–19).

The gospels also associate Jesus with Wisdom images. In Luke, Jesus proclaims his message in the name of Wisdom and his cures are described as the deeds of Wisdom (Lk 7:35; 11:49). In Matthew, Jesus, the teacher of Wisdom, teaches his disciples to listen to his prophetic warnings and share his yoke. In John, Jesus is not only the Word made flesh, the source and sustainer of all things, he is the Wisdom-bearer. Jesus is described in Wisdom images as the bread of life, the light of the world, the good shepherd, and the vine. Like Wisdom, Jesus walks with his people and becomes part of their lives. He is with his disciples all days until the end of time as the revealer of God's plan for the salvation of the world.

Clearly, disciples past and present share in Christ's mission to re-create and rebuild the earth. Today this mission is even more daunting than in the past, given the violence that is done to the earth and its people. The Wisdom tradition reveals the genuine plan of God to save the world, and acknowledges Christ's role in supporting his disciples in their struggle to sustain the earth.

Salvation

From gospel times, Jesus Christ has been recognized as the Savior. The task of the Church is to interpret this message of salvation for each age. Today, it must include saving the earth and its people from environmental disaster. This includes such practical goals as restoring the fishing in Newfoundland and eliminating the practice of dumping nuclear waste in the Russian Federation. It means protection from ultraviolet radiation by preserving the ozone layer, and the promotion of environmental legislation for factories throughout the world. The churches can be a strong and effective voice in the ecological movement provided they see the many links between their teachings and saving the earth.

Traditional approaches to salvation have focused on saving "souls," with little heed to the physical and material things of this world. As a result, salvation became disconnected from life itself, and applied more to a future existence in heaven, far from this "vale of tears." The classical theological debates about salvation dealt with issues such as faith versus good works, and orthodoxy as a way to heaven, but said little about action in the political or social arenas.

If salvation is to regain its relevance, it will have to broaden its scope beyond personal salvation and address the pressing issues of public life. People today want to be "saved" from violence, nuclear threat, terrorism, economic insecurity, oppression, and environmental hazards. If our theology of salvation cannot address these issues, the churches will find it increasingly difficult to hold the interest of their people in contemporary society. As the Evangelical Lutheran Church of America has observed, God's covenant is with all of creation, and Jesus came to "save" the whole of it.

The Hebrews' notion of salvation developed out of a belief that they were specially chosen by God and could count on divine protection. The central experience of such protection was their liberation from slavery in Egypt, the Exodus. This saving process continued as God rescued his people throughout history from exile and persecution. No matter what the crisis, even the terrible Holocaust of recent times, many Jews have placed their trust in God for survival and new beginnings.

Key themes in the Jewish tradition of salvation are confidence in God's saving power, thanksgiving for God's many saving actions, and hope of complete salvation in some future time. Jews celebrate a covenant relationship with God, which expects deliverance from evil forces, and a complete trust in the forgiveness and fidelity of God. This Jewish faith in salvation is broad and inclusive, touching every facet of creation and life.

Jesus' mission was to restore the best of the Jewish tradition of salvation. In his life and teaching he revealed a loving and caring Abba, who loved and protected all of creation. He extended this care to those in need, and demonstrated that God's saving power was accessible to all. The gospel stories reflect Jesus' constant efforts to bring salvation to all people, especially to those who suffered from oppression or rejection. John's gospel proclaims: "Indeed, God did not send the Son into the world to condemn the world, but in order that the world might be saved through him" (Jn 3,17). This is a message of hope and courage for those who struggle to provide the needy with resources, healthy air, and clean water. They share in the Lord's mission to build the earth and not leave our children a legacy of pollution, stripped forests, and depleted resources.

There are new and practical needs for salvation today. Technology, while it has benefited humanity greatly, has also developed weapons that can destroy many people and devastate the environment. Global industry threatens to exhaust the earth's resources and further damage the earth.

The salvation of God has to be somehow relevant to these social, political, and environmental issues if it is to be believable.

Paul's salvation theology

Many of Paul's insights into salvation are adaptable to an environmental theology. Paul often joined creation with redemption, and viewed that latter as a "new creation," wherein God's intentions for the cosmos are revealed and humans are restored to the divine image. Paul told the Corinthians that they could be led by the Spirit to discover their authentic selves and once again be true images of God. He wrote: "Now the Lord is the Spirit, and where the Spirit of the Lord is, there is freedom. And all of us, with unveiled faces, seeing the glory of the Lord as though reflected in a mirror, are being transformed into the same image from one degree of glory to another; for this comes from the Lord, the Spirit" (2 Cor 3:17–18).

Paul was convinced that the materiality in creation was liberated by the power of the Lord. Jesus Christ set free all of creation from its bondage and gave freedom to all of God's children. The redemption of Christ looks toward the ultimate liberation of all creation in the future. Paul writes to the Romans: "We know that the whole creation has been groaning in labor pains until now; and not only the creation, but we ourselves, who have the first fruits of the Spirit, groan inwardly while we wait for adoption, the redemption of our bodies. For in hope we were saved" (Rom 8:22–24).

In Paul's theology, the death of Jesus destroyed forever human solidarity with sin. Jesus' resurrection revealed a new creation, a renewed solidarity in grace between God and humans. For Paul there is now a new world, and we are new creatures who can put sin behind us and rebuild the earth. He is convinced that through the power of Christ the earth can rebound from any catastrophe. Paul writes to the Romans: "neither death, nor life, nor angels, nor rulers, not things present, nor things to come, nor powers, nor height, nor depth, nor anything else in all creation, will be able to separate us from the love of God in Christ Jesus our Lord" (Rom 8:38–39). In Christ, humans are restored once again to "images of God" and are called to represent the Creator as servants of the earth. Paul encourages the early disciples to empty themselves and sacrifice themselves in the image of Jesus. To the Colossians he writes: "For in him all the fullness of God was pleased to dwell, and through him God was pleased to reconcile to himself all things, whether on earth or in heaven, by making peace through the blood of his cross" (Col 1:19–20).

Paul might well have been writing this theology for us today as we face so many crises in our environment. Our earth is indeed "groaning," and we long for Christ to liberate us with a new creation. Christians realize that on their own they cannot overcome the many ecological challenges. But we believe that with the creative power of Christ we can restore the earth and help sustain the earth and its resources. In Eastern Europe, where Communist regimes have left the environment devastated, Christian communities are organizing to restore the quality of their air, water, and land. Taking care of their earth has become part of their Christian mission.

Salvation as liberation

We saw earlier how liberation theology arose out of the cries of the oppressed people of the world. These were cries for salvation from the political and economic forces that were crushing their lives and their hopes. Part of this oppression comes from the lack of clean water and air, the devastation of the forests and land, and the domination of resources by the rich. In El Salvador the rural people are forced to wash their clothes in the dark, polluted water of the rivers, and they suffer from many health problems from drinking the contaminated water from their own wells. In Haiti the poor search endlessly in a barren land for scraps of firewood. The poor have cried out to Jesus as their liberator to free them from these injustices.

As we saw earlier, liberation is at the heart of the Judeo-Christian tradition. The "poor of Yahweh" have always been promised special protection from their Creator, and the prophets have often spoken up for the "little ones" and chastised their persecutors.

Jesus attempted to restore Judaism to its best traditions of liberation. His mission focused on freeing people from sin, disabilities, rejection, and even physical hunger. His miracles and parables often witness to the power of the Creator to free the children of God from whatever might enslave them. In John's gospel, Jesus tells his disciples: "…and truth will make you free.…so if the Son makes you free, you will be free indeed" (Jn 8:32–36). Paul proclaimed this good news of freedom to the churches of Galatia: "Christ has set us free" (Gal 5:1).

Gustavo Gutierrez, one of the founders of modern liberation theology, has insisted that the Christian theology of salvation must link the construction of this world with salvation. The salvation that Jesus brings must include food, a job, a decent place to live, and a healthy environment. These are human rights and the Christian mission must be committed to securing these rights for all.

Liberation theology has gradually turned its attention to environmental issues. Religious leaders worldwide have written persuasive documents indicating how pollution and the depletion of natural resources have become critical problems for their people. In the name of freedom, they have urged developing countries to restrict over-consumption and to pay closer attention to the majority of the world's population who suffer from hunger and poverty. It is becoming more clear each day that our attacks on the earth are at the same time attacks on its people. The bishops of the Philippines have written an extremely significant document pointing out that it is indeed sinful to degrade and exploit the natural world.

The resurrection

We have seen how theologians have restored the resurrection to the center of Christian faith. The resurrection is now much better understood as an action of God that validated Jesus and his teaching, promised eternal life, renewed creation, and revealed both the present and future reign of God.

There are a number of ecological implications in the resurrection of Jesus Christ. First of all, the resurrection affirms the sacredness of the physical, of materiality. In the resurrection stories, Jesus is not described as a disembodied spirit, but as a risen person, transformed but real. These stories seem to be teaching that in resurrection materiality will not be destroyed but exalted. In resurrection, the physical will no longer be subject to suffering or death, no longer limited by time or space. The world will be different, and yet in continuity with the world that we now know.

The resurrection also discloses God's power over death and destruction. What was an apparently hopeless situation of abandonment and despair became triumphant new life. This conquering of death and despair offers hope and courage to those who may feel helpless in the face of the many overwhelming environmental problems that surround them.

Finally, the resurrection reveals the empowerment and solidarity that is available to the disciples. After the resurrection, they were transformed from fearful and doubtful persons into an inspired and courageous community of disciples. This same empowerment is available from the Spirit of the Lord for those who would otherwise be too timid to involve themselves in the mission of building the earth.

We have also seen how the study of the apocalyptic images in the resurrection stories point to its cosmic dimensions. In his exalted state, Jesus Christ manifested victory over chaos and the ultimate fulfillment of all of creation. His transformation into a glorified state points to the future transformation of all the material world. The risen Lord offers hope that our chaotic world can be restored and sustained for future generations. He is now the "heart of the cosmos," the driving force behind the Church's mission to save the earth. In a sense the resurrection promises the accomplishment of God's plan for creation. And yet we know that humans have the freedom to obstruct God's plan for the earth. The resurrection is grounds for hope, but not for presumption. It is in our hands to build the earth. Should we fail, the cosmos can go on as it did for billions of years—without us.

The Cosmic Christ

The term "Cosmic Christ" has its roots in patristic writing, but was first used by John Denney in 1894, and then adopted by German theologians and biblical scholars at the turn of the century. Since then the notion has become integrated into Christology, and, as we shall see, has special relevance to environmental theology.

There are a number of New Testament passages that place Christ in the context of the cosmos. The author of Ephesians writes: "…he set forth in Christ, as a plan for the fullness of time, to gather up all things in him, things in heaven and things on earth" (Eph 1:9–10). In Colossians, the notion of the cosmic Christ is developed with even more sweep and power: "He is the image of the invisible God, the firstborn of all creation; for in him all things in heaven and on earth were created, things visible and invisible, whether thrones or dominations or rulers or power—all things have been created through him and for him. He himself is before all things, and in him all things hold together" (Col 1:15–17).

Teilhard de Chardin rightly linked this passage with evolution, and today it might be equally connected with our environmental concerns. The theology behind the passage is Semitic in that it integrates creation and salvation, and expects salvation to come within history for the whole of creation. This image of the cosmic Christ can serve as a powerful impetus to move Christians to save the earth from exploitation and destruction.

Teilhard saw the Cosmic Christ as a creative and sustaining energy within the cosmos. In his vision, this cosmic Christ, which is in continuity with the historical and risen Lord, exercises a divine power within the universe and draws it toward its final completion and fulfillment. For Teilhard the ultimate convergence of all reality will be brought about by the power of Christ's love. The image of the Cosmic Christ can be extremely useful for an environmental theology. The risen Lord lives among his followers and offers them the vision, energy, and grace to confront the devastation of the earth.

Ecofeminism

Women have joined their voices to those who cry out for the earth. The term "ecofeminism" was first used in 1972 by Françoise d'Eaubonne. She argued that the destruction of the planet was largely the result of the profit motive inherent in male power, and that only women had the sensitivity to nature to bring about an environmental revolution. Others have pointed out that women are most deeply affected by environmental devastation, especially in poor areas. Women are often the ones who have to get up before dawn, travel long distances on foot to gather wood, and wait in long lines for water. In many areas, mothers attempt to feed and nurture their children, who suffer from malnutrition and disease brought on by the pollution of the land, air, and water. Poverty most commonly affects women, and the poor generally live in the most blighted areas.

Scholars also point out that the link between women and the flesh has in part led to the abuse of both by men. Especially in Christian thought there has been a denigration of the physical and an avoidance of matters of the flesh. It is thought that here lies another reason why in a male-dominated world there has been such a strong inclination toward violence against both the material world and women. Such phrases as "rape of the earth" and "virgin forests" point to this connection. In this point of view, domestic violence and violence against the earth arise from the same instincts.

Some ecofeminists call for a new regard for materiality, the body, and sexuality. They understand that a renewed appreciation for the human person and for the incarnation as the entering of God into matter might lead to a deeper respect for both women and the earth. In this mystery, Jesus brings together the human and the divine in oneness and wholeness.

Elizabeth Johnson urges a return to the theology of the Spirit of God as a way of restoring the dignity of both women and the earth. The Spirit is the nurturing, creative, feminine aspect of God. Johnson suggests that the Spirit be perceived as present and active in the world, enlightening and giving the earth warmth and energy. The Spirit of God is the creative origin of life and extends life-giving power to all things. It is the Spirit who heals, re-creates, and renews. This is the Spirit that Jesus promised to send, and this Spirit can lead us to the task of sustaining the earth. Finally, ecofeminists suggest the development of an ethic suitable for ecology. Most search for an ethic of liberation that would free women, the poor, and the earth from oppression. It is the gospel ethic of Jesus that reaches out to the marginalized and recognizes the evils of starvation, deprivation, and degraded living that are often experienced by so many woman and their children today.

Summary

It has often been charged that the Christian tradition, with its notions of domination, has been largely responsible for the damage done to the earth. Some have concluded that Christians have little to contribute to environmental concerns. Our survey of Christology belies this position. Christianity is an extraordinary religion in that it professes that the Creator has actually become one with the world in the person of Jesus Christ. Christians believe that Christ is the savior of the world and that he has brought about the reconciliation of all things and a new creation. The resurrection proclaims that Jesus' material body was transformed and promises the transformation of all creation. And now, Jesus is proclaimed as the Cosmic Christ, the presence of divine grace and power in the world. There is indeed enormous richness here, surely sufficient to inspire the disciple of today to get involved in building and sustaining the earth.

Questions for reflection and discussion

1. What are your major concerns about the environment at the present time?

2. Does your parish or church address environmental issues? What things can you do to get them more involved?

3. What are some of the ways in which the gospels demonstrate that Jesus had a love for creation and saw it as a place where God was present?

4. Discuss some connections that the incarnation, salvation, and resurrection might have with respect for material things.

5. Do you think that there is a link between the abuse of nature and the abuse of women?

Sources

Boff, Leonardo. *Ecology and Liberation: A New Paradigm.* Translated by John Cumming. Maryknoll, NY: Orbis Books, 1995.

Edwards, Denis. *Jesus the Wisdom of God: An Ecological Theology.* Maryknoll, NY: Orbis Books, 1995.

Gebara, Ivone. *Longing for Running Water: Ecofeminism and Liberation.* Translated by David Molineaux. Minneapolis: Fortress Press, 1999.

Hill, Brennan R. *Christian Faith and the Environment: Making Vital Connections.* Maryknoll, NY: Orbis Books, 1998.

Johnson, Elizabeth A. *Consider Jesus: Waves of Renewal in Christology.* New York: Crossroad, 1990.

———. *Women, Earth, and Creator Spirit.* New York: Paulist Press, 1993.

McFague, Sallie. *Models of God: Theology for an Ecological, Nuclear Age.* Philadelphia: Fortress Press, 1987.

Rasmussen, Larry L. *Earth Community, Earth Ethics.* Geneva: WCC Publications, 1996.

Smith, Pamela. *What Are They Saying about Environmental Ethics?* New York: Paulist Press, 1997.

Teilhard de Chardin, Pierre. *Hymn of the Universe.* Translated by Simon Bartholomew. New York: Harper & Row, 1965.

CHAPTER TEN

Savior

The good news of God's salvation has always been at the heart of the Christian tradition. Jesus was a Jewish reformer who preached the saving power of Abba in his parables and decisively demonstrated that same power in his healing miracles. When the disciples witnessed how God's action raised and exalted Jesus, they came to accept him as the Christ, the very embodiment of this saving energy in their midst. Their mission was to spread this good news to all nations.

In the earliest gospel, Mark, Jesus is portrayed as "the Son of God" and is proclaimed as such at his baptism, his trial, and by the centurion after his death. The Markan community clearly recognized the Jesus was the Christ, the messiah, the agent of God's salvation.

In Luke's community, Jesus is linked with the Spirit of God. Mary is told that his conception will be through the Spirit, and at his baptism the Spirit descends upon Jesus and he begins his ministry enveloped by the Spirit. Before his death, Jesus promises to send the Spirit; in the pentecostal experience, the disciples are filled with the Spirit. They experience new life, a peace and wholeness in this life, and a promise to live on in the next.

Matthew's community tells of an angel advising Joseph that Mary's child has been conceived from the Holy Spirit and that his name is to be Jesus "for he will save his people from their sins" (Mt 1:20–21). At Jesus' death, the centurion proclaims Jesus to be the Son of God; after the resurrection, Jesus commissions the disciples to carry on his mission and promises to be with them all days.

John's community believed that Jesus was the Word and that he gave all those who believed in his name the power to become the children of God (Jn 1:12). Jesus tells Nicodemus, "For God so loved the world that he gave his only Son, so that everyone who believes in him may not perish but may have eternal life. Indeed, God did not send the Son into the world to condemn the world, but in order that the world might be saved through him" (Jn 3:16–17). At the last supper, Jesus says: "for I came not to judge the world, but to save the world" (Jn 12:47).

The belief in Jesus as savior is taken up in many other early communities. In Acts, Peter points out that a man has been healed in the name of Jesus Christ and that "there is no other name under heaven given among mortals by which we must be saved" (Acts 4:12). In 1 Tim 2:5–6, Paul is described as saying that God desires everyone to be saved and that Jesus Christ is the one mediator of that salvation. Paul writes the community in Rome that where Adam represents disobedience to God and sin, Jesus stands for obedience and righteousness (Rom 5:12–21). He tells the Corinthians that as all die in Adam, all are made alive in Christ (1 Cor 15:22). Paul tells the Colossians that Jesus is the "image of the invisible God," the first-born of this new creation and that through Christ, God was pleased to reconcile all things to himself (Col 1:15–20). And to the community at Ephesus, a disciple of Paul writes that God has chosen us in Christ to be blessed, holy, and blameless before him in love. He says that from Christ has been heard the word of truth, the gospel of salvation (Eph 1:3–13).

The earliest tradition seems to anticipate an imminent return of Jesus, when the faithful will become the elect of God. It was only gradually that the early Church realized that salvation was already accomplished in Christ and that the end was not soon to come. The carpenter from Nazareth was now understood to be their savior. The saving power of God was now mediated through the Christ. A number of images were used in the New Testament to describe this phenomenon of salvation. Let us examine some of them.

Redemption

The redemption image seems to be derived from a Jewish practice of buying back property that had been confiscated or family members who had been enslaved for unpaid debts. The classic use of this imagery occurs in the redemption of the Hebrew people by Yahweh from slavery in Egypt. Some of the prophets, especially Isaiah, Ezekiel, and Jeremiah, refer to Yahweh redeeming people from their sins.

The New Testament develops this idea in the description of Jesus Christ as redeemer. Early on, God is more at the center of the redeeming process, and the phrases "in Christ" and "through Christ" are used. Later, Christ is given a more active role on his own in the notions of redemption "by Christ" and Christ as the "mediator." This notion of redemption is relevant today to those who have had their property or goods confiscated by oppressive governments. They can look to their God for hope and for the courage to struggle for their rights. Redemption also speaks to those who have become enslaved by drugs or other addictions and who look to God for the power to take their lives back, or to help others do the same.

Ransom

The notion of "ransom" first appears in the gospel of Mark, where Jesus says that he comes to serve and give his life as a ransom for many. This notion seems to underlie Jesus' saying at the last supper that his blood is to be shed for many. Paul points out to the Corinthians that they have been purchased at a price, and in 1 Timothy says that Jesus Christ gave himself as a ransom for many. Only later, in the patristic period, is the figure of Satan introduced as the one holding humanity captive and the recipient of the ransom. This caricature of the redemption prevailed for centuries, until Anselm put it to rest in the Middle Ages.

The "price" that Jesus paid with his own life has inspired people like Gandhi and Martin Luther King, Jr. They too have been willing to give their own lives to ransom their people from poverty, injustice, and prejudice.

Atonement

Jews today still celebrate Yom Kippur, which is a feast of expiation and atonement. Expiation involves purifying oneself of all that is sinful, and being again "at one" with God. In ancient times expiation was done through sacrifice of an animal, whose blood (the source of life) was sprinkled on the people as a symbol of their new life. The sacrifice was also offered up in intercession to God for forgiveness and renewal of the covenant. The killing and burning of the victim in sacrifice represented the radical change that was desired by the penitent.

The writers of the New Testament used this Jewish notion of atonement to explain how Jesus was their savior. Paul wrote to the Romans that they were justified by God's grace through Jesus Christ "whom God put forward as a sacrifice of atonement by his blood, effective through faith" (Rom 3:25). The author of Hebrews uses Temple imagery when he describes Jesus as the high priest who expiates the sins of the people. And John proclaims that God sent his Son to be an expiation for sin (Jn 1:29).

Today, Jesus becomes the model for people like Daniel and Philip Berrigan, who sacrificed much to purify their nation of violence and war. Jesus was the model for Cardinal Joseph Bernardin, who gave of himself to bring the churches and religions together on the common ground of love and respect. At-one-ment empowers many today as they struggle in a world torn by terrorism and human suffering.

Sacrifice

The new sacrifice was that of the cross, but it took time for the early disciples to move beyond the "scandal" of the cross to see it as a symbol of their purification and redemption. In one of the earliest traditions, Paul tells the Corinthians that "Christ died for our sins" and "For our sake he [God] made him to be sin who knew no sin" (1 Cor 15:3; 2 Cor 5:21). The early Christians came to see Christ as "the Lamb of God who takes away the sins of the world" (Jn 1:29). But they knew that Jesus' death was not caused by God, and that he did not die as a passive victim, but as one who overcame the oppression and hypocrisy of his time. He was willing to offer his life out of love, and allowed himself to be sacrificed on the altar of the cross. They gradually came to see Jesus as the prophet-martyr, the suffering servant of God. He became the personification of the loving and forgiving creator.

In our own time, Christ's sacrifice has become the inspiration for Dorothy Day, who devoted her life to giving shelter to the homeless and food and comfort to the outcast. It was the model for Mother Teresa, who offered her life to the poorest of the poor to save them from rejection and oppression. It is important to note that expiation and atonement should not mean that sinners are attempting to appease an angry God. Rather, a gracious and merciful God is here initiating forgiveness and reconciliation. God provides the gift of his own Son, and then accepts that Son's fidelity to his mission, even at the cost of his life, in order to bring all people home to God.

Justification

Justification was often used by the apostle Paul to explain salvation to the early Christian communities, especially in Galatia and Rome. The Hebrews believed that sinful humans could never justify themselves before God. Only God could initiate the process and make it possible for one to be just (holy) in the sight of the Creator. In contrast to this, another more legalistic tradition developed which maintained that one could justify oneself, become "self-righteous" by following the religious laws strictly. Jesus himself frequently found himself in conflict with such legalism. He insisted that loving service was more important than a blind obedience to the law without love.

Paul insists that justification now comes through Jesus Christ and not through the law. In resurrection, Jesus' person and message has become justified before God, and those who follow him receive the gift of justification. Paul writes: "But now…the righteousness of God has been disclosed …through faith in Jesus Christ for all who believe" (Rom 3: 21–22). Believers in Christ are "justified by his grace as a gift" (Rom 3:24).

At the time of the Reformation, justification became an area of serious contention among the churches. Luther's position of justification by faith alone stirred tremendous controversy over such questions as: can salvation be merited? what is the value of good works? need one accept the authority of the Roman Church to be saved? Many of these questions still remain unsettled among the churches today.

Those who currently suffer exploitation and abuse of their human rights can look to Jesus to "justify" them as children of God, people made in the image and likeness of God. This was the message of Gandhi and Mother Teresa to the poorest of the poor.

Reconciliation

Salvation has also been described as reconciliation, where the goal is to restore the covenant between God and the people. Paul told the community at Corinth: "So if anyone is in Christ, there is a new creation: everything old has passed away; see, everything has become new! All this is from God, who reconciled us to himself through Christ, and has given us the ministry of reconciliation" (2 Cor 5:17–18).

Many have been inspired by Christ the reconciler to carry on his ministry: those who work with divorced and separated; those who rehabilitate the homeless and help them get started again; those who serve in family mediation; and those who work at the peace tables of the world. One thinks of Archbishop Tutu and the great efforts he has made toward reconciliation and healing in South Africa.

Liberation

Liberation, or the giving of freedom, is another way of looking at salvation. Early in his ministry, Jesus identifies himself with the prophetic mission to free prisoners and the oppressed. Matthew portrays Jesus as the new Moses, liberating his people in the new exodus of Christian redemption.

Both John and Paul emphasize this theme of freedom. In John's gospel, Jesus tells his disciples: "So if the Son makes you free, you will be free," and assures them that the "truth will make you free" (Jn 8:32–36). Jesus' mission is described as one where he frees many from self-loathing, despair, disabilities, oppression, and sin. Paul develops this theme in his letter to the Galatians when he tells them, "For you are called to freedom" (5:13) and "For freedom Christ set us free" (5:1). He then goes on to tell them that authentic freedom is not for oneself only but for loving service. This model of salvation as liberation has inspired people like Cesar Chavez to liberate many migrant workers from unjust wages and poor living conditions, or like Jean Vanier to free the mentally handicapped from neglect and abuse. This theme of liberation has now taken on new political and social meaning in liberation theology, which will be discussed in a later chapter.

The patristic period

The biblical themes on salvation were developed during the patristic period but were often interpreted in terms of Greek and Roman thought as

Gentiles became more prominent in the church. Some of the major approaches during the patristic period were salvation through the incarnation, victory over Satan, and satisfaction.

Salvation through the incarnation

In the fifth and sixth centuries, theologians were often more concerned about the nature of Jesus Christ than they were about his saving actions. In the councils of this period, the humanity and divinity of Jesus and the saving power of the incarnation were prominent. Many of the church fathers believed that people were saved more by the Logos becoming man than by any event in the life of Jesus. This "high Christology" was expressed by Clement of Alexandria when he remarked that the Logos of God became human so that humans could learn to become like God. This divinization of humans differs from the Western juridical approach to salvation. It is more concerned about being joined to God in eternal life than it is about being saved from sin. The salvation of humans demanded that human nature be united to God. "What was not assumed was not saved" became a slogan of the time.

Recapitulation

Irenaeus' theology of recapitulation is an excellent example of the centrality of the incarnation to salvation. He argued that God's plan of salvation unfolds in three acts: creation, the fall, and the restoration of the world by Jesus Christ. God's purpose in creating was to share divinity with the world and humanity. Adam's fall, which Irenaeus attributes to immaturity rather than malice, disrupted the plan. Moved by compassion, God sent his son to be a new Adam and restore or "recapitulate" the solidarity that God had intended for humans. In assuming human nature, God restored it to its original integrity. The redemption of our nature comes from what Jesus achieved in his life, death, and resurrection. All things are thus summed up in Christ.

Victory over the devil

A common salvation theme for the Fathers was that Jesus was victorious over Satan. They derived their theology from Jesus' struggle with Satan in the gospels, and concluded that the "ransom" was paid to the devil to free humankind. We find variations of this allegorical approach to salvation in Origen, Ambrose, and Augustine. Unfortunately, Satan's holding humans hostage was later on taken too literally, and in fact still is by some evangelicals. The result can be a fearful approach to salvation, where life is viewed as a battle with the devil.

Satisfaction

Tertullian (c. 225), who was deeply influenced by Roman law, was most influential in bringing a more Western juridical slant to salvation theology. He adapted the notion of satisfaction from Roman law, which provided for legal compensations and punishments for offenses. Tertullian did not explicitly connect satisfaction with the death of Christ, but he did teach that the Son of God died for sinners, and thereby saved them from death.

It was Hilary (d. 368) who explicitly connected satisfaction with the death of Jesus, and who viewed this death as a sacrifice that made reparation to God on behalf of sinners. This notion of satisfaction also showed up in the works of Origen, Basil, Ambrose, and Augustine and became one of the prevailing interpretations of salvation until the great medieval theologian, Anselm of Canterbury. This theology still prevails in the minds of many Christians today.

Anselm

Anselm (d. 1109) wrote his famous treatise on satisfaction, *Cur Deus Homo*, in 1098 when he was Archbishop of Canterbury. The work was actually finished during one of the exiles imposed on him by the king for challenging royal authority. Anselm developed a satisfaction theory of salvation that replaced the old "victory over Satan" and prevailed into modern times.

Anselm offered his classic definition of theology as "faith seeking understanding"; he was convinced that he could offer a solid and well-reasoned account of why the cross was necessary for salvation. Anselm used the English feudal system as his model, one that he saw as reasonable and orderly. Anselm taught that creation was similarly designed in an orderly and beautiful fashion. Like an honorable and just feudal Lord, the Creator stood in an honorable position in complete solidarity with his subjects. Addressing his monastic companion (with the unlikely name of Boso),

Anselm related how sin clouds the beauty and order of the universe and offends the honor of God. Because such an offense against God is infinite, it cannot be satisfied by mere mortals. Proper satisfaction can be achieved only by one who can perform infinite satisfaction, namely, the Son of God. It is important to note here that the satisfaction is not being given to an angry God; rather, the satisfaction is offered by Christ to a noble and honorable God, who because of Christ's sacrifice restores harmony, justice, and beauty to a world disfigured by sin.

Aquinas vs. Scotus

A key question for the medieval scholastics was "Why the incarnation?" Thomas Aquinas concluded that the Word became flesh because of the sin of Adam. The entrance of sin into the world, though foreseen by God, was not willed by God in the plan of creation. God sent his Son to redeem the world from its sinfulness. This view has been the classic position held by many Catholics until recent times.

The Scotists disagreed. For them the incarnation was not some sort of "afterthought" on the part of God, but was intended from the very beginning as integrally connected with creation. The purpose of the incarnation is to bring creation to perfection. The Scotists take their lead from Paul's statement to the Colossians that Christ is the first-born of creation, and that he came to reveal the goodness and beauty that God had in mind in creating. Many contemporary theologians are today more influenced by the Scotist position than by Aquinas.

Some Protestant trends

The debate among Protestant theologians over salvation has often focussed on its subjective and objective dimensions. In nineteenth-century Protestantism the subjective dimension was emphasized. Schleiermacher, often called the "father of modern Protestant thought," reacted against the Enlightenment's emphasis on reason and Kant's stress on moral judgment.

It was Schleiermacher's position that salvation must be based on human experience, in particular the "feeling of absolute dependence on God." He rejected the traditional notion of Jesus' death atoning or satisfying for sin.

Instead of Jesus objectively saving others, he serves as an example for others to follow and establishes a community that depends on him and on

God. Here salvation seems to be something that happens to people more than it is a redeeming act of God.

Karl Barth, the great theologian of Protestant orthodoxy, rejected this trend into subjectivity and accommodation to culture. He insisted on the radical transcendence of God and of Christ's message. Salvation for Barth was not rooted in personal experience, but in Jesus and in the revelation of God's gracious election of all people to participate in the kingdom. The atonement of Jesus is a saving work of God, linked to the whole saving process that has gone on since creation. Salvation is objectively gained for all, and can be subjectively received, but only in adherence to Christ in costly discipleship and concern for justice.

Paul Tillich's theory of redemption arose out of the post-war period's existential approach to reality. Tillich rejected the transcendent approach of Barth and proposed instead a theology of culture that would better link salvation to the experience of the world. For him, the need for salvation does not arise so much out of sin but out of alienation from God. God is the "ground of being," and contemporary life has lost its link to the very source of its being and thus is alienated from self and the other. Salvation for Tillich is reunion with the ground of being through Christ, who is the "New Being." Here salvation seems to be more a metaphysical achievement by Christ, rather than a free choice to give himself in life and death for others. In the midst of post-war anxiety and during the alienation of the 1960s, Tillich's stress on the "courage to be" had its appeal, especially to young people.

Contemporary trends

The contemporary person often values individual autonomy and feels no need to be saved from sin or alienation. Theories based on ransom, satisfaction, or re-grounding in being often have little appeal to people of today. At the same time, there are many constraints and dangers from which individuals would like to be "saved." A large percentage of the world's population yearns to be free from hunger, disease, homelessness, unhealthy environmental conditions, political oppression, and violence. Somehow the salvation of Jesus Christ must be relevant to these needs if it is to be "good news." Somehow faith in Christ must offer the needy strength and hope, and must empower Christian communities dedicated to helping them. Jesus' salvation cannot be some mere abstraction, but rather must be a promise that "help is on the way."

There are many in our global society who suffer from addictions, consumer debt, prejudice, terrorism, and exclusion because of their gender, disabilities, ethnic background, or sexual orientation. Christian salvation must in reality offer healing, acceptance, and love to such victims. It must offer a way of life, a community where individuals will be respected, supported, and empowered. Such salvation need not be seen as coming from a remote God who sends a Savior "from above." Rather, salvation today is viewed as coming from a God within, who is part of and present with people in their struggles and suffering. This is a God who was personified in the historical Jesus, the God whose Spirit acts in the risen Christ to bring freedom to people. As Schillebeeckx has pointed out, salvation that is not connected to human experience will soon lose its meaning and usefulness.

Saved by love

In the medieval period, Peter Abelard (d.1142) chose to put love, rather than honor and justice, at the center of salvation. Following the Johannine tradition, Abelard located the human problem in lovelessness, rather than in sin and disorder. Redemption, therefore, comes from Jesus' endurance of suffering out of love. As John writes: "No one has greater love than this, to lay down one's life for one's friends" (Jn 15:13). Jesus tells his followers to love one another as he has loved them, and gives them the power to love themselves and others as his friends and as children of God. Abelard sees the love of Christ as having an enduring effect on the world, existing in his followers as a creative force.

These same themes are taken up by contemporary thinkers. Teilhard taught that love was a universal energy that draws all things to God in Christ. Love is a transforming and liberating force that can transform the world. Along the same lines, Schillebeeckx writes that salvation is substantially love.

To center salvation on love is to move away from an angry God who needs appeasement and satisfaction to the loving Abba described by Jesus. The author of 1 John proclaims: "God is love, and those who abide in love abide in God, and God abides in them" (4:16). The passage goes on to say that in love there is no fear of punishment. Rather, we love because God loved us first, and we perfect this love among us by loving everyone as a brother or sister. Believing in Jesus Christ means to be "born of God," and those so born can conquer the world of sin. One sees this belief in practice in the work of Mother Teresa. She gathered the sick and the dying from the gutters of Calcutta and took them in so that they could experience from her and her followers the saving love of God.

Salvation and religious pluralism

Christians have often held a very narrow and exclusive view of salvation. Starting in the fifth century and continuing even into modern times, the church maintained a position that "outside the church there is no salvation." Christians looked at people from other religions as infidels, heathens, or pagans and made great efforts to convert them, lest they be deprived of salvation. Catholics generally viewed Protestants as heretics, and lumped all of those outside the church as non-Catholics.

At the Second Vatican Council, these exclusive attitudes began to change significantly. Protestant observers were allowed to be part of the process of discussion, and their views were listened to with respect and interest. The truth and saving power of other churches and even other religions were acknowledged, as Catholicism renewed its belief that all are children of God and are called to salvation. The council declared that God's grace and salvation were available not only to Christians, but also to those in other religions and even outside of organized religion altogether. The document *Declaration on the Church* said that to attain salvation people must "sincerely seek God and, moved by grace, strive by their deeds to do His will as is known to them through the dictates of conscience." The Council encouraged dialogue and the study of other faiths, but at the same time it continued to view Catholicism as the one true Church, and Jesus as the universal redeemer.

Recent developments

Four decades have passed since Vatican II, and a great deal has changed. Easier travel, computers, global markets, new communication systems, and many other factors have made the world "smaller" and more accessible. Corporations and educational institutions have come to realize that being "diverse" is to their advantage. People of varying churches and religions find themselves living and working together and needing to better understand each other. Religious conflicts in Africa, Israel, Ireland, Eastern Europe, and other areas gain worldwide attention and call for a better comprehension of the religious issues at stake. Interreligious marriages have become more common, challenging spouses and families to learn about other faiths, and schools are offering more courses on world religions.

After years of extensive dialogue, spokespersons of different faiths, their scholars, and many in their communities have come to understand each other. Much common ground has been established, and there is greater mutual understanding among religions. In the Western world, there has been growing interest and even participation in Eastern religions. Western missionaries often show great deference to indigenous cultures, and they intently study the religions in the areas where they serve. There is more reverence now for African religions, Native American religions, and religions indigenous to Central and Latin America. There is even consideration being given to the likelihood of life on other planets, and questions concerning what implications that would have for salvation.

Is Jesus the only savior?

One of the most hotly debated topics among theologians is the uniqueness of Jesus as savior. Now that Catholics have gained respect and knowledge of Buddhism, Hinduism, Taoism, and Islam, what implications do these religions have for the role of Jesus in salvation? How can one local incarnation of God in Palestine two thousand years ago bring about universal salvation for all time? Is Jesus Christ really the savior of the world, or are there other saviors? If people can be saved in many religions, is that salvation gained through each religion itself or through Christ?

John Hicks, a prominent voice in this dialogue, maintains that in the theology of religion there has been a Copernican shift. No longer does he see Christ at the center in salvation. For Hicks, the incarnation must be viewed as a myth, and God must be seen as the center of salvation. For Hicks, God alone is the source of salvation, and Jesus is one among many saviors. One problem with Hicks's position is that today there is no universal notion of God. Are we talking about Yahweh, Abba, Nirvana, Tao, Allah, or the variety of gods in indigenous religions? Moreover, the savior claims vary from one religion to another. For the Jews, Moses does not stand as a savior. The original Buddhist view did not see the Buddha as a savior, but as the Enlightened One. In the later Mahayana Buddhism, the human Buddha is deified, whereas in Christianity God becomes human.

On the other end of the spectrum are those who maintain that unless one believes in Jesus Christ one cannot be saved. Karl Barth stood for that position on the Protestant side, and disdained other religions. In the past the Catholic view was that outside the Church there was no salvation. Later on, Catholics made some efforts to be inclusive, by teaching that those with "baptism of desire" could be saved, and that Protestants could be saved by virtue that they "pertained to the church." During the 1960s the great Catholic theologian Karl Rahner proposed the notion of the "anonymous Christian" whereby those outside of Christian faith were saved by implicit faith. Ultimately, they were saved by Jesus whether they knew it or not.

Honest and equitable interfaith dialogue called for some new insights and a move from conversion to mutual understanding. Somehow it did not seem proper to come to the table of dialogue and prayer with a Protestant, telling that person that they can be saved in spite of the fact that they are in the wrong church. Nor did it seem appropriate to dialogue with other faiths while holding that they are saved by Jesus when in fact they don't accept Jesus as their savior.

Christian salvation language

We have seen that the early Christian communities use strong language to indicate that Jesus is their savior. Jesus is the Christ, the Son of God, the messiah, the Word made flesh, who came to save the world. For Paul, it is clear that Jesus Christ is the one mediator, the image of the invisible God, the first-born of creation, and that we are saved through Jesus Christ.

Traditionally these statements have been taken at face value as clear expressions of the Christian faith that must remain inviolate throughout the ages. Now, the tools of biblical criticism have made it possible to see these passages in their cultural and historical context. New questions have arisen. Is it possible that these biblical statements are the idealized "love language" of early Christian believers rather than doctrinal positions? Or could such passages be rhetorical statements used to stir the early disciples into action? Others have proposed that these passage were composed in a defensive mode against attackers of the faith, and are thus understandably extreme. For instance, the early conflict with the Jews who denied the messiahship of Jesus moved the disciples to say that in no other Jewish name could they be saved. Others propose that these claims for the uniqueness of Jesus were formulated during a time when the apocalyptic end was expected imminently and their claims were shaped by this urgency. It is possible that historical circumstances pushed Christians into a posture of exclusivity. Possibly today's close encounters with other religions will result in a more open and inclusive posture.

The official Catholic view, as well as that of the centrists in Catholic theology, is that these statements represent the faith of the early Christian communities, are integral to the inspired Scriptures, and cannot be set aside. From this perspective, dialogue then must be approached with the acceptance of differences. We need "to agree to disagree." Catholics don't expect Buddhists to make concessions about the uniqueness of Buddha, nor do they expect Muslims to drop the notion that Mohammed is the final prophet. Jews at the table of dialogue are not expected to downplay the significance of Moses or recognize Jesus' messiahship. If this be true, then why should Catholics be expected to set aside their belief that the salvation of Jesus Christ has somehow affected the entire world and people of all times? As David Tracy maintains, we need a "theology for dialogue" that is true to the tradition, not one where we modify our beliefs so as not to offend our partner in discussion. Religious dialogue aims at mutual enrichment, and this takes place best if each religion brings its authentic traditions to the table.

Some new emphases

All this being said, theologians have proposed new interpretations of Jesus' role in salvation that might assist in dialogue toward mutual understanding among the faiths. These help establish more common ground for the discussion of salvation and can help Christians better comprehend the truth and saving power of other religions.

First, it is useful to reclaim the notion of mystery. The mystery of God is a reality beyond description or understanding. While Jesus Christ is wholly God, he is not the whole of God. Even Jesus does not exhaust the mystery of God. His humanity is a finite and limited expression of God, and his saving power derives its meaning from the universal saving power of God. The saving power of God is fully expressed in the salvation of Jesus

Christ, but is also expressed in other realities and religious movements. As Gandhi observed, God reveals Self through many religions, and it is therefore necessary to listen to them all in order to understand more fully. Each religion has its own unique contribution to make to revelation.

Secondly, a return to the notion of the reign of God as the central teaching of Jesus might help us broaden our understanding of salvation. The reign of God in its broadest sense refers to the dominance of God's love and saving power. Jesus preached that this reign was at hand—healing, forgiving, saving. For Jesus, the reign of God extended beyond his own Jewish people. This became clear in his ministry to the centurion, the Syro-Phoenician woman, the Samaritan woman, and to outcasts of all sorts. In the end, Jesus commissioned his disciples to preach the good news of this reign to all nations. Clearly, the reign of God transcends churches and religions and is present not only among them but in the world at large. As Peter the apostle said to Cornelius: "God shows no partiality" (Acts 10:34). God's saving plan is for all, and this is the same plan that was brought forth in its fullness in the risen Lord.

Another approach to common ground among religions is through the theology of the Spirit. The Spirit of God extends beyond the person of Jesus Christ. The Spirit has been operative from the beginning of creation and has graced the hearts of all of God's children. The Spirit actively reveals and saves within authentic religions and even outside of religion altogether. As Jesus said: "The wind blows where it chooses, and you hear the sound of it, but you do not know where it comes from or where it goes. So it is with everyone who is born of the Spirit" (Jn 3:8). God's ways of saving are mysterious and are not necessarily our ways.

Paul Knitter, who has made major contributions to this debate, suggests that liberation be the central concern among religions. This focuses on the common cause of religions to confront the oppression of people and the degradation of the environment. Rather than look at salvation as a past event, this approach shifts the focus to the future and the struggle to offer peace and integrity of the earth to future generations.

Summary

Jesus' disciples have always proclaimed that he is their savior. Over the centuries, many images and theories have been employed to attempt to understand this mystery of God's saving power. In recent times, Catholicism has moved from an exclusivist position with regard to salvation, and has come to recognize that God's saving grace works within all religions and even outside of religion altogether. The Church has come to better appreciate the truth and saving grace of other religions, and thus has come to be more involved in interfaith dialogue and action.

Questions for reflection and discussion

1. Discuss some of the classic terms for salvation (redemption, atonement, justification, satisfaction). Are any of these terms useful today?
2. What are some of the things that people today want to be saved from? What do they want to be saved for?
3. Where today is salvation most needed in the form of "reconciliation"?
4. Is it possible for people to be saved in every religion? If so, what do you mean when you say that they can be saved?
5. Gandhi said that God reveals Self through all religions and that to hear God, one must listen to all religions. Do you agree? In what ways do you listen to other religions?

Sources

Daly, Gabriel. *Creation and Redemption.* Wilmington, DE: Michael Glazier, 1989.

Dupuis, Jacques. *Christianity and the Religions: From Confrontation to Dialogue.* Translated by Philip Berryman. Maryknoll, NY: Orbis Books, 2002.

Knitter, Paul F. *Jesus and the Other Names: Christian Mission and Global Responsibility.* Maryknoll, NY: Orbis Books, 1996.

O'Collins, Gerald. *Christology: A Biblical, Historical, and Systematic Study of Jesus.* New York: Oxford University Press, 1995.

Pope, Stephen J., and Charles Hefling, eds. *Sic et Non: Encountering Dominus Jesus.* Maryknoll, NY: Orbis Books, 2002.

Schwager, Raymond. *Jesus in the Drama of Salvation: Toward a Biblical Doctrine of Redemption.* Translated by James G. Williams and Paul Haddon. New York: Crossroad Pub., 1999.

Sloyan, Gerard. *Jesus: Redeemer and Divine Word.* Wilmington, DE: Michael Glazier, 1989.

CHAPTER ELEVEN

Liberator

Christology is contextual, in that it arises out of situations, conflicts, and events where new interpretations of the Christ event are needed. The many theologies in the New Testament grew out of struggles with Jewish communities and Roman authorities, out of the experience of martyrdom, and from the increasing ascendency of Gentiles in the early Church. In later centuries, the conflicts over the humanity and divinity of Jesus produced conciliar theologies. In the medieval period, when monasticism flourished, Jesus was known as "Christ the monk," and during the Renaissance he was viewed as "the Universal Man." In modern times, theology is emerging out of the experience of oppression, injustice, and violence. We call its latest forms "theologies of liberation," and they newly reinterpret the gospel tradition to address the needs of those on the margins of society.

Black theology of liberation

In the United States the notion of Jesus as liberator goes back to the days of slavery. Many Christian slaves experienced Jesus as one who had known oppression and shared their suffering. Jesus gave many slaves the courage to endure and hope for freedom somewhere in the future. This Jesus for the slaves stood in opposition to the Christianity of the slaveholders, which ironically saw nothing wrong with owning and exploiting other human beings while at the same time "practicing" the Christian faith. In fact, "liberation" had become so twisted a notion for slaveholders that they really believed they were freeing slaves from the damnation of pagan religions by converting them. Moreover, since Jesus had not opposed slavery and Paul had encouraged it, it was thought that God created some people superior to others and that the condition of bondage was the will of God.

Those who rebelled and escaped slavery saw Jesus standing with them. Harriet Tubman, who made many trips to the South to bring slaves to the North, often prayed to Jesus for the strength and courage she needed to endure the hardships and risks of these journeys. Many slaves saw their communities as the "real church," led by the Jesus who experienced with them the beatings, abuse, and even killing. Like them, Jesus had also been downtrodden and rejected, and yet he carried out a mission to his fellow outcasts and ultimately "overcame." Jesus wanted his people to be free, and his gospel of freedom stood in opposition to the evil of slavery. His cries of abandonment, forgiveness, and love were echoed in their own cries. They identified with his cross as they sang "Were you there when they crucified my Lord?" The cross from the religions that the slaves brought from Africa symbolized the cycle of life, from death to new life, and Christian resurrection taught them that good times were ahead in this life and the next. One thinks of the words of Martin Luther King, Jr., words that are carved on his headstone: "Free at last."

After emancipation

After the Civil War, the slaves were indeed free at last, but many of them were left penniless, illiterate, and homeless. As King once remarked, they were told to lift themselves up by their own bootstraps, but in fact they had no boots! Now free from slavery, the black people of this country were subjected to a new system of oppression—segregation.

For the next century, African Americans were often subjected to two contradictory voices. The prevailing culture told them that they were inferior, separate, even less than human. In addition, the Christianity of the white folks told them that they were descendants of the cursed children of Ham, and not really created in the image of a God who was obviously "white." On the other hand, their own Christian churches told them that they were created in the image and likeness of God, and that they were beloved children of God. They were most especially loved by Jesus, since he knew their plight and had overcome it. Although the black churches encouraged their members to maintain dignity and hope, there was no plan of action for overcoming the indignity of racism and segregation. Love was central to the message, but somehow it did not seem appropriate to become politically active. The "kingdom" was still not of this world.

In 1955 a sea change erupted in the black community. It all started when Rosa Parks, a black seamstress, refused to give up her seat on a bus and move to the rear. This launched the famous bus boycott and the civil rights movement in this country, led by Martin Luther King, Jr., then a young pastor of the Dexter Baptist Church in Montgomery, Alabama.

King began to speak about the "long night of captivity" of African Americans and how they had to reach out for the daybreak of freedom, justice, and equality. He declared that Christianity involved not only love but also justice, and told his people that Jesus was not some utopian dreamer, but one whose mission was to bring freedom. He reminded all Americans that their nation was under God and dedicated to freedom and equality. King instructed the churches that they were not faithful to Jesus' mission if they were not willing to share in his being crucified for God's justice. He challenged the churches of the world to proclaim that Jesus Christ is the hope of all people who cry out for justice.

Though King urged his followers to protest and actively resist segregation, he insisted that they follow the nonviolent commands of Jesus to love the enemy, turn the other cheek, and put away the sword. He promised his enemies that blacks would wear their oppressors down with their capacity to suffer, and that his people would one day win their freedom. King firmly believed that suffering that was unearned and unjustly inflicted had redemptive power. He believed that the cross contained the power of God, and was convinced that all his years of arrests, threats, personal injuries, and agony from the deaths of friends and colleagues actually drew him closer to God.

Black Power

At the same time as King's civil rights movement was gaining momentum, the Black Power movement emerged in the United States. Malcolm X rejected the "white Christ" who stood for the enslavement and segregation of black people. He saw little hope for Christianity in the struggle for racial justice, and he urged his people to love their blackness and to fight for freedom, using "any means necessary."

In 1968, James Cone began to develop a "black theology." He was critical of white theology for ignoring racism and strongly urged that Jesus be looked at as black to symbolize his solidarity with the suffering and struggle of blacks against racism. Cone began to reinterpret the exodus, the crucifixion, and the resurrection in terms of black issues. The exodus became the symbol of a God who liberates slaves, the crucifixion the symbol of divine willingness to suffer with and liberate the oppressed, and the resurrection an event that revealed that liberation was available to everyone. Cone maintained that the Black Power movement was Christ's message to America that blacks must be freed. Cone went along with those who argued that "any means necessary" could be used by blacks to gain their freedom.

Black theology appealed to some in the black community, but others in the churches were cautious of the strident and political tones of this theology. Many blacks had been accustomed to turning to their religion for pastoral care and spirituality, and felt that these areas were being neglected by black theology. Others were critical of the disregard for women's rights and environmental concerns in black theology. They pointed out that women often suffer oppression not only from whites, but from their own families, black communities, and churches. They observed that women of color often lived with their children in the most unhealthy and polluted areas of the cities and rural areas.

More recently, black theologians, especially feminist theologians, have given attention to these issues as well. Kelly Brown Douglas and Jacqueline Grant gave voice to black women who struggle for dignity in their communities and their churches. They speak for the black Christ who stands in solidarity with black women as they raise their children, teach them to hold themselves in high regard, and to resist oppression. This feminist theology arises out of the experience of black women, who pass on the community's wisdom to their children and who nurture their families. Many of them are poor, deserted by their men. So often they grieve for their children who are cut down on the battlefields or in the streets, or who are beaten and dragged off to prison. They are inspired by women like Harriet Tubman, who fought against slavery, Sojourner Truth, who stood up for the dignity of women, Rosa Parks, who wouldn't go to the back of the bus, and Thea Bowman, who valued her African roots and taught her sisters how to sing and suffer with dignity. They turn to the liberating Jesus to help them cope and to give them the courage to protest at any cost.

This Black Christ is viewed as walking in solidarity with lesbians, victims of AIDS, women in prison, the homeless, women working several jobs to make ends meet, women deserted by their men, prostitutes, and so many others of "the least of these." James Cone and others have come to recognize that blacks, especially black women, often suffer from living in degraded areas and that environmental issues are integrally linked to racism.

Liberation in Central and Latin America

In 1968, the very year that King was murdered, the Latin American Bishops held a historic meeting at Medellín, Colombia. The Second Vatican Council had urged Catholics to read the "signs of the times" in order to discern what God wanted them to do for the poor and suffering of the world. The bishops began to read the signs of oppression in their own part of the world. For hundreds of years Latin America had known severe poverty, and many of its people had been subjected to violence, suffering, and poverty.

These bishops recalled the history of their people. In the sixteenth century the Spanish conquistadores waged war on the indigenous peoples of Latin America, brought diseases, plundered their silver, gold, and other resources, and destroyed their native religions. Bartolome de las Casas, a colonial official who later became a courageous churchman, wrote to King Charles I of Spain deploring the horrible atrocities he witnessed. Natives were hunted down by bloodhounds for sport; men were taken from their families and worked to death in the mines; young women were taken from their homes, raped, and forced into the harems of wealthy colonials. At one point de las Casas went to Spain to defend the case that the Indians were actually human beings. He lost the debate, and the Spanish felt justified in taking the lives and possessions of these "semi-human creatures."

The Latin American bishops recognized the dismal situation that existed among their own people. The majority suffered from extreme poverty, polluted water, undernourishment, lack of health care, and unemployment. In many countries the wealth and the land were controlled by a small number of families, while the governments were often dictatorships, funded by the wealthy and by multinational corporations. If the poor complained about their situation or attempted to organize, they could be tortured, "disappeared," or murdered.

The bishops knew well that too often the Church, because of its actions or inaction, had been perceived as being on the side of the oppressors rather than the oppressed. They wanted to move away from a theology that stressed individual salvation and neglected addressing the sinful structures of the world. They admitted that too often their theology had been a sterile doctrinal exercise. The bishops now wanted to adopt a political theology that was concerned with current issues, and a liberation theology, which reflected on "praxis," or the action whereby people lived out their Christianity in the world. The bishops maintained that the purpose of the Christian religion was not to save us from the world but to save the world itself.

The bishops wanted this liberation theology to develop out of their own Latin American context. They no longer wanted to continue to adapt European theology to their needs. Theologians like Karl Rahner had taught them that human experience was the context for doing theology, and so they wanted their teaching to arise out of the human experience in Latin America. It would also be a theology "with an edge," a practical theology that would be critical of the social and political systems that oppressed their people and deprived them of self-determination. The bishops were resolved that the Church could no longer be a silent outsider in political, economic, and social matters. Their Church would now become a vocal and active insider that brought a gospel critique to the table.

The social context for this liberation theology, then, was the widespread misery and poverty that existed among the people of Central and Latin America. The vast majority lacked educational and economic opportunities. The bishops acknowledged that their people hungered and thirsted for justice, and called for a conversion among all their people, in families, organizations, businesses. They encouraged workers to organize and take action for improved education, health care, and economic benefits. They called for the raising of social consciousness, the organization of small base communities, and a Church committed to supporting the downtrodden.

The bishops pointed to the growing frustration among the poor, the repression of protest by those in power, and the rebellion against such repression. They warned that violence was the gravest problem in Latin America; they could see that the oppression, the injustice, the violation of fundamental rights was moving many to violent revolt. They warned the rich, who defended their privileges through violent means, that they were provoking violent revolution. They urged their people to work for peace and justice and avoid the destruction and atrocities of war. As pastors, they committed themselves to defend the rights of the poor and oppressed, and urged governments and the rich to promote equality, peace, and justice.

Theologies of liberation

Gustavo Gutierrez developed the now classic book on Latin American liberation theology, *A Theology of Liberation*. This book proposed a methodology for such a theology and undertook a new interpretation of the Christian tradition in light of the Latin American experience. His work was followed by an avalanche of books and articles, all of which attempted to re-read the gospels in light of the need for action against oppression.

Liberation theology, then, is a "theology from below." Ideally, it is a theology which begins with the experience of those who suffer poverty and oppression. It is a theology that attempts to see God and Jesus in the faces of the children who pick through garbage dumps for scraps to eat, in the mangled bodies of the disappeared that lie naked in the gutters, in the grief-stricken faces of parents who have seen their loved ones arrested, tortured, and killed. It is a theology that asks, Where is Jesus in all of this suffering? What does the cross and salvation really mean here? What relevance does resurrection have to all this apparent hopelessness? What must I do to stop this injustice and repression?

Reinterpreting Christian tradition

Liberation theologians have reinterpreted the Christian tradition in light of the context of poverty and oppression in Latin America. They have re-claimed a God who is in history, liberating people from slavery and injustice. This is a God who speaks through the prophets and denounces injustice. And they see Jesus as the incarnation of that God, a human among humans, denouncing evil and willing to pay with his life for the message. Liberation theologians recover a Jesus who reveals a loving and forgiving God who stands up for the downtrodden.

Return to the historical Jesus

Liberation theologians have shifted away from the Logos Christology of the early councils and focused on the historical Jesus. They point out that this classical Christology, which has prevailed in the Church until recent times, is too abstract and philosophical to be useful in confronting injustice and oppression. They object that such Christology is too concerned with the nature of Christ rather than with his mission. It is too focused on what Jesus Christ is, rather than what he did and continues to do.

Liberation theology shifts from the so-called "high Christology," which depicts God coming from above to enter the world and save it, to a "low Christology," which values the human Jesus, a flesh and blood Jesus who himself experienced poverty, rejection, and suffering. This is a Jesus who gave his life for the poor and the outcast. Jesus is not so much a God becoming man as he is a man becoming God. He was deeply involved in human affairs, and, like everyone else, had to search amidst darkness and ambiguity. This is the Jesus who, in his loving service to others, revealed the possibilities that exist for humans and offered a glimpse of what people can be at their best.

This image of Jesus is one with whom the poor campesinos can better identify. As one walks the back roads of rural El Salvador or Nicaragua, one senses that life here is similar to how it must have been in Galilee in the time of Jesus. The simple lifestyle, the daily hard work, the love and hospitality, the courage in the face of oppression, and the deep faith in Jesus among many of the people somehow connects the distant past with the present. As the people of Latin America often say in their religious celebrations, the spirit of Jesus and the spirits of those who were martyred for the cause of justice are *presente* in their midst. This is a Jesus who is indeed the risen Christ, who walks with them and empowers them in their struggles for peace and justice.

Much as they value the historical Jesus, liberation theologians resist romanticizing Jesus. Most respect the historical-critical approach to the Scriptures and realize the difficulties involved in the search for the Jesus of history. At the same time, they are convinced that Jesus was a man who experienced poverty, oppression, and rejection just like people today, and that he was actively engaged in defending the dignity and rights of all, especially outcasts.

They believe that Jesus was crucified for his opposition to religious and political oppression and that his resurrection stands as a divine confirmation of his mission. They see Jesus' disciples carrying on that same mission of liberation, empowered by the same Spirit of Jesus Christ. For this missionary zeal, many have been martyred throughout history. Today disciples are called to continue this same mission for "the least of these." They too can expect suffering and even death from the powers that are threatened by their efforts.

Was Jesus political?

Since liberation theologians see Jesus as a model for social reformers, they have had to deal with the question of whether or not Jesus was political. It is clear that Jesus was not politically militant in the modern sense. The gospels give us no indication that Jesus was remembered as engaging in disputes about the Roman occupation, or that he devised any sort of revolutionary program. Even though he was sentenced to death as a subversive, we have seen that these charges were clearly viewed as false by the gospel writers. When Jesus was condemned, his followers were not included, as they would have been had he been a rebel leader. There were no uprisings linked to Jesus, and the later revolutions against Rome did not involve Christians. Most scholars agree that Jesus was nonviolent and taught love of enemies.

It needs to be clarified here that religion and politics were much more of a piece in Jesus' times than they are in our era. The Roman occupation was led by an Emperor who was thought to be divine, and the Romans, though tolerant of other religions, expected appropriate tribute to Caesar. Any political opposition to Roman rule had serious religious implications. By the same token, the Jewish Temple was administered by pawns who went along with Roman domination and who were, in fact, appointed by the Romans.

Thus any attack on Temple corruption would have had serious political overtones. And of course many Jews in Jesus' time longed for the restoration of a theocratic form of government, where God and king would be once again linked. Such visions were viewed by the Romans to be seditious.

As we have seen, Jesus grew up in a culture that was charged with religious-political tension. From the beginning his teachings were perceived as being "dangerous," so much so that even early on there were attempts and plots to kill him. He charged Roman-appointed religious leaders with being hypocrites, blind guides, and whitewashed tombs. Jesus publicly defied Herod, calling him a "fox," and told his followers to give Caesar nothing more than the coin of tribute. Jesus challenged the sumptuous lifestyles of the rich Jewish and Roman elite and chided them for laying heavy burdens on the poor.

He deplored the corruption of Temple practices and worship and predicted the destruction of the Temple if greed and violence were allowed to continue. In his public ministry Jesus is portrayed as a person who proclaimed that the poor were blessed and as one who worked to restore their dignity and self-esteem. He extended healing and love to the outcasts of society, actions that no doubt threatened the corrupt religious and political leaders who dominated and exploited them. He revealed a loving, liberating, and forgiving God, which was not acceptable to those who wished to oppress in the name of God. We have seen how the passion stories show Jesus in stark contrast to Pilate, symbolic of the threat to Roman authority. Ultimately, Jesus refused to back down from his confrontational positions, even when threatened with crucifixion. He suffered and died, maintaining his revolutionary teachings on nonviolence, love, and forgiveness throughout his whole ordeal. This is the Jesus who inspires those committed to liberation.

Liberation theologians have reclaimed the prophetic dimensions of Jesus' ministry. They view him as a charismatic figure who challenges and confronts in the tradition of Elijah, Isaiah, and Jeremiah. They point to Jesus' teaching on how inconsistent social disorder is with the will of a just and loving Abba. Central to this theology are Jesus' challenges to abuse of the poor, as well as his condemnation of the idolatry of wealth and power.

The Jesus that many Latin Americans experience in their lives is one who lived a life similar to their own. They endure dire poverty, and are often threatened by imprisonment or death as they stand up for their rights.

They see Jesus Christ walking in solidarity with them, identified with their struggles as their friend. As Bishop Dom Helder Camara once observed, the poor are blessed because God became one of them, experienced their lot firsthand, and continues to support them in the struggle for justice.

Disciples of liberation theology point to Jesus' original call to the poor to be his followers. He called them from attachments to their possessions and families, and ultimately liberated them from even the fear of death so that they could preach his message of love and service. And today, this same Christ is viewed as calling the people of the world to conversion from greed and violent oppression, as well as from the fear of standing up for justice.

The rule of God

As mentioned earlier, the rule of God (the kingdom) is at the center of Jesus' teaching. Many liberation theologians characterize the rule or reign of God as the situation where God's love, mercy, and justice prevail. This rule of God is God's gift and expresses the divine will for the world, a situation wherein God truly belongs to people and people belong to God. It is the kind of world for which people long, a world wherein peace, justice, love, and forgiveness reign supreme. Jesus presented this notion of kingdom as a clear and radical alternative to the oppressive kingdoms of the Herods and Caesars of the world.

Liberation theologians opt for a notion of the kingdom that is both here and beyond, already and not yet. One is able to experience peaceful times, the recognition of human rights, loving relationships, and goodness in the here and now. At the same time, there is always the presence of violence, evil, and oppression. Liberation theologians recognize that Jesus promises that God's rule will ultimately prevail, and that Jesus' disciples are called to clear the way for justice and peace. Gutierrez has observed that the salvation of Christ is liberation from misery and alienation. All people are called to help bring that about in everyday life by seeing that everyone has proper shelter, adequate food and water, health care, safety, education, and employment. God's rule is not some abstraction in the sky, but involves the recognition of human dignity and rights in the present time.

The cross

Since the horrors of suffering and death have been so much more prevalent in the southern hemisphere, liberation theologians have searched for new meanings for the cross. Too often in the past, the cross has meant the patient bearing of oppression as God's will, with the hope of ultimately gaining heaven as a reward. From this perspective religion can well become, as Marx put it, "the opiate of the people," dulling their sense of pain and blinding them to the forces that oppress them.

Liberation theologians interpret the death of Jesus differently from the traditional notion of a sacrifice for sins, or the offering of an innocent victim for atonement. They often view Jesus' crucifixion as an act of cruelty willed by those who hated him, and not as a suffering willed by God. Jesus died for refusing to give up on his message of love and justice, for his dedication to liberating the poor, for his mission to call those in authority to justice. By the same token, Jesus' disciples are called also to put aside their fear of suffering and death, and to give of themselves for the cause of justice.

From the liberation point of view, salvation comes from the life, death, and resurrection of Jesus. It is a vivid demonstration of a loving God who is present in the midst of suffering and willing to give all to save. But salvation is not only for the hereafter: it is also for the here and now, offering God's power to his people in their struggle for freedom.

The resurrection

Liberation theologians have developed many new interpretations of the resurrection. The resurrection, first of all, represents a divine approval of Jesus and his mission. Resurrection offers humankind a glimpse of the new creation, where suffering and death are no more. It represents how the death of an innocent person in the struggle for liberation can be transformed into new life.

The resurrection is more than an event of the past; it is still going on. Ignacio Ellacuría, one of the Jesuits martyred in El Salvador, taught that people should live their lives as risen beings. He said that we help others live as risen people when we heal their suffering and release them from being victims. Those who suffer from rejection, poverty, hunger, and persecution can experience both the crucified and risen Lord within their hearts. That experience can give them the power to go on in their struggle for a new life.

The ongoing process of resurrection is within the very real struggle for health care, good food, safe shelter, clean water. Resurrection indicates that

Jesus Christ and his followers are committed to building new life for people who walk in the valley of death. It is a source of hope for victims and a source of power to their defenders. The resurrection offers a reason to overcome despair, fear, doubt, and cowardice. It holds out a hopeful future for which to work, and engenders trust in a God whose rule ultimately prevails.

The resurrection transforms Jesus into the Christ. Jon Sobrino cautions that the titles given to Jesus (Lord, Messiah, Son of God, Mediator) should not be used to justify domination or exploitation. Nor should Jesus Christ be so titled that he appears above the problems of the world. No matter what the title, Jesus must be seen as friend and brother, as one who reveals a loving, caring, and divine presence in the world. He is the suffering servant, not one who "lords it over," "plays God" or has a "messiah complex." He is the humble Lord, the "foot washer," the beloved Son of God, and the one who mediates justice and peaceful solutions.

Oscar Romero

Archbishop Oscar Romero has become the icon of liberation theology. Early on, he was a traditional churchman, who viewed his work for Jesus to be spiritual and loving but excluded involvement in political or social justice issues. Romero trusted that institutions like Church and state had God-given authority and would eventually work things out. He was critical of liberal interpretations of the Medellín Conference on liberation, and strongly chastised the resistance work of some Jesuits and his own clergy as too radical or even Marxist.

The brutal assassination of Romeo's close friend, Jesuit Rutilio Grande, was a turning point for Romero. He began to understand the prophetic side of Jesus' mission, and in his own ministry became directly concerned with issues of social and political justice. He began to speak of Christian liberation and to openly confront his own government for the repression of his people.

Romero came to realize that the reign of God was in everyday life and that work for God's reign included action for human rights. Romero saw the crucified Jesus in the faces of refugee children, victims of death squads, and parents who had lost their loved ones among the disappeared. He saw the resurrection going on among his people as they struggled for a new creation and a new life. Toward the end of his life, Romero offered a new theology of resurrection when he said: "If they kill me, I will be resurrected in the Salvadoran people." Visitors to El Salvador today can experience the truth of this statement. The small house where he lived, the chapel where he was shot while saying Mass, and the crypt in the cathedral where he was buried have become shrines to his living memory and an inspiration to those who continue his mission for the oppressed.

The liberation theologies of Latin America have reached a new turning point. The revolutions in Central America have ended, the collapse of the Soviet Union has diminished the fear of communism, and the events of September 11th, 2001, have shifted the world's focus to the threat of terrorism. The flood of books on liberation theology from Latin American has slowed to a trickle. Yet the same poverty, inequities, unemployment, oppression of women, and abuse of human rights that brought about liberation theology still exist in the region. The spirit of liberation still lives in the hearts of many base communities, and the dream of freedom remains in the hearts of the poor. The question now is, will more church leaders like Oscar Romero come forth to lead the Church's mission for justice in all parts of the world?

The growing numbers of "the other"

Prevailing Latin American liberation theology has been criticized for its neglect of women's liberation. Latin American women theologians charge that with all this talk of freedom, there is little consideration given to the still prevalent "macho" attitude that views woman as sex objects and toys. With all this writing about liberation, why is no thought given to the phenomenon of desertion, where many men start families and then move on? Where is the protest against husbands who are often controlling and unfaithful? Where are women's rights in the Church considered?

Some of the women of Latin America look for a praxis that is caring and a theology that is more combative. They look for a liberation theology that listens to and is focused on the poor and illiterate in their countries. They present a "mujerista" theology that connects Jesus to the cries for freedom heard from Latinas. The women of Latin America are reclaiming their story: of how they were "discovered" in their nakedness and innocence, pressed into slavery, forced to bear children for the work force. They had to watch as their men were worked to death, tortured, and driven into drink, gambling, and suicide. They and their children had a religion forced upon them which justified domination, slavery, and exploitation.

Women's liberation theology in Latin America calls for the equality of women. It stresses that both females and males have been created in the image and likeness of God. There is a conviction here that God is both Mother and Father, and that Jesus subverted the patriarchal, social, and religious order of his time. This perspective points to Mary, as the model of a poor woman who gave birth to the liberator. She was one of the women who shaped his life and shared in his mission.

Ivone Gebara speaks of liberation in the context of her native Brazil, where there is a great disparity between a rich minority and a poor majority, and where most women experience the oppression of machismo. She sees two women's forces operative. First, there are the many illiterate women who have natural gifts of leadership and strong powers of intuition and problem solving. Secondly, there are the religious sisters who have brought education, spirituality, and empowerment to many women. Women are now entering into Latin American history in a new way and are becoming a force in the freedom movement. She points to the Madres de Plaza de Mayo who stood against repression in Argentina, and their counterparts in Bolivia, El Salvador, and Nicaragua. She points to the peoples' church in the base communities, where the women share authority and ministry.

Many of today's Latinas lead vital Christian communities in worship and action. They organize neighborhood groups to struggle for better health care clinics. They extend caring to abandoned and disabled children in poorly funded institutions. Some have participated in revolutions, where they have been maimed or even killed. There are growing numbers of Latinas who see their love for Jesus and his gospel as a call to leadership and ministry in the Church.

The spread of liberation theology

The desire for liberation is universal and at the heart of the Christian message. As the world's consciousness opens up to the notion of liberation, the list of "outsiders" grows. The poor and oppressed are awakening in many different political, social, economic, and religious contexts throughout the world: political prisoners, victims of sex abuse, those addicted to drugs and alcohol, victims of terrorism, racism, ageism, homophobia, or environmental degradation. People of all nations and faiths are experiencing God as their liberator, and are looking to religion for support. A growing number of Christians see Jesus as their liberator, walking with them in their struggles for freedom. In the following pages we will look at examples from Africa and Asia.

Liberation theology in Africa

Africa is a vast continent with venerable cultures, rich resources, exotic beauty, and diverse tribal and religious traditions. Africa only recently emerged from a colonial period, where centuries of domination and exploitation devastated the native customs and religions as well as the self-esteem of the African peoples. The people of this vast continent are now struggling in a period of emerging nationalism, where corrupt leadership, bloody coups, tribal and ethnic disputes, and civil wars have brought extreme deprivation and suffering to many.

In this period, neo-colonialism in the form of economic domination by the United States, Europe, and Eastern Asia has brought poverty and unemployment to Africa. In the northeast, drought, famine, and civil wars have been devastating. In South Africa, efforts to overcome inequities and rebuild the country after apartheid have had mixed results. In central Africa, the plague of AIDS is spreading out of control and destroying social structures. In the midst of all these challenges live warm-hearted, spirited people who long for freedom. Some are turning to Jesus the liberator.

Christ in Africa

There are many images of Christ in Africa. These include the images of Jesus in the ancient churches of Egypt and Ethiopia, images that predate those of Europe. There are the creedal images of Christ brought by European missionaries. For many Africans, this Christ is a distant figure not connected with their culture or with everyday life. There is also the Jesus of the independent churches, the Jesus who has been incorporated and interpreted by native religions. For some, Jesus is the Elder, the Ancestor, the Master of initiation into life. For others, he is the Tribal Chief or the Healer (medicine man). Throughout this continent, where there is one of the fastest growing Christian populations in the world, some are turning to Jesus the healer, who can free them from evil spirits, magic, and from disease, especially AIDS. Others view Jesus as the Black Messiah in solidarity with their struggle against white oppression.

Liberation in Africa

In South Africa, Christian leaders like Archbishops Desmond Tutu and Denis Hurley, as well as theologians like Albert Nolan, developed versions of liberation theology as they struggled against apartheid. This theology was influenced by both black theology from the United States and liberation theology from Latin America, and was uniquely applied to the African context. Generally, this approach advocated nonviolent confrontation and active resistance to oppression.

There is in African liberation theology a tendency to deliver Christ from all the Western institutions, practices, and theology that make him a stranger to the African. Instead, native values are used to help Africans in their efforts to reinterpret Christology. Many Africans are on a quest for their true identity, which was for so many centuries obliterated by colonialism. The goal of some African religions (for example, the Ewe-Mina) is to be fully human, and eventually to be united to the life of the Supreme Being. They can appreciate Jesus as one who sets the ideal for human wholeness and, moving beyond that, to divinity. In this perspective, the individual is always linked to the human community and to the cosmos, and this enables some Africans to view Jesus as the founder of his unique community of disciples and to see themselves as linked to all of creation. They are making efforts to see Jesus Christ as being in solidarity with those who suffer and yearn for wholeness in both personal and communal life. The Christ who attracts many Africans today is one who accompanies them in the midst of hunger, poverty, disease, oppression, and environmental crisis. This is a Jesus who knew these realities of life himself, and whose Spirit now accompanies and empowers them in their efforts to be liberated.

Since Africans generally place a great value on community, they are drawn to an image of Jesus who is part of their daily community life, an elder brother who supports and empowers them. Often African religions view life as a natural passage to new life, and this enables Africans to integrate the death of Jesus with his resurrection.

Many Africans see themselves caught in a new kind of slavery. At first, there was the slavery of colonialism, and now there is slavery of neo-colonialism. They continue to search for identity, self-esteem, security, and a sense of wholeness that has been lacking for hundreds of years. Laurenti Megasa, a theologian from Kenya, maintains that the only Jesus who could have broad appeal to Africans is one who calls them to freedom from voice-lessness and lack of dignity. Only a Jesus who is in solidarity with the struggles of the poor can win their trust and hope. The Jesus who knew humiliation and suffering and rose above it can be the savior of the African. Likewise, the only Church that can gain credibility is one that proclaims and carries out Jesus' mission to diminish poverty, malnutrition, lack of medical care, and religious and civil corruption. This is a Jesus who calls everyone, rich and poor alike, to detachment, generosity, love, peace, and justice.

The voices of women

Most African women don't have the time or education to write liberation theology. But many of them live it day to day as they carry heavy burdens of water and firewood, tend the farms, care for their children, prepare food, do laundry, and many other tasks. Most African women are marginalized by their native religions and are not taken seriously by men. Yet the African religions are holistic, so African women can experience the supernatural as part of everyday life. If Jesus is to be real, he has to be present to them in their joys and hardships; he has to help them conquer the evils around them, assist them in the struggle for respect and equality, and empower them to be whole. Jesus has to empower them to address the abuses of domination and exploitation in their villages, homes, and churches.

Jesus the liberator inspires women to get better education, fair wages, and safe working conditions. African women want a Jesus who is embedded in a community, a real and dynamic person who cares for them and supports them. Jesus' presence in his community must give women the courage to tolerate police harassment as they sell their wares in the cities; help them resist being forced against their will into polygamous relationships; enable them to face the hardships of rural life with humor and good spirits; and resist the abuse that is often directed at single mothers. The African woman expects Jesus to cast out the demons from her society as he did in his own day. And yet many African women see so many contradictions in Jesus' "good news." They know that they must live in the belief that through the power of Jesus they can triumph in the face of overwhelming odds.

Liberation in Asia

Christians often have to be reminded that Jesus came from Western Asia, and that the church originally spread through the Middle East and other parts of Asia. When the colonial powers brought Jesus back to Asia, it was often as a symbol of domination and wealth. Today there is a growing effort to reclaim Jesus' Eastern roots and reinterpret him in light of the many diverse political, economic, and religious contexts of Asia. One aspect of this new perspective is the view of Jesus as liberator of those who struggle for survival throughout Asia, where more than half the world's population lives.

Often this Asian approach to Christology does not so much return to the historical Jesus in Galilee, but reflects Jesus as he exists today side by side with other venerated figures such as Buddha, Krishna, and Confucius. Since Christians are a small minority in these regions, the challenge is to sustain a unique identity for Jesus, an identity that will not be swallowed up by the dominant religions. Let us look at a few of these efforts.

Some of the first important reflections on the Asian Jesus come from a group of Indian Hindus, who drew parallels between Jesus and figure in the Hindu pantheon. Jesus was perceived as one who in new ways taught the truths of the East. Gandhi, for instance, viewed Jesus as the Supreme "Satyagrahi," or lover and fighter for truth. Gandhi kept Jesus' picture in his room, was inspired by the Sermon on the Mount, and looked to Jesus as a model for nonviolent protest against oppression of the children of God.

Interreligious dialogue is much more common in the East than in the West, and this new image of Jesus is evolving from such dialogue. Jesus is seen as one who became enlightened to the ultimate in a fashion similar to Buddha. Jesus gradually became the Christ, just as Gautama became the Buddha. And where the Buddha liberated through knowledge, Jesus liberates through love. Confucian thinkers have attempted to find parallels between the yin and yang notion of progress and Jesus' teaching on conversion. Islamic scholars, who already have images of Jesus in the Koran, have attempted to link their notion of Jesus' prophetic role with that of Christians.

Jesus the liberator

Hindus and Christians have found common ground in the notion Jesus and Krishna both came from God for the welfare of humanity. For many in both religions today, the liberation of the poor is the central goal. Both are involved in the movement to liberate the *dalits* of India, migrant workers who move from place to place at the mercy of their landlords and middlemen. In part, that is why Mother Teresa of Calcutta was able to gain such reverence from Hindus. She recognized that 200 million people live in absolute poverty in India, and through her services she provided concrete proof that God loves all of these people.

Much common ground is also shared by Buddhists and Christians on the subject of liberation. The Dalai Lama of Tibet has described Thomas Merton as a bridge between Eastern and Western spirituality. The two men became friends in their search for links between Buddha and Jesus, and both have been strongly committed to peace and justice in their respective countries and in the world.

Both Jesus and Buddha are alike in their purity of nature, their simplicity, and their commitment to overcome suffering in life. Both promote the value of contemplation, humble and compassionate service to the poor, and social transformation. Jesus and Buddha require total commitment from their followers to achieve the final goal of human liberation (the kingdom of God/nirvana), and yet both taught that ultimately such fulfillment is beyond the power of human effort. Buddha strives for the achievement of the non-self in the service of freedom, whereas Jesus defines the ideal in terms of selfless giving to the other. Both Buddha and Jesus loved the suffering masses (the *minjung*).

None of these parallels is perfect, for there are enormous differences between Buddhism and Christianity. At the same time, these similarities do provide some common ground for united action toward the liberation of the oppressed. Indeed, the liberation of all people can be the shared goal for both Buddhists and Christians. Freedom becomes the central focus of a dialogue that accepts diversity in beliefs but firmly stands for unity in commitment.

Asian women

There is a growing Christology among Asian women. Rather than being bothered by his maleness as are many feminist theologians in the West, Asian women accept that Jesus' maleness gave him the authority he needed in his culture to fight for the equality of all and to liberate the poor. Some point out that the fact that Jesus was a man is accidental to salvation, since salvation was achieved through Jesus' humanity and not his masculinity.

Christian women theologians in Asia often view Jesus as an Asian person, who preached an inclusive reign of God, and a divine preference for liberating outcasts (in their context this includes teeming millions of the poor, especially women). They point to Jesus' denunciation of hypocrisy and abuse of power, and they treasure his unique calling of women disciples. They view him as a young Asian person who was willing to give his all, even his life, so that all people might be free.

The liberation of women in Asia highlights many concrete situations of oppression: the plight of Indian women who often have to endure public taunting, a widespread and oppressive dowry system, and the choice of suicide after rape so as to not shame the husband. In the context of the lives of Asian women, Jesus' life, death, and resurrection disclose a loving God who stands against such abuses and offers women the courage to resist. Some Asian women propose a shift from the image of Jesus who suffers quietly with resignation to the Jesus who stands bravely before oppressors and is willing to sacrifice himself for the freedom of others.

Such views on liberation are critical of the hierarchical, male-dominated Church that had fostered exclusivity and inequality. Some Asian women theologians point out that the churches and Eastern religions need to be freed from doctrines and practices that prevent women from achieving human wholeness. They encourage their churches and religions to reclaim Jesus' prophetic role and denounce sexism, racism, economic injustice, and ecological devastation in their cultures.

One of the most common images of Jesus for Asian women is that of "the suffering servant." For many Asian women, obedience and suffering is their lot in life, and they see Jesus as an empathetic figure. Many see Jesus as a person who is loving and faithful to them amidst the common experience of male abuse, battering, control, and desertion. For these women, Jesus represents revolutionary standards toward women: dignity, fidelity, equality, and discipleship. And yet Asian women often hear from their churches and religions that they should be patient with abuse and obedient to rigid authority. They struggle for an image of Jesus that is liberating, a loving comrade who empowers them to both endure and resist.

Jean Zaru, a Christian Palestinian woman, values this image of Jesus as she inveighs against the violence and degradation imposed upon her people by the Israeli government. Korean theologian Choi Man Ja distinguishes between suffering as a result of oppression and that which arises from exposing those who oppress. For her, redemptive suffering does not mean submission to evil but the exposure of evil. Jesus as suffering servant empowers many Asian women to condemn the suffering of the innocent and to struggle for freedom.

Other Asian women have reinterpreted Jesus' title of "Lord." No longer is this title acceptable to justify colonial or neo-colonial domination, or male control in society or the home. Here Jesus is Lord of the poor, the Lord who condemns evil and frees the oppressed. He is the Lord of justice who frees women from male domination. He is the Lord who not only frees sinners but who also liberates those who are sinned against.

The incarnation is also important to many Asian women for it points to both the divinity and humanity of Jesus Christ. In his divinity, Jesus reveals a God of forgiveness, love, and healing. In his humanity, Jesus reveals a new humanity where all are free and equal. This is an incarnation from below where a human person becomes God and shows the unlimited possibilities of development for women. Jesus was the fully liberated person, whose Spirit now empowers the many movements of liberation.

Jesus the liberator is a dangerous and yet increasingly attractive image for Asian women. Asian women who exposed the use of hundreds of thousands of women as "comfort women" for the occupying Japanese forces during World War II were ignored and threatened. Vietnamese women who exposed the use of young women and girls for "rest and recreation" of American soldiers received a cold reception from the American government. Women who confront the massive sexual tourism industry in Thailand have been repressed. Filipino women in their struggle for self-determination have been arrested, raped, tortured, and imprisoned. Korean mothers have suffered the anguish of seeing their sons and daughters taken off by the secret police for their efforts against oppression. Young Sri Lankan girls who endlessly pluck tea leaves without ever dreaming of going to school are attracted to Jesus' power and courage. His liberating presence is felt by women factory workers, farmers, and street vendors; by those standing in lines for a ration of food for their children; and by women forced into prostitution to survive.

Jesus the liberator inspires some Asian women to resist the contemporary Western call to become sex objects and consumers. Jesus the liberator has empowered women throughout Asia to organize, become politically active, and resist the injustices inflicted on them. They have organized theological conferences and published theological journals. Though Christians make up but three percent of the Asian population, and only a few women gain advanced degrees in theology, Christian women are becoming a voice for liberation.

In formulating their own version of liberation theology, Asian women have resisted adapting the Western feminist approach. Many Asian women hold that the feminist view is that of white middle-class women who do not share the Asian woman's experience. They point out that traditional feminists tend to focus on patriarchy and the domination of men over women, and often ignore racism, ethnic superiority, neo-colonialism, the violence of women against women, as well as religious pluralism and many other factors in the Asian woman's experience.

An Asian women's liberation theology must then come from the Asian experience, which is diverse and which puts unique demands on the Christian tradition. Many Asian Christian women are not satisfied with a theology that seems to them an overly academic exercise, when so many are starving and suffering. They look for a Christian theology that will act for freedom. This will require new lines of theological inquiry and a new integration of Christianity into the heart of the many Asian cultures and religions. Here the Bible and Christian tradition need to be reinterpreted, not only through feminine eyes, but through the eyes of women from the diverse experiences of Asia. At the same time, Asian theologians are turning to the indigenous religions in order to reclaim, reinterpret, and update ancient beliefs. It is clear that an intense period of interfaith dialogue and action is going on, which should bring a rich harvest for the future of Asian Christianity.

Summary

A new theology of liberation has emerged "from below" in the last century from those enslaved in America. In this century, it shifted to the call for freedom from segregation. Then in South and Central America the call for freedom came from those oppressed and brutalized by their own governments. Today the call for liberation has spread to Africa and Asia, and is heard from those who experience poverty, hunger, and injustice in these areas. Most recently the voices of women have been heard, crying out for themselves and for their children. The recognition of Jesus as the liberator of the poor and abused continues to spread throughout the globe.

Questions for reflection and discussion

1. What does it mean to say that liberation theology comes "from below"?

2. In what sense was Jesus a liberator in his own day?

3. Did Jesus allow his followers to use violence to achieve liberation? Do you think that violence can have a role to play in liberation today?

4. Are there still areas in which women need to be liberated today? How can the gospel teachings be useful here?

5. In what sense are the poor considered to be blessed? In what ways can Christians bring liberation to the poor?

Sources

Aquino, Maria Pilar. *Our Cry for Life: Feminist Theology from Latin America.* Maryknoll, NY: Orbis, 1993.

Balasuriya, Tissa. *Mary and Liberation.* Harrisburg, PA: Trinity Press International, 1997.

Brackley, Dean. *Divine Revolution: Salvation and Liberation in Catholic Thought.* Maryknoll, NY: Orbis, 1996.

Cone, James. *Risks of Faith: The Emergence of a Black Theology of Liberation.* Boston: Beacon Press, 1999.

Dear, John. *Jesus the Rebel: Bearer of God's Peace and Justice.* Franklin , WI: Sheed and Ward, 2000.

Douglas, Kelly Brown. *The Black Christ.* Maryknoll, NY: Orbis, 1994.

Erskine, Noel Leo. *King Among Theologians.* Cleveland: The Pilgrim Press, 1994.

Gebara, Ivone. *Out of the Depths: Women's Experience of Evil and Salvation.* Minneapolis: Fortress Press, 2002.

Grant, Jacqueline. *White Women's Christ and Black Women's Jesus.* Atlanta: Scholars Press, 1989.

Hayes, Diana. *And Still We Rise: An Introduction to Black Liberation Theology*. New York: Paulist Press, 1996.

King, Ursula (ed). *Feminist Theology for the Third World*. Maryknoll, NY: Orbis, 1994.

Pui-lan, Kwok. *Introducing Asian Feminist Theology*. Cleveland: Pilgrim Press, 2000.

Schreiter, Robert J. (ed). *Faces of Jesus in Africa*. Maryknoll, NY: Orbis, 1991.

Sobrino, Jon. *Jesus the Liberator*. Maryknoll, NY: Orbis, 1993.

———. *Christ the Liberator*. Maryknoll, NY: Orbis, 2001.

Sugirthaajah, R.S. (ed). *Asian Faces of Jesus*. Maryknoll, NY: Orbis, 1993.

Tamez, Elsa. *Through Her Eyes: Women's Theology from Latin America*. Maryknoll, NY: Orbis, 1989.

Thumma, Anthoniraj. *Dalit Liberation Theology*. Delhi: ISPCK, 2000.

Williams, Delores S. *Sisters in the Wilderness: The Challenge of Womanist God-Talk*. Maryknoll, NY: Orbis, 1993.

CHAPTER TWELVE

Early Doctrines:
Development and Critique

The church's official teachings about Jesus Christ were defined in early councils in the fourth and fifth centuries. Beliefs concerning Jesus Christ's humanity and divinity first appeared in the oral stories of the early disciples, as they remembered Jesus of Nazareth and interpreted his teachings and actions in the light of post-resurrection faith. These interpretations employed new imagery, meaning, and theological depth as they were written down in the form of Scripture. Then the Fathers of the early Church developed these doctrines further, often in response to current controversies. Once Christianity was accepted as the religion of the Roman Empire, it became possible to organize councils that could make definitive statements about Jesus and exclude those who disagreed as "heretics."

In this chapter we will look at some of the main stages in the development of these doctrines about Jesus. We will begin with a brief overview of the early statements about Jesus' humanity and divinity. Then we will look at some of the first controversies, and how they were answered by the early apologists and church fathers.

We will examine the great debates over Jesus' divinity and humanity and show how they were addressed by the Councils of Nicaea in 325 CE and Chalcedon in 451 CE. Finally, we will discuss the strengths and weaknesses of these definitions, and overview more contemporary approaches to Jesus' divinity and humanity.

Divinity and humanity in the Scriptures

The gospels leave no doubts that Jesus of Nazareth was truly human. Underlying the gospel stories are memories of Jesus' human reactions. Jesus is portrayed as crying over the death of a friend, indignant over tricky questions, outraged by hypocrisy, and compassionate toward the disabled and outcast. He was amazed at the faith of the centurion, upset with the ingratitude of the lepers he healed, and admitted ignorance with regard to the last days. At one point, Jesus asked his disciples about his reputation with others. Jesus had to grow and develop, and struggle with the same human drives and appetites, like everyone else. At the very end of his short life, Jesus displayed great excitement and sorrow over his last meal with his followers. During his passion and death, he experienced many human emotions, including abandonment, frustration, love, and forgiveness. The gospels, for all their flourishes of imagery and theology, nevertheless leave no doubts about the humanity of Jesus.

The Scriptures also proclaim the divinity of Jesus. Mark highlights Jesus' baptism with a proclamation "You are my Son, the Beloved; with you I am well pleased" (Mk 1:11). Matthew has Peter proclaim his profound faith in Jesus: "You are the Messiah, the Son of the living God" (Mt 16:16). In Luke's nativity story, Gabriel announces to Mary that her child "will be great, and will be called the Son of the Most High" (Luke 1:32). And, of course, John's gospel stands out in stressing the divinity of Jesus. Here, Jesus has "the glory of the Father's only Son," and doubting Thomas confesses to Jesus: "My Lord and my God"(Jn 1:14; 20:28). Even though all these statements represent post-resurrection faith, the fact that they are read back into the life of

Jesus indicates an early awareness of Jesus' special union with God.

Paul the apostle, who chooses to bypass the gospel traditions of Jesus' human life, stresses Jesus as the Christ. He writes to the Galatians that "God sent the spirit of his Son into our hearts" (Gal 4:6) and reminds the Colossians that Jesus "is the image of the invisible God" (Col 1:15). Paul often writes of Christ Jesus Our Lord but says little about the human life of Jesus, other than that he was crucified. He does point out that Jesus was like us in all things except sin, but Paul's interest is in the risen Lord and not in Jesus of Nazareth.

The post-scriptural writers also emphasize the divinity of Jesus Christ. At the end of the first century, Clement of Rome preached: "We ought to think of Jesus Christ as God." The early martyrs were willing to die rather than give up the worship of Christ. In the second century, Ignatius of Antioch described Jesus as God in a human being, and the *Didache* spoke of Jesus as Lord and Son of God. While it is true that the early Fathers recognized that Jesus was human, they all regarded him as a perfect man, a divine man, or a being with divine power and knowledge.

Even the Romans observed this unique faith in the followers of Jesus. Pliny the Younger reported to the Emperor that "Christians" gathered before sunrise to sing "a hymn to Christ as though to a god."

Challenges to orthodoxy

Challenges to both the divinity and humanity of Jesus emerged early on. Jews converting to the Jesus movement sometimes found the claim of Jesus' divinity to be a challenge to their firm belief in one God. The Ebionites were such a group of Jewish-Christians. They were willing to believe that Jesus was an elect of God and a true prophet, but did not find either the virginal conception or the pre-existence of the Son to be acceptable because it implied that Jesus was God.

Those from a Hellenistic background, where God was considered to be unchangeable, also objected to the notion of God becoming man. The Monarchists stressed a "monarchy" in God, which allowed for no distinction between Father and Son and thus gave little consideration to Jesus' humanity. The Adoptionists took the position that since God was one and unchangeable, Jesus must have been a mere adopted son and not really divine.

Gnosticism was a significant movement in the early centuries and seriously challenged the humanity of Jesus. The Gnostics were dualists: they maintained that the material world was from an evil source, and that the body imprisons the spirit and leads it away from its true destiny. It was inconceivable to them that God would become enfleshed and take on a human existence. For many Gnostics, the human Christ was really a shadowy figure who accompanied the real Christ. They believed that Christ was exempt from suffering and death because he was divine. For some Gnostics, the human Christ was simply a phantom, who only appeared to live and die as a human being.

For the Docetists, Jesus wore his humanity as a costume, and thus only appeared to suffer and die. Clearly, versions of this thought still exist in Christian churches today. Many contemporary Christians have little awareness that Jesus led a truly human life.

The notion of "Logos"

The notion of "Logos" (Word) was central in early discussions about Jesus. For the Jews, the Logos was the aspect of God through which God entered history to exercise divine power. The Word was the creative agent in Genesis, the prophetic agent in the prophets, the source of Wisdom. For some of the early fathers, the Word meant a timeless and eternal substance in God. This enabled them to establish a concrete link between the Word and Jesus' divinity.

For the Greeks, the notion of Word was more metaphysical, and pertained to the order and rationality of being. Especially for the Greek Platonists, who profoundly influenced early Christological debates, reality was dualistic. The visible phenomena of the physical world rested on eternal essences, and it was these essences that had the highest value and reality. This led many theologians of the time to emphasize Jesus' divinity (the essence of Jesus) over his humanity.

The early apologists and fathers commonly used the notion of the Logos to link the Son of God with the humanity in Christ. They identified the Son with the Logos, and then proceeded to link the Logos with Christ. Precisely how the Logos was the Son and in what manner the Logos was linked with Christ would be a matter of heated debate for centuries. The notion that the Logos was not equal to God or that it was even "created" would constantly inform the discussions and would be the crux of the question in the classical debate with Arianism. Let us examine how some representative apologists and fathers dealt with these questions.

Early apologists

In the second century, a group of Greek apologists defended Christianity against various movements of magic, Gnosticism, and heresy. By that time, the Christians had broken from Judaism and its members were predominantly Gentiles. New concepts had to be used to explain Jesus Christ, and Greek philosophy became a major resource.

Justin Martyr, an outstanding teacher in Rome, was one such apologist in the middle of the second century. Justin was well-versed in Greek Platonism, and spent his career attempting to harmonize Christianity with Hellenic culture. In his Christology, Justin taught that the Logos is identified with the Son of God. He maintained that the Logos is a derivative of God, but not the first and ultimate deity. The Logos lies between the divinity of God and the non-divinity of creatures. In Jesus, the Logos, or principle of reason became incarnate in order to overcome the demonic forces of "unreason." Justin's views would become extremely influential in subsequent debates. His views on the Logos as being "less than divine" led some to deny the divinity of Jesus, while it led others to neglect his humanity.

Irenaeus (d. 200), the bishop of Lyons, was another apologist who was and still remains today an influential theologian. Irenaeus insisted on using the gospels as a main resource for Christology. He vigorously opposed the Docetist position that Jesus only appeared to be human. He also repudiated Marcion, who rejected the God of the Hebrew Scriptures as the one who created evil and humanity. Irenaeus accepted only the God of love of the Christian Scriptures, and maintained that this was the God made known by Christ. Irenaeus attacked Marcion's dualism, which in effect produced two Gods (evil and good), as well as two Christs (heavenly and earthly).

Irenaeus' main contribution was his integrated and holistic approach to Christian belief. For him creation and redemption, matter and spirit, were continuous. He preferred to use the Hebrew notion of the Logos, seeing it as the communication of God, though not quite equal to God. It was through the Logos that God entered creation and history from the beginning, always wanting to share Self with all of creation. The incarnation, then, is the climax of creation and sums up, or "recapitulates," what God had intended for the world all along: the union of the divine and the human. In Christ a new humanity has begun, and through this new humanity sin has been overcome. Irenaeus has to be credited with establishing the foundation of incarnational theology, which sees the world not as a place to be avoided, but as God's world, where peace and justice will prevail.

Early theologians

Clement (d. 215) was a Greek philosopher who converted to Christianity and became one of its earliest theologians. He went on to become the main instructor at the great center for Christian scholarship in the powerful church of Alexandria, Egypt. Clement taught that God was revealed to the philosophers as well as to the prophets. He held that all revelation comes through the Logos, which in time became incarnate in Jesus Christ. It is this Word, "clothed in human flesh," that reveals God to humans and leads them to God. Clement's Platonism rendered Jesus' humanity vague and placed emphasis on the teaching of the Word, rather than on the concrete life and death of Jesus. Clement's approach to Jesus Christ would be most influential in the school of Alexandria, which emphasized Jesus' divinity.

Origen (d. 253) succeeded Clement in the prestigious school of Alexandria. Origen made significant contributions to the Christological debate, even though his views were regarded as unorthodox by some church authorities. Origen applied Platonic thought to the questions about Jesus, and used the Logos to describe Jesus as mediator between God and humans. Origen taught that God was completely transcendent, and so the divine never gets very close to the flesh. The divine must then be mediated through the soul, and therefore the soul is the point of contact for the Logos. This would indicate that divinity was in Jesus' soul, but not in his body. Origen, like many of his contemporary Greek thinkers, ascribed to the Logos a lower degree of divinity than the Father.

We can see from this brief overview that there was a tendency in this early thinking to render the Logos either unequal to God, derived from God, or an image of God, but not fully God. In fact, the true divinity of Jesus was being challenged by many of these views. But the approach was kept on such a philosophical and Platonic level that orthodoxy did not yet seem to be threatened. It was only when Arius (d. 336) stepped over the line and boldly declared that Jesus was a creature that a crisis exploded.

Arius

Arius was a tall, austere priest of Alexandria. He was extremely charismatic and had many disciples, especially among women consecrated to the church. Arius apparently was influenced in his thinking about Christ by earlier views that the Logos, and therefore Jesus, was less than God. Arius was rigid in his belief that since God created everything out of nothing, the Logos was also a created reality. True to Greek philosophy, he maintained that God was transcendent, absolute, and indivisible, and therefore could not possibly enter into the created world. Whatever is outside of God was created, and that, of course, included the Word, which ultimately became flesh in Jesus.

Arius often quoted Proverbs 8:22 in its description of the birth of Wisdom: "The Lord created me at the beginning of his work, the first of his acts of long ago." This led Arius to conclude that the Logos is a kind of demi-God that intercedes between God and the world. The Word is a superior creature, even one worthy of worship, but is still a creature. It was through this created Word that God made the Son as well as Christ. Therefore, Arius concluded, Christ is a creature suspended between God and the human. "There was a time when he was not" was a classic phrase of Arius. Christ did not pre-exist as the Word, nor was he truly God.

Reaction came swiftly from the bishop of Alexandria, who called a meeting of his priests and asked Arius to recant. When Arius refused, a meeting of the bishops of Egypt and Libya was called in 320. Arius was condemned and sentenced to exile, but he fled to Caesarea in Palestine, where his friend Eusebius (d. 340), the bishop there, offered him refuge and where he continued to make converts.

This dispute was raised to imperial level by Constantine. In 313 the Emperor gave legal status to Christians, in part hoping that this now widespread religious movement would give much needed stability and unity to the Roman Empire. The heated debate over Arianism was standing in the way of these goals, and so Constantine wanted the dispute to be resolved. He decided to make an unprecedented move: to call an official council and order the bishops to resolve the matter immediately.

The Council of Nicaea

Constantine, who regarded himself as the divinity of earth with the power to preside over matters both material and spiritual, called the bishops of the Empire together in 325 in Nicaea (present-day Isnik in Turkey). About 250 bishops gathered in the imperial summer palace, most of whom were from Eastern sees. There was great enthusiasm as the emperor delivered the opening address and ordered them to resolve the Arian dispute. There must have been irony in the air, since some of these bishops had been tortured and oppressed by previous emperors. Now they were being regaled by the Emperor himself!

After much argument, Arius' teachings on the created nature of Jesus Christ were condemned. A creed was formulated to express the official position, and this creed is still recited today at Catholic Masses. It reads: "We believe in one God the Father Almighty, Maker of all things visible and invisible; and in one Lord Jesus Christ, the only Son of God, eternally begotten of the Father, God from God, Light from Light, True God from True God, Begotten, not made, of one substance with the Father, through Whom all things were made."

The Nicene creed left little wiggle room for the Arians. Clearly, Jesus Christ was begotten, not made, was truly God, and was of the "same substance" as God. The Greek word for the same substance (*homoousios*), is a slippery word that can mean the same essence, the same being, even the same "stuff." In other words, whatever God is made of, Jesus is made of the same. The council did not elaborate on what precisely this "stuff" was, and as a result the way to more confusion and debate was left opened. The decree on the doctrine of Christ's divinity was signed by all but three bishops, and these men were deposed and banished from their sees by the Emperor.

There are several important points concerning this conciliar gathering in Nicaea. First, this was a clear exercise of imperial authority to settle a doctrinal matter in the church. The churches, once persecuted by the Empire, were now accepted as officially part of the imperial culture and structures. But there was a price to pay in that the churches were now beholden to the Emperor and became associated with a "kingdom" far different from that which Jesus had preached.

Secondly, in composing its Christological creed, this council relied more heavily on Greek philosophy than on Scripture. This would lead the churches to move more toward a "high Christology," which described God coming from heaven in the form of his Son to save the world. This approach to Christology would for centuries emphasize the divinity of

Jesus at the expense of his humanity, his earthly life, and his ministry to human need. This emphasis on the divinity of Christ would also deeply affect the celebration of the liturgy, shifting focus from a communal meal to that of a worship service.

Antioch and Alexandria

After Nicaea, two major schools of thought about Jesus gained strength in the churches of Antioch in Syria and Alexandria in Egypt. Sorting out these two schools is no easy matter because the views on each side are extremely complex. The fundamental differences spring from two conflicting approaches to God. The Antioch school postulated a double reality in the one God, whereas the prevailing view in Alexandria was that God was a single reality.

The Antiochenes believed that if Jesus was to be the Savior he had to be fully human. This view stressed the indwelling of the Logos in Jesus in such a way that his humanity was not diminished. To safeguard the humanity of Jesus, the Antiochenes developed a "Word-man" theology wherein the Logos dwelled in the man Jesus as in a temple. They favored a "low Christology," which starts with the gospel life of Jesus rather than with the pre-existing Word. Jesus' life is viewed as a gradual assent to the Father, and salvation is viewed more as an imitation of the life and ministry of Jesus than as a process of becoming divinized through the incarnation. This "low Christology," as we have seen, has become the predominant approach among many contemporary biblical scholars and theologians.

The Alexandrians developed a "high Christology," where the Word of the one God descended into Jesus. They maintained that in order to be Savior, Jesus had to be fully divine. The school of Alexandria developed a "Word-flesh" theology, which stressed the oneness of the union of the divine and human in Jesus. The Alexandrians supported the earlier approaches of Clement of Alexandria and Origen, which emphasized the divinity of the Word that divinized the flesh of Jesus. In their efforts to preserve the divinity of Jesus, the school of Alexandria often neglected Jesus' humanity, as well as his life and ministry. This "high Christology" informs the beliefs of many of the Christian faithful today.

Athanasius

Athanasius (d. 373) was a short, dark man from a poor Coptic family in

Egypt. Sometimes called "the Black Dwarf," Athanasius had been a deacon at the Council of Nicaea, and later became a brilliant theologian and a major player in the Arian dispute. As bishop of Alexandria, he opposed Arius even to the point of being banished numerous times by the Emperor, who often tried to appease Arius in order to keep peace in the Empire.

Athanasius was firm in his commitment to the Alexandrian school, and held to the full divinity of the Word. God alone saves, and the purpose of the incarnation was to save fallen humanity and restore it to the image of God. His position became a slogan for the East: "God became human so the human might become God."

The Alexandrian emphasis on the divinity of the Word precipitated another question: How could God suffer on the cross? Athanasius answered by distinguishing between the Word in itself, where there is no suffering, and the Word in Jesus' body, where there is suffering. In this view, however, the Word seems to replace the human soul of Jesus and he is portrayed more as a heavenly man than a truly human being.

Climax of the conflict

The dispute between Alexandria and Antioch came to its climax when Cyril, the patriarch of Alexandria (d. 444), crossed theological swords with Nestorius, the patriarch of Constantinople (d. 451). Nestorius was an Antiochene, and insisted that two natures in Christ remain distinct. The divine Logos could undergo no change upon entering Jesus, and so in Jesus Christ we have the man Jesus and the Son of God. Nestorius' conclusion from this separation in Jesus was that Mary was the mother of Jesus the man but not the mother of God. The Alexandrians were outraged by this "heresy," for they had long described Mary as "the mother of God," and celebrated this belief in a treasured liturgical hymn. The battle between Cyril and Nestorius was drawn.

Cyril attacked Nestorius' position swiftly and vehemently. Many think that politics played a role in Cyril's indignation. After all, Constantinople was vying with Rome for power in the Church, and so both Antioch and Alexandria promoted their man for the patriarchate of Constantinople. If Nestorius could be eliminated as Patriarch of Constantinople and declared a heretic, this would be a victory for Alexandria. Cyril wrote to Nestorius that his position reduced Christ to that of an inspired man who was awarded divine status. Cyril urged him to recant and affirm that in Jesus the Logos and the human were "hypostatically united." When Nestorius refused, Cyril reported him to the Emperor and then called for a council to refute Nestorius.

The council met in 431 in Ephesus, a city in Asia Minor. Nestorius remained at home but sent his followers, who were so late on arriving that Cyril began without them. The council predictably condemned Nestorius as a heretic and deposed him. When Nestorius' supporters arrived, led by John of Antioch, they organized a rival council, had Cyril declared a heretic, and reinstated Nestorius. Amidst a great deal of shouting and confusion, the Emperor intervened and had both Cyril and John arrested. Subsequently, an agreement was struck that favored Cyril's council and condemned and exiled Nestorius to Petra, a desolate area in Palestine. He died there a broken and abandoned man. Cyril's position on the hypostatic union of the divine and human in Christ was confirmed and it was defined that Mary was the mother of God.

There was more to come in this time of political and theological feuding in the church. In 449, Flavian, the Patriarch of Constantinople, called a synod to condemn Eutyches, a monk who taught that Jesus only had a divine nature. Eutyches appealed to the emperor and to Dioscorus, the Patriarch of Alexandria. Dioscorus organized a council to condemn Flavian and exonerate Eutyches. Diorscorus had rigged the debate, and when Flavian objected to the procedures, Diorscorus feigned being attacked and called in police and some hired thugs to give Flavian a fatal beating. The council condemned those who taught that there were two natures in Christ, with the bishops shouting: "Cut him in two who divides Christ." Ultimately the pope called this council a band of robbers, and the Emperor called another council to return to more orthodox views. Eutyches was imprisoned in a monastery, and the bishops of the "robber council" recanted. These were colorful times indeed in the history of doctrinal development!

Council of Chalcedon

In 451 a new council was called by the Emperor to settle the ferocious debates surrounding Jesus' divinity and humanity. Hundreds of bishops were in attendance along with papal delegates and, of course Dioscorus and his unruly followers. Amidst shouting matches and the occasional fist fight, Dioscorus and his followers were condemned for their views on the single nature of Jesus. After much heated debate, the council denounced all theories which implied a double sonship, confused the two natures of Christ, or suggested that Jesus' humanity was only a pretense. The bishops reiterated the creed of Nicaea and went beyond that to define that Jesus Christ was "truly God and truly man." Compromising with both Antioch and Alexandria, they stated that Christ has "two natures, without confusion, without change, without division, without separation." Each nature, the human and divine, was affirmed in one person, one center of unity.

Critique of the Councils

The Councils of Nicaea and Chalcedon were milestones in the development of Christology. They settled serious disputes within the Church and made definitive statements about the divinity and humanity of Jesus Christ. The doctrines indicate that the churches had moved from a Jewish milieu into a Greco-Roman world, and had adopted new systems of thought and interpretation. The historical contexts of these councils reveal how political and social as well as religious issues deeply influenced the development of doctrines concerning Jesus Christ.

Today, sixteen centuries later, the Church finds itself in a much larger and more diverse world. Christology exists in a new context, one characterized by advanced scientific understandings of the cosmos and nature, a variety of psychological and social perspectives on the human personality, and a more analytical approach to history. In this complex and ever changing global context, there are urgent demands to link the study of Christ with human liberation, the sustaining of the earth, and the beliefs of other religions. A wide variety of cultures and contexts requires new images of Jesus Christ that will help in the human struggle to survive and gain freedom.

Many contemporaries find the philosophical perspectives of these early councils to be foreign and even irrelevant to the religious needs of our global society. Western Christians, with some acquaintance of Aquinas, may have some understanding of the issues, but Christians from Asia and Africa find the definitions to be puzzling indeed. The Christological language of the early councils must strike many as antiquated and esoteric.

Nicaea declared that Jesus was of the same "stuff" as God, but never explained what this "stuff" is. Many believe that we are left with a solution to the problem of Jesus' identity that is no solution at all.

Criticism of these early conciliar formulations is growing among contemporary theologians. These councils present an abstract, dualistic, and ahistorical approach to reality that is foreign to today's believer. The theological debates surrounding these councils seem to be more concerned with the Logos than they are with Jesus himself. In this perspective, so often the Logos, with a pre-existence that defies contemporary thought, seems to take over a humanity that remains passive and not open to human development. The notion of salvation, so central to these debates, concerns itself with divinizing a fallen world and humanity, rather than saving a graced people on the earth from the real problems that threaten to take away peace and justice.

It has been suggested that when the churches get together for the next ecumenical council, Jesus Christ should be the main agenda. The Second Vatican Council mainly focused on church reform in the modern world. The next council should reclaim the person who is central to the Church, Jesus Christ. Just as so much of the thinking in the first half of the twentieth century prepared the way for Vatican II, much of the Christology of the last fifty years has now cleared the way for fresh perspectives on the person of Jesus.

A new context

Christian beliefs are shaped by the contexts or "signs of the times" in which they appear. As we have seen, the early doctrines on Jesus Christ came at a time when first the divinity and then the humanity of Jesus were being challenged. With Gentiles now prominent in the Church, thought patterns shifted from Jewish to Greco-Roman. The Empire's center relocated to Constantinople, which gave the Eastern churches dominance over those of Rome and the West. A Christian Church, which had lived in the shadows and suffered persecution from time to time, was now emerging as the official religion of the Empire. The Church was now under imperial pressure to make definitions, yet at the same time was beginning to gain a powerful authority of its own. Christian doctrine was of concern to the ordinary citizen, so much so that riots and violence could break out in the streets over theological arguments. As we have seen, disruption even overflowed into the official councils of the churches. The definitions of Nicaea and Chalcedon were shaped by the times in which they were debated and formulated.

Our times are most certainly far different from those in the early centuries of the church. We live in an age of information, where we place great value on facts, sound scientific research, and competent scholarship. At the same time, we are in a period when "post-modernism" often relativizes the study of history and personhood. Many Christians today have moved beyond the Jesus of popular piety and want a Christology that is based on thorough historical and biblical study. A century and a half of archeological discoveries, biblical studies, and research into the religious, social, and political background of Palestine has provided diverse and yet consistent portraits of the historical Jesus. The focus today is on Jesus' life and ministry, on what he did and continues to do, rather than on his metaphysical make-up, his persona and natures. New and fresh images of a historically real and presently active Jesus Christ have helped his followers more closely connect his person and teachings with their daily struggles for freedom, peace, and justice.

A shift to the human

Today's interest is primarily in Jesus' humanity, for it is here that people can identify with Jesus. Human beings can take comfort in the knowledge that Jesus understands their struggles, weaknesses, feelings, and experiences because he too led a genuinely human life. As we saw earlier, the historical Jesus especially holds interest for the millions who struggle for liberation from deprivation and oppression. The man Jesus knows their experience of suffering and death and, now that he has been raised, gives them hope and power for a better future in this life and the next. Many believers value the image of this Jesus that can be recovered behind the scriptural forms; but they also accept and attempt to live out the post-resurrection faith in the presence and power of Jesus' Spirit.

Modern psychology and anthropology have revealed much about the human person. Today Jesus is looked upon as a human person, since "person" now refers to a center of consciousness and not a philosophical center of unity as it was understood in the early councils. We now understand how serious God was in wanting to live a human life, with all its questions, limitations, hopes, and setbacks. Jesus is generally not viewed as a divine man, but as a human person who had to learn, discover his identity and purpose in life, make choices, and suffer and die like all other human beings.

Today's approach to divinity

Today, the Christian approach to Jesus' divinity differs considerably from that of the ancient world. The early councils, with their "from above" approach to God, emphasized the transcendence of God. God was understood in Hellenic terms: omniscient, eternal, unchanging, and far removed from the world. Today's biblical studies have reclaimed the immanent God of the Hebrew Scriptures, the "Abba God" revealed by Jesus. This is a God within history and life—a God who singularly blesses the poor and the outcast; a Creator who heals, forgives, and saves.

This is not a divinity who masquerades as a human but a God who is fully revealed in the life and work of the human person Jesus. It is a God who raised Jesus, and revealed that he was and is the Christ, the beloved Son of God. Here Jesus is wholly God, but not the whole of God. Divinity does not overwhelm or render Jesus' humanity passive, as in earlier thinking and even in some contemporary theology. Rather the divinity is revealed from what Thomas Merton called "the true self" of Jesus; or, as Karl Rahner maintained, divinity is revealed through the human experience of Jesus. (Rahner once observed that the more we know about our humanity, the more we learn of God.) This is a God who is found within joys and hopes, as well as the crosses and suffering of life. This is not the premodern metaphysical God, vaguely described in terms of "stuff" or "essence." Rather it is a postmodern God wrapped in mystery, beyond description but somehow experienced in history and within the human struggle for freedom and peace.

A more holistic context

We have seen how the past conciliar context for discussing Jesus was more philosophical and reflected the abstraction and dualism of Greek thought. Jesus was portrayed as a static divine persona, with two natures side by side. Today's anthropology is much more dynamic and evolutionary, more concerned with process. The contemporary accent is not on being, but on becoming; not on essence but existence; not on nature alone, but on nature that is constantly growing. Many prefer to see Jesus as a human person becoming divine in his awareness and experience, rather than as a divine Logos being incarnated into a human being. Jesus was a person of faith who completely opened himself to divine mystery, and who attempted to reveal this uniquely intimate experience of God to others.

A global context

Technology, rapid means of travel, a worldwide economy, and the growing intermixture of peoples have produced what is now a global society. The dominance of military and economic superpowers, the prevalence of wars and holocausts, the devastation of the earth, and the growing number of refugees have created a growing divide between the haves and the have-nots. The majority of the world's people suffer from a scarcity of food and water, a lack of proper shelter, and the growing devastation from disease. The outcasts of Jesus' time have grown into the billions, while most of the wealthy and powerful enjoy a luxurious lifestyle and are blind to the grow-ing squalor and poverty throughout their world.

The oppressed and deprived of the world are not so much concerned with the nature of Christ as they are with his mission and presence, and with how he can sustain and support them in their struggles for wholeness and freedom. Many are not so much interested in the hereafter as they are with the here and now, the daily challenges to survive. They look to a Spirit of the Lord within their lives and hearts who can give them the strength to keep going, as well as the courage to stand up to injustice. Their interest has shifted from the ancient question of whether we are saved by Jesus' divin-ity or humanity, to the "how" and "when" liberation will come to God's people through Jesus Christ. And they want to know what role they are called to play in this liberation of the poor, of women, of homosexuals, of prisoners, of AIDS patients, and of many others who desire freedom in the Lord. More and more we hear of the intense search for Christ from people of color, feminists, womanists, *mujeristas*, the migrant workers of India and Mexico, the homeless from the inner cities, the indigenous people of Central and Latin America and Africa, and the oppressed in Asia.

An interfaith context

In our time, the world's religions are commonly recognized as authentic instruments of God's revelation and saving power. Christians today generally have more knowledge of other religions than was the case in earlier centuries, and encounter them with a deeper understanding, more respect, and sometimes with a real participation. Missionaries are not as concerned with converting others as they were in the past. Rather, there is more effort on integration, authentic witness to gospel life, and participation in respectful dialogue.

As we have seen, interfaith dialogue has presented new challenges to Christology. Christians are attempting to put aside the triumphalism and exclusivity of the past and to be open to the saving powers in other religions. Biblical scholars reexamine the scriptural titles of Jesus and reinterpret these titles within a new framework of interfaith exchange. Churches are still intent on not giving up doctrinal integrity for the sake of dialogue, but at the same time they want to come to the table with an authentic Jesus who does not diminish other religious figures.

A environmental context

There is growing alarm at the devastation that the people of the earth continue to inflict on their environment. Air, water, and land are being polluted. The earth's protective shields are being disturbed, resulting in increased exposure to ultraviolet rays and severe changes in weather. Resources are rapidly being depleted, and there is an extraordinary amount of waste.

The environmental crisis grows more serious yearly, and yet the world's religions seem reluctant to address these problems and move their people to action. As we have seen, there has been some movement among the churches and religions to connect religious faith with ecology. Some Christian environmentalists look to Jesus for his "sacramental" appreciation of creation as a way to discover the reign of God within. Others suggest that Jesus' spirit of simplicity and detachment needs to be followed by his disciples today in order to stem rampant consumerism and greed. Some turn to the Cosmic Christ as the Spirit we need to inspire us to build the earth and pass on a healthy environment to future generations.

Jesus as symbol of God

Roger Haight, a Jesuit theologian, offers one of the most insightful suggestions for reinterpreting Jesus for the contemporary context. He points to the past use of symbolic language, such as Logos, and observes that often these symbols were taken too literally and became objectified. The Word, rather than being a symbol, came to be understood as a pre-existent reality. Haight reminds us that symbols point to reality, and that when they point to God are always limited in what they can convey of this Mystery.

Haight points out that in our era, symbols should not be drawn from philosophical abstractions, but must arise dynamically out of human experience. Religious symbols are mediums through which God offers Self, gives Self to people in their lives. They are powerful conveyors of God's revelation and power. From this perspective, Jesus can be understood as a medium or symbol through which God gives Self to the world. Jesus brings about salvation by making the saving God present in the world. He is also a unique and powerful symbol of who God is: a creative, loving, healing, and forgiving Creator. Jesus' life and mission reveal human life at its best, as completely open to God, and utterly free in its choice of God's will. As Haight observes, we are most human when we are the most open to God. In sacramental terms, we might say that Jesus is the primary sacrament, the prime way through which God shares life with others. Jesus is divine in the sense that he makes God present.

This symbolic approach begins with the historical Jesus, who in his life, death, and resurrection made present God's gift of self. Then Jesus is viewed as the Christ who continues to bring a loving and merciful God to a people and an earth that seek liberation. Christ dynamically reveals a God who saves people in their individual and communal contexts, where they search for dignity and freedom.

Summary

The affirmation of both the humanity and divinity of Jesus Christ is essential to Christian doctrine. The New Testament clearly professes both dimensions of the Christ, and early councils made definitive statements in this regard. Today theologians confront the limitations of these ancient doctrines. They attempt to formulate new and fresh understandings of Jesus' humanity and divinity that will better resonate with disciples in our contemporary world.

Questions for reflection and discussion

1. Discuss some of the gospel stories that demonstrate that Jesus was truly human.

2. Do you think that Jesus was aware that he was divine? Were his disciples aware of his divinity?

3. Why did so many early Jews find it difficult to accept that Jesus was divine?

4. What are some of the main contributions of the early councils concerning the divinity and humanity of Jesus? What are some of the limitations of these definitions?

4. In your religious education was there much attention given to the humanity of Jesus? If so, cite examples.

Sources

Behr, John. *The Way to Nicaea.* Crestwood, NY: St. Vladimir's Seminary Press, 2001.

Davis, Leo Donald. *The First Seven Ecumenical Councils (325–787): Their History and Theology.* Collegeville, MN: Liturgical Press, 1990.

Haight, Roger. *Jesus, Symbol of God.* Maryknoll, NY: Orbis Books, 1999.

Macquarrie, John. *Christology Revisited.* Harrisburg, PA: Trinity Press International, 1998.

Norris, Richard A. Jr., trans. and ed. *The Christological Controversy.* Philadelphia: Fortress Press, 1980.

Pelikan, Jaroslav. *The Emergence of the Catholic Tradition (100–600).* Vol. 1 of *The Christian Tradition: A History of the Development of Doctrine.* Chicago: University of Chicago Press, 1971.

Seitz, Christopher, ed. *Nicene Christianity: The Future for a New Ecumenism.* Grand Rapids: Brazos Press, 2001.

Index

Lightning Source UK Ltd.
Milton Keynes UK
UKOW06f0629140116

266389UK00002B/167/P